FORMING THE PUBLIC

THE HISTORY OF COMMUNICATION

Robert W. McChesney and John C. Nerone, editors

For a list of books in the series, please see our website at www.press.uillinois.edu.

FORMING THE PUBLIC

A CRITICAL HISTORY OF JOURNALISM
IN THE UNITED STATES

Frank D. Durham and Thomas P. Oates

UNIVERSITY OF
ILLINOIS PRESS
Urbana, Chicago, and Springfield

Library of Congress Cataloging-in-Publication Data
Names: Durham, Frank D. (Frank Dallas), author. | Oates,
    Thomas Patrick, author.
Title: Forming the public : a critical history of journalism in
    the United States / Frank D. Durham and Thomas P. Oates.
Description: Urbana : University of Illinois Press, 2024.
    | Series: The history of communication | Includes
    bibliographical references and index.
Identifiers: LCCN 2024023350 (print) | LCCN 2024023351
    (ebook) | ISBN 9780252046506 (cloth) | ISBN
    9780252088599 (paperback) | ISBN 9780252047817
    (ebook)
Subjects: LCSH: Journalism—United States—History. |
    Journalism—Social aspects—United States. | Press and
    politics—United States.
Classification: LCC PN4855.D87 2024 (print) | LCC PN4855
    (ebook) | DDC 071.3—dc23/eng/20240605
LC record available at https://lccn.loc.gov/2024023350
LC ebook record available at https://lccn.loc.gov/2024023351

Contents

Acknowledgments

No book comes into print solely through the labor of its authors. We have benefitted from many people whose contributions helped make this book possible. We thank Danny Nasset at the University of Illinois Press, who has been an excellent steward of this project from the beginning. Mariah Schaefer and Tad Ringo worked closely with us to refine the manuscript. John Nerone provided helpful feedback that shaped the book.

The reviewers and readers of this book in its various forms helped refine its arguments, and our colleagues helped to create a nourishing community that made writing it a joy. Special thanks to Brian Ekdale, Naomi Greyser, Jennifer Sterling, Melissa Tully, Eric Vazquez, Travis Vogan, Stephen Warren, and Rachel Young for their interest in and support of this project. John Haman, Qi Ling, Subin Paul, Christina Smith, David Tuwei, Tammy Walkner, Xianwei Wu, and Andrea Weare also shaped this book with their feedback and suggestions. Thanks to Liz Cecil, Laura Kastens, Michele Ketchum, Laura Kerr, Brittany Ogden, and Lindsay Vella for their help with logistics.

Finally, this book would never have existed without the help and inspiration of our families and friends who provided crucial logistical and emotional support. We are indebted to you for this book and for so much else. We owe everything to those at the center of our support networks: Gigi, Sonali, Maya, Rebecca, and Eleanor.

FORMING THE PUBLIC

Introduction

Journalists usually describe their work as central to democracy. Because democracy requires that governments reflect the will of the public, the thinking goes, the public would be poorly prepared to govern itself without the independent information journalism provides. At the heart of this formula lies the question of just what and who the "public" has been in the history of American journalism. The historian James Carey calls that organizing idea journalism's "God term . . . , the term without which the entire enterprise fails to make sense."[1] Carey's metaphor emphasizes that the many facets of journalism need a unifying concept. The public is that concept.

In this history of American journalism, we define the public from moment to moment within these chapters by showing the actions of many politically active citizens who used journalism to lay claim to life in American democracy. They presented themselves as Americans by writing and so by thinking publicly. They shared their ideas, named their challenges, and spoke their dreams of joining that public. Constructed through the changing practice of journalism, the broader discourse of the "public interest" has always carried complex and often conflicting issue agendas.

Like all histories, this one reflects choices about how to fit into the spaces and gaps left by the existing scholarship. It is part of a collective effort to account for the contributions to American civic life made by journalism that has taken a variety of shapes. The point of this book is to offer a more rounded history of journalism by focusing on key struggles to define and redefine the public, its problems, and its interests. We do this not by examining the dominant, mainstream leaders of the public interest—as many histories of journalism do—but by offering a history that emphasizes the constant, ongoing, and everchanging struggle to expand the definition of American life. This history insists on the centrality of power in these struggles by describing how the mainstream has been shaped and transformed by *outsider* uses of journalism that challenged the status quo and the public with it.

Rather than describing American journalism as the accomplishment of a series of apparently inevitable stages of institutional growth, we present American journalism as a changing practice that has been a site of cultural and political struggle since the colonial era. Employed by both cultural outsiders and insiders, it has been used either for supporting or rejecting emerging social changes. Journalism thus became a central site and a process for social change. In that idea-driven contest to either conserve, reform, or overthrow social meanings, historian David Mindich sees the interplay between renegade and mainstream voices as the "process" and the daily news pages of mainstream newspapers the "site" of the ongoing contest to define "the public."[2]

From their positions in the margins of American life, the voices of abolitionists, suffragists, and activists in the labor and civil rights movements have countered definitions of American democracy that has left them out. Within each group were writers taking up a range of rhetorical strategies—news stories, dramatic anecdotes, data-rich reports, satire, hoaxes, and, sometimes, outright disinformation. In doing so, they acted as critical "counter publics," engaging through what one scholar calls "poetic worldmaking" from outside the mainstream.[3] Counter-public voices often appropriated the routines and voices of mainstream journalism. They did so to challenge the developing principles of social, cultural, and political life that mainstream journalism was helping to develop and maintain.

Mainstream and counter-public journalisms have so often been affected by some form of propaganda. This book presents discussions of that in chapter discussions of the anarchist labor movement, the commercial press of the late nineteenth and early twentieth centuries, the rise of public relations and advertising after World War I, and the Second Red Scare under McCarthyism as challenges to the use of journalism as the basis of a liberal democracy.

More traditional histories have approached the task of describing and explaining the growth of American journalism by collecting categorical narratives, including accounts of the "African-American press, women in journalism, immigrant periodicals," according to the scholar Jane Rhodes. There is a risk of what Jane Rhodes has called the "add and stir method," which produces a compensatory tokenism, instead of a more holistic historical account.[4] In an attempt to avoid that, this book locates struggles between the mainstream and the margins within the broader historical contexts of events and shows the development of the mainstream press as a conservative institution against which movement and outsider journalists worked.

More often than not, the mainstream press has served as a gatekeeper of access to a version of democracy that privileged the white mainstream and white middle- and upper-class men in particular. The history of journalism cannot be reduced to their efforts, however. It is instead more properly and comprehensively understood as an ongoing struggle to define who belongs in "the public," what their interests are, and how they could be controlled.[5]

Much of this book documents what political scientist Michael Rogin called the "countersubversive tradition" in US political culture. The chapters highlight how mainstream journalism has frequently been a site for the use of political demonology by mainstream leaders and writers. To examine this cultural flow and counterflow, we show examples of mainstream journalism engaged in the "inflation, stigmatization, and dehumanization of political foes" whom it believes to be a threat to all that is authentically and unquestionably American.[6]

Race has loomed large in this tradition, although, as this book will show, the concept has always been unstable and fuzzy. Unlike today, the idea of race formerly did not depend on skin color or other physical features, but on national origin, language, religion, and culture as they differed from Anglo-American norms. So, a typical Irishman who would be judged to be "white" today based on his appearance would have been seen by Anglos in the nineteenth century as belonging to a lower racial status because of his national customs, including dress, dialect, and diet.[7] Against the racial other, those with access to power constructed the notion of "whiteness." Though also ill-defined and changing, the concept has nevertheless been applied ever since by those who wished to "conserve" a mythical, white vision of the past. Over time, threads of this exclusionary vision would include often imaginary or magnified threats to the status quo by the labor, suffrage, women's, and civil rights movements. The mainstream press has often posed shifting ideas of race to answer the question of "[W]ho gets to be 'American?'" in terms that left their power and influence undisturbed.[8]

The Organization of This Book

To help readers understand the essential details of these struggles, this book includes substantial sections of text as they appeared in the journalism of the day. Rather than summarizing their arguments or excerpting small passages, as existing journalism histories do, wherever possible, *Forming the Public* presents extended excerpts of news stories that have helped to form mainstream political culture in the United States. Confronting historical texts can be challenging. In some cases, the language can be difficult to penetrate, and references can go over the heads of many readers. Wherever possible, we have attempted to help the reader with contextualizing information. The arguments included here may seem outdated, even shocking, while other themes will feel eerily familiar. By presenting such detail, we hope that readers will be able to appreciate not only *what* was argued, but precisely *how*. In the process, we hope to offer a richer understanding of both the past and the present.

The two and a half centuries covered in this book have witnessed several changes in the structure, economics, scale, and organization of mainstream journalism. Newspapers in the United States began as small operations run out of single rooms, often by a printer and his assistant. These small presses have not gone away; indeed, they remain staples of the alternative journalisms proliferating in today's digital media.

In the eighteenth century, the practice of journalism was tied to the business of printing. As mainstream news organizations grew in size, they adopted a series of organizational strategies in pursuit of audiences that were devoted to subtly different values. Although such changes gave shape to the narratives, newer approaches to the production and meaning of journalism are not typically evident in the narratives themselves. So, to make sense of these shifts, we present four often-overlapping stages in the development of the mainstream press. We detail them below and use them as a guide to organize the book.

The Early Partisan Press

From the beginning, the notion of the public created by the Constitution was a severely limited one. Voting was limited to white male property owners, who accounted for a minority of the total adult population. Even these voters could not vote directly for their senators, who were elected by state legislatures until 1913, nor could they vote for president, who was chosen by a small group of electors (a system that remains, in modified form, to this day). Patriarchal laws barred women from the rights guaranteed to men, and slavery denied millions of people any of the benefits of citizenship. In 1790, Congress passed the Naturalization Act, which made US citizenship contingent on whiteness.

But, despite these severe limitations, there were also signs of an almost radical commitment to facilitating public discourse and deliberation. The First Amendment offered protections to speakers and publishers that were extraordinary for the time. When Congress passed the Post Office Act of 1792 subsidizing the delivery of correspondence and newspapers, it was serving a nation of newspaper readers. Making sense today of these parallel developments at the nation's founding helps to illustrate one of this book's central themes—that the course of news and journalism emerged, not from some unified spirit of the age but as the result of struggles over the nation's future.

The press's role in the contest to define the public began to diversify in the early nineteenth century as new political parties took shape against each other, often through party-owned newspapers. Writing in 1835 of his travels in the nascent American society, the aristocratic French diplomat Alexis de Tocqueville highlighted the unusual, perhaps unique, civic life of the nation. Despite the exclusion of women and people of color, which the author took for granted, Tocqueville saw in the United States an unusually decentralized and freewheeling democracy. Unlike the aristocracy of his native France, he saw that in America "all parties are prepared to acknowledge the rights of the majority, because all hope some day to exercise those rights." Especially at the local level, power was up for grabs in the United States in ways that impressed (and occasionally alarmed) Tocqueville.[9]

Tocqueville saw newspapers playing a central role in this emerging civic culture. "Because it is easy to start a newspaper, anybody can do it," he noted with only some exaggeration. Indeed, in part because of newspaper subsidies and a well-funded postal system, the United States had three times as many newspapers per capita as Great Britain. But, Tocqueville was quick to add, journalism was not a route to wealth or respectability. Most papers were kept afloat by subsidies from political parties and often pursued a bareknuckle style. There Tocqueville saw a tendency for any one newspaper editor to "appeal crudely, directly, and artlessly to the passions of the people he is addressing, forsaking principles in order to portray individuals, pursue them into their private lives, and lay bare their weaknesses and vices."[10]

Nevertheless, Tocqueville clearly saw a link between the interest in journalism and political participation. "Newspapers make associations, and associations make newspapers," he observed. "Of all the countries in the world, America is the one with both the most associations and the most newspapers."[11] Because these newspapers were funded by local political parties ("associations") and because those local parties were relatively autonomous, the partisan press presented a wide mixture of voices. "To be sure," Tocqueville noted, "all of the Union's political papers are either for or against the administration. But they attack and defend it in a thousand different ways. Therefore, newspapers in the United States cannot create currents of opinion so powerful that not even the formidable dams can withstand them."[12] At the same time, as an institution, journalism was a force. "The press wields enormous power in America," he concluded. "It carries the currents of political life into every section of this vast country."[13]

The Commercial Press

As the nineteenth century came on, the nascent American economy and the press with it grew more complex. During this time, for example, newspaper publishing shifted from the colonial apprentice system of training print-ers as publishers to a commercial model that was built by industrialism. Tracing changes in circulation methods shows how this growth happened. Instead of using the colonial postal service, whose circulation depended on merchant-publishers, through the middle of the nineteenth century, the newly developed partisan presses reached wider audiences. Early jour-nalists developed their presence in the cities by accessing the industrially driven national printing and postal systems that had been developed and subsidized by Congress. Presenting a variety of political positions intended to build coalitions among the more literate elites, urban newspapers often "reflected bitter disputes, but also argued eloquently the respective positions of different parties."[14]

At the same time that partisan journalism was emerging, a handful of newspapers in large cities turned to the newly available resource of com-mercialization. By the 1830s, the ability to reach larger readerships opened the way to the more formal business of newspaper publishing. To attract more readers, publishers dropped the price of a newspaper to a penny or about three dollars today. Although partisanship would remain a feature of the news for the rest of the century, many American readers soon found themselves and their interests represented in the newly "depoliticized" com-mercial press. The first such newspaper was Benjamin Day's *New York Sun*, which began publishing in 1833. It was followed the next year by that city's *Evening Transcript*. James Gordon Bennett's *New York Herald* followed in 1835. Soon, this new form of newspaper had been adopted by newspapers in Boston, Philadelphia, and Baltimore.[15]

Into the 1890s, the growth of the penny press entwined several key trends. By embracing the immigrant millions as readers, publishers were able to break from the political and business elites they had adhered to before 1830. As a result, the news included a greater diversity of voices. In this moment, the commercial press cultivated its readers as consumers who could be delivered as a salable commodity to advertisers. The effect of this development was to broaden popular access to the news and, therefore, to readers' active participation in mainstream public opinion.

The Industrial Press

Commercial development of nineteenth-century newspapers was enhanced by industrial advances in technology. By midcentury, fast steamships and faster transcontinental trains were aided by new kinds of printing presses and, above all, by the coast-to-coast telegraph in ways that changed the scope and scale of the newspaper business.[16] Changing publishing practices also changed the nature of their news. Whereas earlier newspapers had copied and borrowed content from a variety of sources, newspapers began creating their own content—changing from "printers and collectors" of news to its "producers and creators."[17]

Based in the nation's booming larger cities, mainly in New York, their new economic scale brought a more formal editorial structure to the production of news. To address this newfound scale of business, publishers hired managing editors and reporters to create content for the masses, including the millions of immigrants who arrived from 1880 through the end of World War I. In this moment, we can see that commerce fueled by industry drove a still-partisan press to new organizational heights. Bigger, faster, and richer than ever, the early structure of the media industry took shape. In particular, Joseph Pulitzer's *New York World*, founded in 1883, and William Hearst's *New York Journal*, founded in 1895, developed "within a growing infrastructure of content providers—wire services and features syndicates," as well as the booming entertainment industry.[18] In Pulitzer's genius for capturing the attention of his city's massive immigrant readership, he created a popular form of content—easy to read, sometimes fabricated, but always enticing—that came to be known (for reasons explained in this book) as "yellow journalism." Hearst copied it all, and soon their front pages were filled with bold headlines, color pictures, and lurid details of stories real or imagined.

Even as the masses bought these later-style penny papers, the result was hardly democratic. Instead, operating at the expense of Americans' place in public opinion, Hearst, along with a complicit Pulitzer, was able to promote the public's support for a war between the United States and Spain in 1898 just to increase newspaper sales. Today, we call such propaganda "fake news." While the *Journal* and the *World* sold a fraudulent war to the mass of new arrivals, most of whom voted Democratic, the smaller *New York Times* objected to their crass commercialism. Founded in 1851 by publisher Adolph Ochs, the *Times* wrote for the Anglo-Republican business class, more often with evidence-based reporting.

The Professionalizing Press

The trend toward professionalism in journalism had begun in the 1880s with the "proto-professionalism" of the "muckrakers." As progressive investigative reporters, they pursued the "journalism of exposé" by investigating governmental and corporate corruption.[19] Their work, often republished in book-length versions, highlighted the growing position of the journalist between the public and political culture. No longer a reflection of Thomas

Jefferson's "bucolic" smalltown America, the daily press at the beginning of the twentieth century produced more distance between the individual and the individual's sense of public opinion than ever.

The question of how individuals could engage in self-government in the new mass society came to a head just after World War I ended. Writing in 1920, media theorist and critic Walter Lippmann launched a critique of who the public was and what its members should do—or even could do—to maintain their places in a participatory democracy. Lippmann challenged the myth of Jeffersonian democracy as invalid in the new mass society of the twentieth century. Instead, his concept of democracy called for a strong press to connect individuals to the state in an active, if occasional, participatory process that could still be called public opinion.

While he advocated for better-educated and better-paid reporters to challenge the massive lying and propaganda that had followed the United States home from the war, he also called for a public that could use such a reformed, science-based journalism to see the empirical differences that reporters could show between one's own individual perceptions and the world as it truly was. His influential writing on the subject fully supported key aspects of a professionalizing press corps, including the continued establishment of journalism schools, higher salaries, and the development of professional codes of ethics—all features of corporate journalism through the mid-twentieth century.

Describing the institutional development of the field, the historian John Nerone explained that "In the first half of the twentieth century, the 'press' claimed a place alongside other institutions like the military, the legislature, banking and organized religion as part of the apparatus that maintained the social order."[20] That status created more distance between the news and its consumers. Through their expertise, the modern journalist "inserted her or himself in between the flow of information and the ordinary citizen."[21] Whereas the nineteenth-century partisan press had defined its readers as part of the public by representing those whose opinions it could incorporate into its version of the "news," by 1920 the increasingly professionalized institutional press was working in a much bigger, more commercialized, and more industrialized version of America.

The prevalent lack of journalistic professionalism coupled with the vastly larger scale of life in the nation's major cities actually widened the gap between those who wanted to get into the public and those who were admitted to it. That change was exactly what had frustrated Lippmann's hopes for bridging the gap between individual citizens and their potential involvement in American democracy.

In the 1920s, the rise of radio seemed to offer to unify the nation through its expansive broadcast reach. But not all observers were convinced. Faced with regulating the new medium, President Herbert Hoover warned that "Radio lends itself to propaganda far more easily than the press."[22] By the late 1930s, both projections would become true. Various broadcasters would mount a national campaign of anti-Semitism in support of the Third Reich. And, at the same time, by 1939 radio would capture 25 percent of the news market as the most trusted source of news for Americans, a number that would rise to as much as three quarters of the general public by the mid-forties. Many believed that radio was "more objective than the newspapers."[23]

The expectation that broadcast media could corral the nation's attention continued through the 1980s, as the three private television networks—the American Broadcasting Company (ABC), the Columbia Broadcasting System (CBS), and the National Broadcasting Company (NBC)—developed to overtake radio as the nation's primary news source. Media scholar Dan Hallin describes this moment as one of "high modernist" unity.[24] Five nights a week for fifteen minutes and, later, for thirty minutes at dinnertime, the three television networks' nightly news broadcasts presented a limited agenda of mainstream content. By excluding nonmainstream subjects from their newscasts, however, they also practiced a tradition of limiting access to membership in the public.

In the 1980s, new media platforms began to change the place of the individual in what had become a global public. In the United States, newspapers gave way to the rise of cable television and the internet, a result largely of a business model that failed in the face of increasing demands for stocks-based returns and increasing monopolization.

Throughout American history, the dynamic of public opinion has tilted in different directions and the press has tilted with it. Jefferson held that the (white and male) individual could fully participate in public opinion in 1787.[25] Tocqueville saw community associations as the basic unit of social organization in 1835.[26] At every overlapping stage, the grasp of the individual American on his or her place in society grew less Jeffersonian and more reliant on the press.

By the early twenty-first century, digital algorithms were changing the shape of news again. Still, today the concept of an American public held together by journalism persists. At this writing, it seems clear that the role of local print and television as either a primary source of news or as a gatekeeper to the public has been altered, even sidelined, by competing content on digital mobile devices and their constantly reformulating social media platforms. Because the present and the recent past cannot be treated as history, we will have to wait to draw firm conclusions not just about the place of the individual sustained by democracy and a thirst for freedom, but of the continued existence of American liberal democracy, at all.

To tell the history of outsiders struggling against mainstream public opinion in order to join it, this book is organized chronologically. In each case, we have described the prevailing characteristics of these alternate moments in terms of the shifting professional, legal, technological, economic, and cultural forces that made the daily press dominant and the movement presses viable.

Chapter 1 describes how colonial journalism, both prorevolutionary and loyalist, contributed to the constitution of American national identity by serving as the site of debates over the limits and nature of citizenship in the new nation. In chapters two through four, we show how the partisan and commercial presses variously opposed—and, thereby, shaped—the challenges to mainstream status posed by abolitionism, woman suffrage, and immigrant labor, respectively. Chapter 5 examines the evidence-based development of objective journalism in contesting mainstream attempts to justify the national epidemic of lynching. Chapter 6 details the struggle over whether the United States should pursue an empire at the beginning of the twentieth century, and chapter 7 explores the struggle by Tejanos to define themselves both as citizens and as members of a transnational people. Chapter 8 considers the contest between truth and propaganda in the rise of public relations and the "crisis of liberalism" in the post–World War I era. Chapter 9 traces the Second Red Scare and its disruptive effects on professional journalism. Chapters 10, 11, and 12 trace how social movements sought to utilize both movement media and the mainstream to advance their goals.

The aim of this book is to deepen an appreciation for the many ways journalism has been deployed in US history—both for good and for ill—as well as for the common threads of continuity that run through that history. From pamphlets to television, the news has been organized and delivered in different ways and with different effects. But one constant has been the struggle to define the public—who belongs to it, who threatens it, and what it demands. Rather than simply serving the public, journalism has been an important way that the public has been defined in the first place. That reality calls on us all to consider how some people have used journalism to create a more expansive and inclusive polity, while others have sought to "protect" democracy from those they deem unworthy. Of course, these struggles continue to be urgent in our present. Our future will depend in part on how well we learn the lessons of the past.

1

Creating an American Public Interest

The thirteen British colonies that became the United States of America endured a century of British misrule that matched royal neglect with the sudden overbearing demand that the American colonists pay for the empire's broken budget without representation in Parliament. Tensions came to a head in two prominent crises: the Stamp Act of 1765 and the Boston Massacre of March 5, 1770. The ways in which Samuel Adams and Thomas Paine wrote about these events to the colonial public gave breath to the revolution. Their work also helped form the colonial press by using the persuasive techniques of propaganda effectively.

The timeline from the British Empire's financial ruin to the American Revolution spanned from the mid-1750s to July 4, 1776. From 1754 to 1763, the British fought and won the French and Indian War, so called because the Americans were fighting both at the same time. By then, the British had fought a series of wars with the French for control of Indians' lands and their wealth of natural resources.

The British government had overextended itself by prosecuting a war "that spanned the globe from Bengal to Barbados, drew in Austria, Portugal, Prussia, Spain, and Russia," leaving the British nearly ruined.[1] While they were busy defending the empire, the colonists—particularly those born in the colonies—began to act and think as Americans, even as they remained loyal to the Crown. As the colonists became caught between old loyalties and their growing identities as Americans, the growing differences between the two cultures became apparent when the two armies were combined to fight the French a year into the war.

In 1755, a year after the war started, the British sent some 1,500 British and American troops to join American soldiers. To the dismay of the Americans, the battle-hardened British soldiers commandeered homes and property along their way to push the French back from the Ohio frontier. Soon, there would be 45,000 soldiers, half British and half American.[2] As the war dragged on, animosities grew between the American soldiers and the better-seasoned and better-provisioned British troops.

The cultural differences between them were stark. The British, for example, were fully invested in military rank and its privileges. They criticized their American counterparts for their lack of training, their lack of discipline, and their disregard for rank and class. In turn, the Americans resented the vulgarity, arrogance, and brutishness of the British. Worse, at the beginning of the war, the colonists had been promised by William Pitt, the new secretary of state in the British colonial government, that the Crown, not the colonies, would foot the cost of the expensive war.

When the British broke that promise by taxing the colonies without allowing them to represent themselves before Parliament, the colonists found themselves in a crisis. The Crown's move to tax the colonies to support the failing empire tested the Americans to the limit. Most colonists were loyal, if deeply disappointed with the Crown. Inciting the colonists to fight and win the American Revolution would take the strategic writing of Boston-based Sam Adams. In his newspaper, *Journal of Occurrences*, he developed a writing style that mimicked the real journalism of the day, though it was not. Instead of news based on verified facts, Adams published false and exaggerated stories about the British. How did this disinformation campaign help the Revolutionary cause? And, more generally, how did other forms of writing from the era appeal to the already growing sense of an American identity? To show the beginning of the colonial press and its relationship to propaganda, this chapter starts with Benjamin Harris's *Publick Occurrences*.

Defiant Beginnings: *Publick Occurrences*

In 1690, the first newspaper published in the American colonies met with disapproval from the British governor of Massachusetts. Although its publication was stopped after its initial issue on September 25, 1690, Benjamin Harris's *Publick Occurrences Both FORREIGN and DOMESTICK* showed how the dominant white Anglo-Saxon and Protestant (WASP) cultural values would define the American mainstream.

Harris makes it clear that British people (including those in the colonies) did not see the indigenous people as equals. Defining indigenous people in terms of their differences of race, language, dress, and even foods offered British a logical way to claim power over them and to take land from them. He held that the British colonists were the true American natives—not indigenous people, not the many enslaved Africans brought to the colonies as property, and not even other apparently "white" Europeans (mainly the French), whom they regarded as ungodly and inferior. The concept of white, Anglo-Saxon, Protestant supremacy is an ideal that remains part of American political life today.

We can see these dynamics at work in how Harris framed who belonged to the colonial public and who stood outside and threatened it. Harris's report on the first Thanksgiving seemed friendly enough. It read, "The Christianized *Indians* in some parts of *Plimouth*, have newly appointed a day of Thanksgiving to God for his Mercy in supplying their extream and pinching Necessities under their late want of Corn & for His giving them now a prospect of a very *Comfortable* Harvest. Their Example might be worth mentioning."[3] The apparent gratitude Harris described in his account of the Wampanoag people's generosity did not last long. Further down the single page of *Publick Occurrences*, Harris referred to other indigenous people who were fighting with the French against the British as "Barbarous."[4] The distinction that Harris was making between Christians and Catholics advantaged Protestants of the Church of England against Catholics. One historian described him as "a rabid anti-Catholic with an eye for the sensational." Harris reported an alleged sex scandal involving a "Popish priest . . . who . . . had occasion to make use of his Ladies Chamber maid," foreshadowing the sensationalism of the gossipy tabloid press by almost two centuries.

Although American journalism did not start free of British governance, its early practitioners did begin with a sense of a new founding mission. They also adhered to very strict libel laws governing who could sue the press. In this way, colonial journalists assumed that they could and should define the American outlook. They did so in terms that would help to set the main issues, belief systems, and resulting debates over the next two and a half centuries.

Establishing Press Freedom: The Zenger Trial

In the early American struggle for press freedom, the most significant test came in 1735 when printer Peter Zenger was tried for "seditious libel" in New York. Zenger had printed a newspaper, the *New York Journal*, for New York colonial governor William Cosby's political enemy, Judge Lewis Morris. According to colonial printer and historian Isaiah Thomas, "In December 1734 a writer in Bradford's *Gazette*, the oldest newspaper in the province, accused Zenger of publishing 'pieces tending to set the province in a flame, and to raise sedition and tumults.'"

Indeed, Morris had used the *Journal* to publish "strident articles and mock advertisements" ridiculing Governor Cosby for suing the previous governor to enrich himself. For publishing that unseemly fact, the governor sued Zenger, not Morris, for "seditious libel." According to historian Douglas Lee, "Seditious libel was defined as the intentional publication, without lawful excuse or justification, of written blame of any public man or of the law, or any institution established by the law." In a move that shows the importance of colonial printers to early journalism, Cosby apparently thought that striking at the printer would work best to undermine the newspaper. So he had Zenger jailed for eight months while waiting for his trial.

Aside from this early test of free speech, at stake in the Zenger trial was the principle of truth as a defense for libel. Although Cosby believed that the *Journal* had injured his reputation, what Morris wrote and Zenger printed was true. Therefore, Cosby was not just embarrassed by the *Journal's* harassment. He was within the traditions of English custom and common law, which held that "The greater the truth, the greater the libel." In this light, the law held that "truthful information could be even more dangerous than lies, because it was more believable."[5]

In Zenger's trial in August of the next year, in keeping with English law, the prosecutor, New York attorney general Richard Bradley, argued that the truth of the words published was not a valid defense. At a time when criticism of the government—*especially* legitimate criticism—was treated as a threat to the public order, the undemocratic goal of such laws was to maintain control, regardless of the faults of the government officials. Andrew Hamilton took a novel approach: he countered that publication alone should not be the standard for libel. Instead, he told the jury that the text must be false to constitute libel. Although his argument contradicted the established legal standard, Hamilton's appeal to his fellow New Yorkers prevailed and Zenger was acquitted. This victory did not change the law, but it allowed the colonial press to act with more freedom, because authorities, fearing similar contempt for the law, became hesitant to bring sedition cases to trial.[6] Never completely settled, the issue of sedition would be used as the basis of suspending free speech in moments of perceived threats to the United States from "aliens" or non-American citizens.

The Stamp Act: Growing Discontent in New England

In 1763, when the British defeated the French in North America and in India in the Seven Years' War, as the French and Indian War was known in England, their victories came at significant expense to the empire: Britain was nearly broke. As a result, many British political leaders saw the need for the American colonies to produce more revenues. In order to afford the expense of these faraway colonies, Parliament decided that the American colonists should bear the costs of the war, as well as the outlays for defending the still-expanding empire.

To raise revenues from the American colonists, Parliament passed a series of laws between 1764 and 1773 known as the Revenue Acts. They included the Plantation or Sugar Act of 1764, the Currency Act of 1764, the Stamp Act of 1765, the Townshend Acts of 1767, and the Tea Act of 1773. While each of these measures taxed a key part of the colonial economy, the Stamp Act affected printers most, because it placed high tariffs on paper of all kinds, especially newsprint.

British citizens at home were used to that kind of tax; a similar assessment had been in place in Britain for more than fifty years without complaint. But the colonists, who had no such law, objected. Above all, they were incensed at being taxed by an absentee government in London without having a voice in the matter. Their opposition to the Stamp Act took shape in the vigilante group known as the Sons of Liberty, a vigilante group led by Sam Adams to harass the British.[7]

The Tea Act produced the infamous Boston Tea Party, but other acts had greater reach through the trade routes between the American northeast and the Caribbean. The Sugar Act was intended to stop the smuggling of molasses by making the cost of molasses competitive with the black market that had undercut legitimate merchants. George Grenville, who represented the British ministry in the colonies, required that every shipment to and from American ports be documented. At first, the colonists were pleased when the Sugar Act reduced the duty imposed on molasses by half. A separate provision gave jurisdiction over smuggling cases to the admiralty courts, who were more likely to find the accused smugglers guilty than the colonial courts had been.

When the colonists learned of the Stamp Act in late May 1765, most of the colonies' twenty-five newspapers reacted against it. In particular, colonial merchants resented the imposition of "taxation without representation." As one historian pointed out, the tax on printing fell most heavily on printers and lawyers, the two groups most "capable of doing harm to the mother country."[8]

On October 31, 1765, the *New-Hampshire Gazette and Historical Chronicle* published an issue full of complaints about the Stamp Act. Above its masthead read the legend "This is the Day before the never-to-be-forgotten STAMP ACT was to take place in America." In the middle of the title banner sat the seal of George III, with the royal legend in French, "Dieu et mon Droit," or "God and My Right," the motto of the royal Arms of Britain expressing allegiance to the Crown.

The ambivalence of this presentation reflected the split among American newspapers over how to react to the Stamp Act. Some printers went out of business in the face of the tax. Others, like John Holt of the *New York Gazette and Post-Boy*, promised to defy the law through an available loophole: If a newspaper did not publish under its masthead, it could not be considered a taxable newspaper.[9]

The principle of freedom of the press had been articulated in 1755 by the *Boston Gazette* as the right of the press to monitor and report on the abuses of power of government in a way that was "essential to and coeval with all free Governments." That is why, ten years later, printers generally reacted to the Stamp Act as if their press freedoms were under assault. In one article reprinted in the *Boston Post-Boy* from the *Pennsylvania Journal and Weekly Advertiser* on October 7, 1765—just three weeks before the Stamp Act was to take effect—the colonists' willingness to break with the British Crown was apparent. The author signed himself "A True American" because anonymity was required to avoid British censure. He wrote, "In this time of complaint when the genius of America seems to droop her head under the weight load imposed on us by parliament, I think it my duty to say a word or two upon this much canvassed subject."

The author wrote several hundred words on the subject as an argument against the British demands of more money from the colonies to finance the empire. He claimed that the colonies were equally impoverished by the war, or, more nearly, that the absence of the cash flow that the war had brought to American merchants was in itself too dear. He argued, "During the last war, when armies were collected in America, and trade carried on briskly, we had plenty of money, but now, the causes of this being removed, we are almost quite drained of our cash, and left, by the late acts of Parliament, and new regulations with respect to the Spanish trade, destitute of the means to pay our debts."[10]

The article made a case for the colonies' own financial predicament. It read, "It is the misfortune of this country (Britain) to have an expensive turn beyond its circumstances; to remedy this requires much care and wise conduct." As he calculated the ballooning trade deficit faced by the colonies—from £300,000 in 1765 to a projected £3 million in ten years—the author suggested that "it might have been prudent in the Parliament to have provided some method by which we might have been enabled to pay our portion of the tax, at the same time it was passed." But that opportunity was gone, and the American sense of independence from Britain was growing.[11]

While "True American" was making a nuanced case for the opportunity missed by the Crown to direct "taxation *with* representation," he was also establishing the dual American objections to British taxation: It trampled the colonists' right of self-determination, and it interfered with American capitalism. The two principal types of colonists affected by the Stamp Act—lawyers and printers—were likely less idealists in the defense of the rights of man than merchants in defense of the right to earn money.

The *Boston Gazette* also provided a prominent forum for objections to the Stamp Act. Isaiah Thomas reports that the most distinguished revolutionary patriots in Boston, several years before 1775, frequently convened at the *Gazette*'s office and also at the *Massachusetts Spy*. He wrote, "It may be truly said, that in those meetings were concocted the measures of opposition to the British acts of Parliament for taxing the colonies—measures which led to, and terminated in the independence of our country."[12]

Most of these writers wrote anonymously. We do know that Sam Adams, Benjamin Edes, and John Gill figured prominently among the writers who militated for home rule. Adams, alone, was responsible for hundreds of political essays and news articles, often under the pen name of "Vendix the Avenger," although he used dozens of other made-up names.

In addition to news stories about current events, Adams wrote broadsides—poster-size declarations—against the British, which could be posted in public houses, on tree trunks, and in other public places. Because many colonists could not read, broadsides were meant to be read aloud. Adams also wrote and distributed pamphlets for the cause. Taken together, these three forms of writing—news stories, broadsides, and pamphlets—are described as his "journalistic strategy" for reaching the various reading audiences he wanted to incite.[13]

To quell the colonists' resistance, in 1768, the British government decided to send detachments of royal troops from all over the empire to Boston. Dickerson writes, "The sending of troops to Boston was a most serious episode in the history of the empire." Indeed, the Stamp Act and the British decision to garrison, or house, the troops in the homes of local residents incited Adams, as well as the majority of Bostonians. They believed that the British had broken their social contract with the colonies by taxing them unfairly and by imposing military rule. There was now real concern in London that the colonies might revolt.[14]

The *Journal of Occurrences*

To take advantage of this tipping point, Sam Adams and his rebel cadre of journalists weaponized a new kind of American journalism against the British by writing and distributing the *Journal of Occurrences*. A venue for early form of fake news, the newspaper was also published as the *Journal of Transactions* and a *Journal of the Times*. Throughout, the paper's brief, provocative posts built outrage against the British among the colonists. From 1768 until the next year, when the British withdrew from Boston scorned and defeated, the *Journal of Occurrences* presented diarylike entries breathlessly, falsely, and believably—each nugget describing another mistreatment of Bostonians by the king's soldiers.

On October 2, 1768, the daily entry closed with the italicized assurance that "The above *Journal* you are desired to publish for the general satisfaction, it being strictly fact." But that was not so. Rather, the "news" it presented about the misbehavior of the British troops was often exaggerated or fabricated by Adams and others.[15] Where the term *journalism* suggests accurate news reports based on evidence, Adams's writing represented, instead, a basic kind of propaganda. His strategic lies and disinformation were intended to incite the colonists against the British.

In the *Journal's* accounts, the offensive nature of the British occupation of free Boston in support of the Stamp Act was topped only by their violent behavior. Having experienced the violent behavior of the English army during the French and Indian War, the colonists may have had a negative image of the British military. Certainly, Adams was prepared to play on that historical memory.

In Boston, although the events reported there actually happened, Adams and his colleagues colored their accounts freely. Sometimes they invented quotes, a serious sin in journalism. Part of this decidedly unjournalistic behavior reflected the ways in which any march to war makes the enemy so dehumanized that their lives may be taken for a strategic purpose.[16] So it was after the Boston Massacre on March 5, 1770, that the *Journal's* propaganda defined the British as the problem and primed the colonists for a revolutionary war. Two themes dominated the newspaper's reports: The menacing behavior by the occupying troops, particularly against women, and the corruption of the Customs Commissioners who mismanaged the collection of taxes in Boston.[17]

A "news" entry on December 12, 1768, presented an example of the fears that the writers at the *Journal* created for the unassuming reader: "A married lady of this town was the other evening, when passing from one house to another, taken hold of by a soldier: who other ways behaved to her with great rudeness; a woman near Long Lane was stopped by several soldiers, one of whom cried out seize her and carry her off; she was much surprised, but luckily got shelter in a house nearby." To be sure, the suggestion that a British soldier might sexually assault a colonial woman was not beyond belief.

At its close, the story also showed the colonists' developing position against the beastly British. It read, "The inhabitants (the colonists) however still preserve their temper and a proper decorum; in this we have doubtless disappointed and vexed the enemies. . . . We cannot but flatter ourselves that Administration must soon be convinced of the propriety and necessity of putting affairs upon the old footing, which experience now demonstrates to be best for both countries." The story's final words, which refer to the "enemies" and to "both countries," showed Adams's goal of giving the colonists a way to see themselves fighting for independence.[18] Story by story, he was coaching Americans to free themselves from George III. In this sense, Adams's *Journal of Occurrences* became a site for forming a sense of a distinct American public.

Persuading the colonists to break with the Crown depended on getting the word out. Colonial newspapers regularly reprinted content from other newspapers as an economy and as a way to broadcast shared views. In this effort, Adams had help from John Holt, publisher of the *New York Journal*, who reprinted the first entry of the *Journal of Occurrences* on September 29, 1768.[19] Marking a significant development in substance of the early American newspaper, the *Journal* was the first to publish politically charged descriptions of events in the colonies. Moreover, it was the only source of news then available to London about the most important colonies in the Empire.[20]

By distributing the *Journal*'s news copy to other newspapers throughout the colonies where it could be reprinted, the news of the day could go viral. In more formal terms, the network established by Holt worked very much like the wire service system we now know as the Associated Press, which reports and sells news from all over the nation to today's news outlets.[21]

Ambivalence and Turning Points

Deciding to break away from England was difficult. Many were still looking for a way to mend the relationship. By the time that they had thrown off the Stamp Act in 1765, many Americans felt that they had been grossly misrepresented to the British government by the British colonial officials. In their own defense, they "planned an extraordinary campaign to supply the King, both houses of Parliament, the British public, and the people in other colonies with a truer picture of actual conditions." In what amounted to a public relations promotional campaign, the Americans employed all kinds of writing to explain themselves. Of course, their challenge to anti-British public opinion depended on their strategic use of taxable paper, which included "personal letters, newspaper articles, resolutions, and representations of town meetings and of the House of Representatives, and even the protests of a great convention of delegates from the Massachusetts towns." Still, writing to the public did not mean reaching the entire public. Many colonists were illiterate and were read to by their peers. But that was normal. The average colonist had no reluctance about asking a literate friend what a broadside poster or a newspaper said.[22]

Expressing their desire to be considered full-fledged citizens—especially with regard to representation in the Parliament—colonial leaders turned to a culture of writing. The pen and the press were their tools for conveying the gravity of the problem to the wider American public. As this circumstance tightened, the Americans increasingly expected to be represented in Parliament. And as popular opinion turned against the Crown, they increasingly depended on Adams's propaganda as the one channel that could connect their aspirations to political rights and, ultimately, to independence.

When British troops fired on an unarmed group of colonists in Boston on March 5, 1770, Samuel Adams, Benjamin Edes, and John Gill seized the chance to inflame events for the colonial cause in the Boston *Gazette*. When a group of six British soldiers confronted a rowdy crowd of locals assembled to protest what they had read in Adams's newspaper, the violence left five colonists dead and three others mortally wounded. This street fight that had flared into mayhem that evening effectively sparked the Revolution. Afterward, much of what actually happened and why was questioned, but the impact of Adams's genius was not in dispute after he and his allies had told the story in the eyepopping language of a scandal sheet.

As shown in the *Boston Gazette* on March 12, 1770, they used vivid language in "diarylike" bursts to incite public opinion against the British, first by calling the battle a "massacre." The emotion and alarm conveyed to the readers of the *Gazette* and the three-dozen other colonial newspapers that might have reprinted such stories mattered far more than the facts. Distributed as "news," this highly effective propaganda sounded the call to arms.[23]

Parliament had portrayed the colonists as given to "mob violence." Writing to his superior in England, Lord Hillsborough, Massachusetts governor Francis Bernard complained bitterly about the colonists' rudeness and disloyalty. He angrily decried the "collection of impudent, virulent, and seditious lies, perversions of the truth and misrepresentations" that appeared in Adams's paper.[24]

Unimpeded by facts or, perhaps, reaching for a higher kind of truth, the *Gazette*'s highly animated account began by setting the scene of a soldier recklessly flashing a large sword as four boys came by: "A few minutes after nine o'clock four youths, named Edward Archbald, William Merchant, Francis Archbald, and John Leech, jun., came down Cornhill together, and separating at Doctor Loring's corner, the two former were passing the narrow alley leading to Mr. Murray's barrack in which was a soldier brandishing a broad sword of an uncommon size against the walls, out of which he struck fire plentifully."

The narrator tells how quickly the nameless soldiers found their many weapons, including a "broadsword," "tongs and a shovel," "drawn cutlasses, clubs, and bayonets." No sooner had they met than the soldiers attacked the lads who had come to see what was happening:

> A person of mean countenance armed with a large cudgel bore him company. Edward Archbald admonished Mr. Merchant to take care of the sword, on which the soldier turned round and struck Archbald on the arm, then pushed at Merchant and pierced through his clothes inside the arm close to the armpit and grazed the skin. Merchant then struck the soldier with a short stick he had; and the other person ran to the barrack and brought with him two soldiers, one armed with a pair of tongs, the other with a shovel. He with the tongs pursued Archbald back through the alley, collared and laid him over the head with the tongs.

With a crowd rushing to the scene, the mismatch was on:

> The noise brought people together; and John Hicks, a young lad, coming up, knocked the soldier down but let him get up again; and more lads gathering, drove them back to the barrack where the boys stood some time as it were to keep them in. In less than a minute ten or twelve of them came out with drawn cutlasses, clubs, and bayonets and set upon the unarmed boys and young folk who stood them a little while but, finding the inequality of their equipment, dispersed.

When another local, Samuel Atwood, challenged the soldiers, they cried for murder, attacking him brutally:

> On hearing the noise, one Samuel Atwood came up to see what was the matter; and entering the alley from dock square, heard the latter part of the combat; and when the boys had dispersed he met the ten or twelve soldiers aforesaid rushing down the alley towards the square and asked them if they intended to murder people? They answered Yes, by Gd, root and branch! With that one of them struck Mr. Atwood with a club which was repeated by another; and being unarmed, he turned to go off and received a wound on the left shoulder which reached the bone and gave him much pain. Retreating a few steps, Mr. Atwood met two officers and said, gentlemen, what is the matter? They answered, you'll see by and by. Immediately after, those heroes appeared in the square, asking where were the boogers? where were the cowards?

The real cowards, Adams claimed, were the British soldiers who had attacked innocent American teens. The British were nothing but howling bullies out of control. In their bloodlust, they went on a rampage against innocent bystanders:

But notwithstanding their fierceness to naked [unarmed] men, one of them advanced towards a youth who had a split of a raw stave in his hand and said, damn them, here is one of them. But the young man seeing a person near him with a drawn sword and good cane ready to support him, held up his stave in defiance; and they quietly passed by him up the little alley by Mr. Silsby's to King Street where they attacked single and unarmed persons till they raised much clamour, and then turned down Cornhill Street, insulting all they met in like manner and pursuing some to their very doors.

As the violence attracted a much bigger crowd, Adams described the British militia fixing their bayonets for battle:

Thirty or forty persons, mostly lads, being by this means gathered in King Street, Capt. Preston with a party of men with charged bayonets, came from the main guard to the commissioner's house, the soldiers pushing their bayonets, crying, make way! They took place by the custom house and, continuing to push to drive the people off pricked some in several places, on which they were clamorous and, it is said, threw snow balls.

And then it happened! Guns were fired! Men were down! And to show how high the stakes were and how little the British cared, Adams wrote, "The Captain commanded them to fire; and more snow balls coming, he again said, damn you, fire, be the consequence what it will!" By dramatizing this pivotal moment, the *Journal's* writer knew that the "consequence" would be a revolt.

From there, the scene deteriorated as a "townsman" struck back at the soldiers: "One soldier then fired, and a townsman with a cudgel struck him over the hands with such force that he dropped his firelock; and, rushing forward, aimed a blow at the Captain's head which grazed his hat and fell pretty heavy upon his arm. However, the soldiers continued the fire successively till seven or eight or, as some say, eleven guns were discharged."

This sudden taste of blood or, at least, a fictionalized version of it, must have carried the *Journal's* readers away with its adrenaline-fueled chaos. To top it all, when help for the victims of this unprovoked "massacre" came, Adams reported that the British had attacked them, too! He relayed his imagined description, writing, "By this fatal manoeuvre three men were laid dead on the spot and two more struggling for life; but what showed a degree of cruelty unknown to British troops, at least since the house of Hanover has directed their operation, was an attempt to fire upon or push with their bayonets the persons who undertook to remove the slain and wounded!"

Having orchestrated a version of the fight that wholly demonized the troops, their officers, and the empire in general, the *Gazette's* writer began the work of canonizing the nation's first martyrs to the colonists' now rolling cause. In graphic detail, he described the wounds of the fallen, giving the reader a sense of the crimson American blood spilled in the pure snow of King Street: "Mr. Benjamin Leigh, now undertaker in the Delph manufactory, came up and after some conversation with Capt. Preston relative to his conduct in this affair, advised him to draw off his men, with which he complied. The dead are Mr. Samuel Gray, killed on the spot, the ball entering his head and beating off a large portion of his skull."

Significantly in a colony where many white citizens enslaved people, the first death reported in the revolution was an African American:

A mulatto man named Crispus Attucks, who was born in Framingham, but lately belonged to New-Providence and was here in order to go for North Carolina, also killed instantly, two balls entering his breast, one of them in special goring the right lobe of the lungs and a great part of the liver most horribly.

Mr. James Caldwell, mate of Capt. Morton's vessel, in like manner killed by two balls entering his back.

Mr. Samuel Maverick, a promising youth of seventeen years of age, son of the widow Maverick, and an apprentice to Mr. Greenwood, ivory-turner, mortally wounded; a ball went through his belly and was cut out at his back. He died the next morning.

A lad named Christopher Monk, about seventeen years of age, an apprentice to Mr. Walker, shipwright, wounded; a ball entered his back about four inches above the left kidney near the spine and was cut out of the breast on the same side. Apprehended he will die.

A lad named John Clark, about seventeen years of age, whose parents live at Medford, and an apprentice to Capt. Samuel Howard of this town, wounded; a ball entered just above his groin and came out at his hip on the opposite side. Apprehended he will die.

Mr. Edward Payne of this town, merchant, standing at his entry door received a ball in his arm which shattered some of the bones.

Mr. John Green, tailor, coming up Leverett's Lane, received a ball just under his hip and lodged in the under part of his thigh, which was extracted.

Mr. Robert Patterson, a seafaring man, who was the person that had his trousers shot through in Richardson's affair, wounded; a ball went through his right arm, and he suffered a great loss of blood.

Mr. Patrick Carr, about thirty years of age, who worked with Mr. Field, leather breeches-maker in Queen Street, wounded; a ball entered near his hip and went out at his side.

A lad named David Parker, an apprentice to Mr. Eddy, the wheelwright, wounded; a ball entered his thigh.[25]

The *Boston Gazette*'s vivid tale of the massacre applied the format and appearance of journalism to create the propaganda needed to persuade Americans and otherwise loyal British colonists to commit fully to a war for independence.

Noting that the eighteenth-century reader was familiar with conspiracy theories, historian Peter Messer explains the strategic advantage gained by Sam Adams and his band of patriot agitators through them. By spreading conspiracy theories linking the massacre to a much bigger, if unspecified, plot against Boston by the British, Adams produced a surge of political power for his Sons of Liberty and other patriots through the fear and confusion he sowed in the *Gazette*.

Looking for a way to start a revolution, Adams had found what he needed in his suspicious readers. Much like many Americans today, they believed in fictional political conspiracies and were prepared to defend them violently. Historian Peter Messer explained that "any action for which no observable cause could be identified must be the result of an unseen conspiratorial hand pursuing some malicious, hidden end." Adams saw a strategic opening in their confusion and ignorance. The chance to lead a public investigation of the incident would lend him more authority than the violent mobs of the day. Besides, he could write the story his way. In this sleight of hand, Adams the propagandist, trickster, and politician gained an enormous advantage over the British, whom no American would believe again in the face of Adams's useful lies.[26]

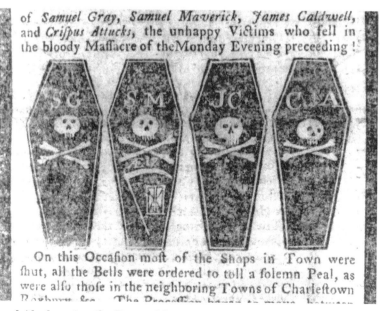

A broadside decrying the Boston Massacre.

Thomas Paine's *Common Sense*

By 1774, the colonies were putting together the committee structures needed to form a government of their own. In the spring of 1775, the Crown recognized the rebellion, and the war began in earnest. Thomas Paine, a struggling British tradesman, who had previously been a corset maker and tax collector, had recently met Benjamin Franklin in London. Inspired by Franklin to move to Philadelphia, Paine began his writing career there in January 1775 as editor of *Pennsylvania Magazine*. Although Franklin had recommended him, his employer, Robert Aitken, thought his writing against the British—and, especially, against the king—was too inflammatory. He was soon out of work.

At a time when many colonists were still cool to the idea of a break with the British, Paine revised the work that Aitken had found too strong. Published as a pamphlet, *Common Sense*, his argument called for a revolt against George III and his government. Although Paine's form of persuasion differed from Adams's—he dealt in facts—his intention to incite public opinion matched Adams's aims completely. As inspiration, Paine's use of unifying symbolism compared to the prose drafted for the Declaration of Independence by Adams, Thomas Jefferson, and Franklin. Because the population of the colonies was about 2.3 million, Paine's work had even more immediate influence. As many as 120,000 copies of *Common Sense* were published and distributed in January 1776. By the end of the war, more than 500,000 copies were in print, an unheard-of figure at the time.[27]

In bold language meant to shock the complacent into action, *Common Sense* directly rejected the right of the king to rule the colonies. Paine argued instead that governments that rule least rule best. Under the heading "ON THE ORIGIN AND DESIGN OF GOVERNMENT IN GENERAL, WITH CONCISE REMARKS ON THE ENGLISH CONSTITUTION," he made his not so "concise" case for "self-rule." By attacking the validity of the monarchy, the British constitution, and the Houses of Lords and Commons, he made his mark and more. No one had ever dared to write publicly against the king before.

As he railed against the idea of government. Paines's informal political theory struck original chords of libertarianism, conservatism, and even anarchy that would surface in American political life to come. His main point held that the British government was not only not the solution to the colonists' needs for "happiness" and "security," but, according to Paine, all governments were the source of individuals' problems. He began: "SOME writers have so confounded society with government, as to leave little or no distinction between them; whereas they are not only different, but have different origins. Society is produced by our wants, and government by our wickedness; the former promotes our happiness POSITIVELY by uniting

Title page of the *Common Sense* pamphlet.

our affections, the latter NEGATIVELY by restraining our vices. The one encourages intercourse, the other creates distinctions. The first is a patron, the last a punisher."

Describing the rule of any government as a symptom of the inevitable moral failings of the individual in society, Paine struck a utopian tone. If it were beyond the individual to be moral in a natural state, then it would be better to have no government at all. In his disgust, he identified the British government as not just an empty solution to the deficits of colonial life, but an aggravation to it.[28] Worse, that same, disabling government made the colonists pay for its inadequate services through unrepresented taxation—an issue every colonist understood.

Lamenting this unjust state of affairs, he wrote,

Society in every state is a blessing, but Government, even in its best state, is but a necessary evil; in its worst state an intolerable one: for when we suffer, or are exposed to the same miseries BY A GOVERNMENT, which we might expect in a country WITHOUT GOVERNMENT, our calamity is heightened by reflecting that we furnish the means by which we suffer.

Government, like dress, is the badge of lost innocence; the palaces of kings are built upon the ruins of the bowers of paradise. For were the impulses of conscience clear, uniform and irresistibly obeyed, man would need no other lawgiver; but that not being the case, he finds it necessary to surrender up a part of his property to furnish means for the protection of the rest; and this he is induced to do by the same prudence which in every other case advises him, out of two evils to choose the least.

Allowing that, at least in principle, some monarchies might be useful, he indicted the British government for what he saw as its complete incompetence. He took the government in London to task part by part. First, the constitution was a bloated, archaic mess. Second, the "peers," or the House of Lords, served royal tradition and, therefore, themselves only. And, third, the "new Republican" House of Commons inspired little more confidence than the first two. Next, Paine wholly ridiculed the king amid this circular system of fools:

As the same constitution which gives the Commons a power to check the King by withholding the supplies, gives afterwards the King a power to check the Commons, by empowering him to reject their other bills; it again supposes that the King is wiser than those whom it has already supposed to be wiser than him. A mere absurdity!

There is something exceedingly ridiculous in the composition of Monarchy; it first excludes a man from the means of information, yet empowers him to act in cases where the highest judgment is required. The state of a king shuts him from the World, yet the business of a king requires him to know it thoroughly; wherefore the different parts, by unnaturally opposing and destroying each other, prove the whole character to be absurd and useless.

Having shifted from logic to name-calling—shocking, but attention-getting to the American ear—Paine continued his essay for forty pages or more, demolishing the king and the Parliament at every turn.

Because he wrote in a style geared to the common reader, he struck a nerve. *Common Sense*, the nation's first bestseller, became the topic of discussion into the summer of 1776. Rebel patriots championed his message, while loyalists published counterarguments and challenges to Paine's case for independence. The reach of the pamphlet was amazing. One copy was sold for every 12 people living in the American colonies.[29]

Once the war had begun, George Washington enlisted Paine to write a series of twelve essays to inspire the troops. Published as "The Crisis Essays," their poetical language has been familiar even to schoolchildren ever since: "These are the times that try men's souls. The summer soldier and the sunshine patriot will in this crisis shrink from the service of his country, but that he stands it NOW, deserves the love and thanks of man and woman."[30] Paine's extensive body of work spanned the intellectual and political universe of the day.

Yet, for all of his services to the nation, he died an outsider. Having lost or alienated most of his friends through his controversial political positions—he had opposed slavery and championed the French Revolution, among other partisan points—Paine died discredited and shunned on June 8, 1809, at the age of seventy-two in New York. Just six people attended his funeral.

A Legacy of Dissent

The whole question of freedom of the press remained a point of contention, even after the First Amendment was ratified in 1791. Its language, which mandated that "Congress shall make no law . . . abridging the freedom of speech or of the press" was called into question when the Federalists under President John Adams passed the Alien and Sedition Act of 1798. The restrictions on press freedom there reflected the government's fear that non-Americans, principally French and Irish immigrants, might undermine the United States by bringing their own revolutionary ideas to our shores. The Sedition Act represented the Federalists' impulse to stifle free speech in order to silence these foreign influences. Arguing that the First Amendment only forbade censorship, not punishment after publication, the act made it illegal to

> write, print, utter or publish, or cause it to be done, or assist in it, any false, scandalous, and malicious writing against the government of the United States, or either House of Congress, or the President, with intent to defame, or bring either into contempt or disrepute, or to excite against either the hatred of the people of the United States, or to stir up sedition, or to excite unlawful combinations against the government, or to resist it, or to aid or encourage hostile designs of foreign nations.[31]

As far back as the Zenger case and its focus on seditious libel, the notion of sedition illustrates the ever-unsettled meaning of the free press, even among those who enshrined it in the Bill of Rights.[32] These moments, which have typically seen civil rights and press freedoms reduced, include the 1789 Alien and Sedition Acts in reaction to the French Revolution, the 1918 Sedition Act in reaction to the Russian Revolution, and the 2001 Patriot Act in reaction to the attacks on the World Trade Center and the Pentagon on September 11, 2001.

Free speech is not the norm for journalism worldwide. In America, the idea grew in part from conditions that allowed the colonial press to function with less oversight than in Europe. That lack of control allowed early colonial newspapers to go as far as encouraging rebellion against the government. This is precisely why most governments worldwide did not—and do not—tolerate freedom of the press.

2

Writing against Slavery

The Abolitionist Press

The practice of slavery was wedged into the Constitution of the United States in 1787 when northern anti-slavery federalists reached a "three-fifths compromise" with their southern, pro-slavery counterparts. At stake during the Philadelphia Constitutional convention was how to plan a new American government. Solving this problem opened a complex debate over how to address the hard-won opportunities produced by the revolution itself, namely the need for taxation under a system of equal representation. Although the word, "slavery," did not appear in the Constitution, the debate also called for balancing the interests of large and small states, as well as those of southern states where slavery was central to the economy, and their northern counterparts.

Several objections quickly arose. On the one hand, counting enslaved people (and small landowners) would have meant giving more congressional seats—and power—to the southern states. They would have paid more federal taxes, as well. On the other hand, the southern states objected to a system proposed by northerners that was based on a state's free population, alone. Within this mix, enslaved people were considered to be property by southerners.

The establishment of the Senate gave the smaller states equal footing with more populous states at that key level. Out of this dealmaking, slavery would remain legally protected and enslaved people would count for three-fifths of a person in the population-based drawing of Congressional districts.

Although some framers of the Constitution hoped that slavery would gradually diminish in importance and disappear as a result of economic choices, it would not. Instead, technological innovations made the cultivation of cotton increasingly lucrative and slavery became even more deeply entrenched in the southern states where the crop was grown. Powerful economic forces coalesced in defense of the institution of slavery and defended its legal legitimacy. Before 1850, all but two US presidents and most Supreme Court justices owned slaves. Auctions of enslaved people were routinely held within sight of the US Capitol building. Rather than becoming more marginal, the question of slavery was at the very heart of US economics, culture, and politics.

Forerunners of Abolitionist Strategy

Beginning in 1827 with *Freedom's Journal*, newspapers published by Black people offered slaves and freedman a redemptive idea of their place within the "chosen nation." Their writing offered a way for formerly enslaved people to reclaim themselves and their devastated families and communities from the traumas of slavery. The Black experience of America was and remains deeply affected by the longtime experience of slavery. As the historian Benjamin Fagan explained, "The suffering that Black Americans endured in the United States solidified their own connection to the biblical Israelites as God's chosen nation." Expressive of their genuine desire to join the wider public, the inspirational idea of "chosen-ness" upended the original, seventeenth-century notion of a white-governed America as the "new Jerusalem."[1]

Because of their experience with slavery, Black Americans' version of exceptionalism was entirely different from the uncritical beliefs of most whites. At the time, the white mainstream believed that slavery was a normal business practice, even the natural order of the world.[2] By sharp contrast, in an 1833 speech, Black activist Maria Stewart described the nation as "a seller of slaves and men's souls." Unable to reconcile slavery with the wider claims of America's God-given favor, Stewart called the nation, instead, "the "great city of Babylon." She knew that her audience would appreciate her Old Testament reference to the wickedness of that ancient city. Far from accepting the America of her day as favored by God, she was calling out the immorality and hypocrisy of America's enslavement of some four million people.[3]

Stewart's use of religious language came out of a broader, evangelical millennial movement in the country known in the 1820s and 1830s as the "Second Great Awakening." Its followers accepted the popular Protestant belief that Jesus would return to this world when the people showed their "purity." Some believers set 1840 as the year of Jesus's return. Samuel Cornish, by then the editor of the *Colored American,* "expected the arrival of a millennium brought about by the reformation of earthly institutions and cast the fight for Black freedom as part of this larger effort."[4] Further, according to Fagan, "Being Black, more than any other factor, qualified one to be part of God's chosen nation."[5]

For believers, the spiritual horizon of Black chosen-ness initially seemed unlimited. Given "Blackness as the marker of chosen-ness, and by extension, of a special destiny," millenialists—those waiting for the end of the world and the beginning of heaven—were set "to lead the world to holy perfection." Coming as it did from the depths of slavery, this collective hope went beyond abolition. It led slaves to expect "the transformation of the American nation into a place where they finally, fully belonged."[6] When Jesus failed to return to "destroy their captors as he had destroyed those who had enslaved the Israelites," as *The Colored American* had promised, the newspaper "began imagining the United States not as the representative of the chosen American nation but as its oppressor."[7]

As Fagan explained, "From 1827 on . . . Black newspapers, such as *Freedom's Journal* and the *Colored American*, offered antebellum Black Americans outlets in the most important medium of the era."[8] Coinciding as it did with the early abolitionist movement, this moment of self-recognition also gave Black Americans their own space at the start of the predominately white-led abolition movement. As the historian Stephen Kantrowitz concluded, while "colored citizens failed to remake the nation as they had hoped . . ., they nonetheless left it forever changed."[9]

Early Forms of the News

Apart from the small Black press, the mainstream news delivery system that would make the abolition movement possible developed during two key periods. The first had begun in 1783, the year in which the Americans won the Revolutionary War. At that time, postrevolutionary newspapers were edited by local printers for local consumption. Without reporters, whose role would not develop for several decades, news from the world abroad came in the form of reprinted articles, shipping schedules, essays, and letters. At the time, political conflicts over how the new nation would govern itself were pulsing through the roots of the postal delivery system. This early information network depended on printers in different parts of the country making gatekeeping choices about which opinions to reprint to fill their newspapers.

The American postal system was designed as the delivery system to support the nation's growing number of newspapers supplying information to fuel a growing democracy. The farsighted Post Office Act of 1792 provided for a "massive federal program" to build the roads that would carry mail across the country. The internet of its day, this intentionally overbuilt infrastructure combined the bureaucratic scale needed to build out such a giant plan with the ability to connect each individual voter with the rest of the nation and the world. Like the World Wide Web but with roads, its designers could not have predicted who would use it. But nineteenth-century media-savvy political actors of all stripes joined in, from the expected newspaper editors and printers to Andrew Jackson's early partisans, William Lloyd Garrison and his abolitionists, and others.

The democratic goals that drove the postal plan was to "produce a kind of geographic equality that would match the nation's political equality." The word *equality* had its limitations, of course. Still, for the first half of the nineteenth-century, this early distributive network gave every white male property owner access to a national information network that linked him to the government and to the press.

The Postal Act "massively and intentionally subsidized newspapers" by lowering postal rates for newspapers even below the cost of mailing letters and by providing free mail services among all newspapers nationwide. This pair of built-in advantages created an information subsidy for newspapers through the first half of the nineteenth century.[10] The act allowed printers and editors to send and receive the content they typically reprinted from other papers regularly at very low cost.

This environment meant that no newspaper was truly local. Rather, the Postal Act enabled individual newspapers to access and reprint national and international news economically. The cross-fertilization gave printers and editors a powerful role in selecting their content and readers access to content from the wider world, whether from friend or foe. It did not, however, foresee the use of this powerful and wide-open system by social movements and political parties to advance their agendas.[11]

For political partisans of the late eighteenth century, the hot issues of the day were how much authority to give the federal government, how to finance federal debt, and what position to take in the ongoing political contest between France and Britain. To this list, Garrison sought to add—or more accurately, to popularize through moral force—the abolition of slavery. Garrison began this work in the 1820s, when partisan editors developed the circulation strategy using the postal delivery system to target inflammatory political messages to regional and even local partisan newspapers—the hotter, the better—to get readers' attention. Garrison would adopt this strategy. The openness of this system to party candidates willing to write dramatic, even violent, columns and essays would be apparent in Garrison's revolutionary style just a decade later.

By the election of 1824, perhaps no one appreciated the strategic advantage of distributing heated political writing through the postal service more than Andrew Jackson. By 1822, when he was first nominated for the presidency, he had already found strong newspapers to represent his rough, populist image and platform issues. Moreover, he had identified strongly partisan editors who would represent his positions to voters. Jackson more than anyone else of his day understood how to use the partisan press. A specific talent came from being able to mobilize different messages to different constituencies within a single political campaign. As a media strategist, he was years ahead of the field.

Beginning at about the same time, Garrison would view the narrow scope of that kind of journalism as a moral failure. Where Jackson injected customized political messaging into the postal system to attract specific voters, Garrison had just one issue and one goal: He felt the weight not just of American abolitionism but of the international basis of abolitionism. He was particularly sensitive here, because England had abolished slavery in 1833. For that reason, in the *Liberator*, the partisan press became a target. Garrison saw that the partisan press was guilty of supporting even pro-slavery news instead of adhering to the strict abolitionism he knew. Yet he also saw a way to take advantage of that fault, because he knew how the party press took strategic advantage of the federal postal distribution system. He saw that supporters nationwide would reprint his anti-slavery commentary as the moral truth. He understood that his opponents would reprint the same articles as lies. Either way, he got the cause of abolition much-needed attention. He also knew (or at least hoped) that the abolitionist press would be as temporary as the movement.

Early Abolitionists as Journalists

Never one to shrink from conflict, Thomas Paine observed that the colonists were fond of saying that taxation without representation amounted to their enslavement."[12] Paine helped to found the first anti-slavery society in America on April 14, 1775, in Philadelphia. But it would be decades until a national abolition movement would gather momentum. The effort would be aided by a rising abolitionist press and the abolition of slavery in the state of New York in 1827. In 1831, Garrison founded the *Liberator* in Boston and, two years later, the American Anti-Slavery Society in Philadelphia. By 1840, there were two thousand chapters nationwide with as many as two hundred thousand members.[13]

The national movement had been anticipated and influenced by the work of two Black journalists. In 1827, Samuel Cornish (1795–1858) and John Russwurm (1799–1851) became coeditors of the first African American newspaper in the nation, *Freedom's Journal*, which they published for two years in New York. Cornish later edited a paper, *The Weekly Advocate*, which was renamed *The Rights of All*. In 1837, he assumed the coeditorship of the *Colored American* along with the locally well known Reverend Charles B.

WALKER'S

A P P E A L,

With a Brief Sketch of his Life.

BY

HENRY HIGHLAND GARNET.

AND ALSO

GARNET'S ADDRESS

TO THE SLAVES OF THE UNITED STATES OF AMERICA.

The frontispiece and title page of David Walker's *Appeal*, 1848.

Ray (1807–86). Although limited in their scope and reach, these newspapers showed the wide diversity of beliefs about slavery that was held among African Americans just before the founding of the Anti-Slavery Society. In 1833, for example, the establishment-oriented Cornish, a Presbyterian minister, rejected efforts to help runaway slaves remain in the North. Yet he joined Garrison in founding a New York branch of the Anti-Slavery Society.

In 1829, Russwurm had joined the campaign by the American Colonization Society to send enslaved people—most of whom were born in America—to the newly formed nation of Liberia on the western African coast.[14] David Walker (1796–1830), an African American subscription agent for *Freedom's Journal*, fiercely rejected the colonization effort. He explicitly challenged the dominant belief among whites that slaves were racially inferior. In his pamphlet, "*Walker's Appeal, in Four Articles; Together with a Preamble, to the Coloured Citizens of the World, but in Particular, and Very Expressly, to Those of the United States of America, Written in Boston, State of Massachusetts, September 28, 1829,* Walker called for African Americans to fight the racialism of slavery at all costs. In *Appeal No. 2*, he wrote, not asking, but demanding the recognition of the apparent injustices of slavery:

> Are we MEN!!—I ask you, O my brethren! are we MEN? Did our Creator make us to be slaves to dust and ashes like ourselves? Are they not dying worms as well as we? Have they not to make their appearance before

the tribunal of Heaven, answer for the deeds done in the body, as well as we? Have we any other Master but Jesus Christ alone? Is he not their Master as well as ours?—What right then, have we to obey and call any other Master, but Himself? How we could be so *submissive* to a gang of men, whom we cannot tell whether they are *as good* as ourselves or not, I never could conceive. However, this is shut up with the Lord, and we cannot precisely tell—but I declare, we judge men by their works.

As he continued to describe the terrible past and the uncertain future of violence by white Americans against black Americans, he charged that "[T]he whites have always been an unjust, jealous, unmerciful, avaricious and bloodthirsty set of beings, always seeking after power and authority.[15]

If white violence against black citizens would not stop, the abolitionist press would not concede. Elijah Lovejoy (1802–37), a Presbyterian minister, newspaper publisher, and ardent abolitionist, began his newspaper, the *St. Louis Observer*, in St. Louis, where his unrelenting moral attacks on slavery had made him an outcast.[16] By moving across the Mississippi River from St. Louis, Missouri, a slave state, to Alton in the free state of Illinois, Lovejoy sought to escape the censure of mainstream, pro-slavery newspapers, as well as the white mob violence they incited. Like most newspapers of the day, these pro-slavery papers were controlled by the Whig and Democratic parties, both of which skirted the issue of slavery as a risky political topic.

One St. Louis newspaper, the *Daily Commercial Bulletin and Missouri Literary Register*, described a July 1837 meeting of concerned citizens about Lovejoy. They called on the "citizens of Alton" to renounce Lovejoy for violating his "pledge" to avoid the subject of abolition while in "exile" there. Beneath the headline "ANTI-ABOLITION MEETING," the article complained about "the course pursued by the Rev. E. P. Lovejoy in the publication and dissemination of the highly odious doctrines of modern abolitionism." The report described a public meeting in St. Louis that had been called to stop Lovejoy from publishing abolitionist news in Illinois.[17]

But "free" Illinois proved to be far more dangerous for Lovejoy than slaveholding Missouri had been. Encouraged by the mainstream, pro-slavery press, rioters followed him from St. Louis. It was no surprise. He had come to expect the violence. By the time of his death, Lovejoy had seen four of his printing presses thrown into the river by racist mobs. Until the last, Lovejoy would not back down. In defiance after his third press was dumped into the river in September 1837, he had responded by founding the Illinois Anti-Slavery Society in Alton. While each act of destruction prompted contributions for replacement presses from abolitionists across the nation, the mounting violence only led Lovejoy to tighten his embrace of Garrison's demand for the immediate end of slavery.

William Lloyd Garrison (1805–79), photographed in 1870.

On November 7, 1837, the lynch mob that destroyed Lovejoy's fourth printing press murdered him. After setting his house on fire, they waited until he had to run from the flames. Then they shot him dead. He was two days shy of his thirty-fifth birthday. His murder galvanized the national abolition community to follow his example by working to end slavery at all costs. The shock of his lynching shocked the national abolition movement, even as his death gave the movement its first martyr to inspire them.

Out of the intensifying national argument to define slavery as a blessing or a sin, one young journalist emerged to lead the movement. Growing up in Newburyport, Massachusetts, Garrison (1805–79) began his career as a journalist by apprenticing at the local *Herald*, where he soon began writing under the pen name "Aristides." A devout Christian, Garrison sought to reform society in strict agreement with what he understood to be sound biblical moral principles against one person owning another.

Yet, early on, he stumbled while trying to ground his moral direction. In the late 1820s, he had aligned himself with the American Colonization Society, which worked to repatriate enslaved people to a "home" in Africa that few, if any of them, knew. The newly founded African state of Liberia had been created as a place to send enslaved people. Not at all a gateway to American freedom, the strategy was designed to reduce regional tensions about the number of slaves being held in the South. Quickly realizing his objections to the society's actual goals, he renounced his position, arguing, instead, for an unconditional and immediate end to slavery. As a result, he announced his rejection of "any scheme of expatriation, which pretends to aid, either directly or indirectly, in the emancipation of the slaves, or to be a substitute for the immediate and total abolition of Slavery."[18]

Founded in 1831, Garrison's newspaper, the *Liberator*, promised to end slavery as a means of "defending the great cause of human rights." The radical newspaper energized and focused the abolition movement until the end of the Civil War in 1865. In the newspaper's inaugural editorial, Garrison had warned mainstream slave owners and those in the slave trade that he would be uncompromising in pursuit of divine justice:

> I am aware, that many object to the severity of my language; but is there not cause for severity? I will be as harsh as truth, and as uncompromising as justice. On this subject, I do not wish to think, or speak, or write, with moderation. No! no! Tell a man whose house is on fire, to give a moderate alarm; tell him to moderately rescue his wife from the hand of the ravisher; tell the mother to gradually extricate her babe from the fire into which it has fallen;—but urge me not to use moderation in a cause like the present. I am in earnest—I will not equivocate—I will not excuse—I will not retreat a single inch—AND I WILL BE HEARD."[19]

Two years earlier, on December 4, 1833, Garrison had led the founding of the American Anti-Slavery Society. Under his leadership, the society declared its intention to use journalism to reach those who lived beyond the bounds of its activist membership.

Ringing with Garrison's apocalyptic voice, the society's inaugural "Declaration of Sentiments" read "We shall organize Anti-Slavery Societies, if possible, in every city, town and village, in the land. We shall send forth agents to lift up the voice of remonstrance, or warning, of entreaty and rebuke. We shall circulate unsparingly and extensively, anti-slavery tracts and periodicals. We shall enlist the pulpit and the press in the cause of the suffering and the dumb."[20] With just a few hundred copies per issue, the *Liberator* needed a way to promote Garrison's cause nationwide. The rapidly changing party presses of the time inspired Garrison. In particular, he saw how they had just years before taken advantage of the increasingly widespread postal exchange system to promote their positions.

From his position as the society's president, Garrison attracted adherents with a wide range of religious, social, and political views. He and his followers had a broad agenda, calling for support for women's rights, while criticizing pacifism, nonresistance, and some religious sects as supporters of the evil institution of slavery.

Incensed by such challenges to their mainstream privileges, pro-slavery Americans often resorted to violence to make their case, so much so that

Garrison called their hostilities toward abolitionists "a reign of terror." In 1835, during a rally in downtown Boston in support of southern slavery, the crowd got word that abolitionists—maybe even the infamous Garrison himself—were nearby. When they found Garrison, a mob chased him through Faneuil Hall, stripping him bare and threatening to lynch him. Only the help of "two burly Irishmen not known as abolitionists" prevented his murder.[21]

For his part, Garrison was so radical that he called for abolitionists to leave the Union. In a pamphlet published by the society in 1844, he announced that

> At the Tenth Anniversary of the American Anti-Slavery Society, held in the city of New York, May 7th, 1844—after grave deliberation, and a long and earnest discussion—it was decided, by a vote of nearly three-to-one of the members present, that fidelity to the cause of human freedom, hatred of oppression, sympathy for those who are held in chains and slavery in this republic, and allegiance to God, require that the existing national compact should be instantly dissolved; that secession from the government is a religious and political duty; that the motto inscribed on the banner of Freedom should be, NO UNION WITH SLAVEHOLDERS.[22]

Still, not all abolitionists were so forceful. Some other anti-slavery activists called themselves "Christian abolitionists." Like the Garrisonians, these northern abolitionists criticized pro-slavery Christians in the North and in the South, as well as northern Christians who opposed slavery but did nothing about it. Unlike Garrison's creed of abolition at all costs, the Christian abolitionists sought to reform the pro-slavery beliefs of American religious and governmental institutions rather than destroy them in order to end slavery.[23]

In countering the half-steps of compromise, part of Garrison's genius came from his ability to understand and to install recent changes in the growing business of journalism. At the national level, he had watched Andrew Jackson understand how to use the contemporary partisan press to mobilize different political allies. But for the cause, Garrison found that niche-specific kind of journalism to be an obstacle to the important support that came from the international cause of abolitionism. This was particularly true of England, which would abolish slavery in 1833.

From Garrison's arch perspective, the American party press was guilty of supporting shades of pro-slavery positions in pursuit of their own political interests instead of joining his jihad against slavery. Nonetheless, he also knew how to co-opt the system. He saw that when abolitionists nationwide reprinted his anti-slavery commentary in order to criticize it, they inadvertently publicized his vehement anti-slavery arguments against slavery as well.

Faced with a white-majority public that believed that slavery was moral and even natural, Garrison's gift for developing media strategy would face bigger obstacles. For much of the time between the Revolution and the Civil War—seventy-eight years from 1783 to 1861—abolitionist journalists had worked against an array of often religiously based cultural and political beliefs to reframe slavery as immoral. From his positions as editor of the firebrand *Liberator* and as head of the American Anti-Slavery Society, Garrison also knew that he could not represent the enslaved himself. He was going to need the authentic voices of people who had experienced or witnessed slavery firsthand in order to recruit members to the society and to raise money for the campaign against this national sin.

He quickly recruited a roster of speakers from a range of experiences to provide his mostly white northern audiences with the one thing that he lacked in this epic battle to persuade northerners to act: firsthand testimony to bring the horror of slavery home to his audiences. Among those activists were Frederick Douglass, Maria Stewart, Angelina Emily, Sarah Moore Grimké, Theodore Weld, Mary Ann Chapman Shadd, and Henry Bibb, all of whom follow in this chapter.

Frederick Douglass and the Diversity of Abolitionist Tactics

Few people understood the sticky metrics of social position, race, and gender in the abolition movement better than Frederick Douglass (1811–95). An escaped slave, Douglass became Garrison's protégé after their first encounter at an American Anti-Slavery Society meeting at Nantucket in August 1841. Douglass had been encouraged to speak there about his life as an enslaved person. Garrison was so impressed that he engaged Douglass as a regular speaker for the society and in 1842 as a writer for the *Liberator*. Douglass's fiery speeches often shocked his audiences, especially when he stripped off his shirt to show his audiences his scars from whippings, confirming northern abolitionists' grimmest concerns about slavery.

In the preface to Douglass's first autobiography, published in 1845, Garrison endorsed his friend's first-person account of slavery, writing,

> Mr. DOUGLASS has very properly chosen to write his own Narrative, in his own style, and according to the best of his ability, rather than to employ some one else. It is, therefore, entirely his own production; and, considering how long and dark was the career he had to run as a slave— how few have been his opportunities to improve his mind since he broke his iron fetters—it is, in my judgment, highly creditable to his head and

heart. He who can peruse it without a tearful eye, a heaving breast, an afflicted spirit,—without being filled with an unutterable abhorrence of slavery and all its abettors, and animated with a determination to seek the immediate overthrow of that execrable system,—without trembling for the fate of this country in the hands of a righteous God, who is ever on the side of the oppressed, and whose arm is not shortened that it cannot save,—must have a flinty heart, and be qualified to act the part of a trafficker in slaves and the souls of men.

I am confident that it is essentially true in all its statements; that nothing has been set down in malice, nothing exaggerated, nothing drawn from the imagination; that it comes short of the reality, rather than overstates a single fact in regard to SLAVERY AS IT IS.[24]

For Garrison, making an authentic case to the public depended on promoting Douglass's life story. In this dynamic, which made Garrison a kind of talent manager, Douglass quickly became a star speaker for the society. In the *Liberator*, Garrison described his protégé as having given "a fresh impulse to anti-slavery."[25] Because Garrison had already mastered the movement's use of the national postal distribution system to promote the *Liberator*, Douglass enthralled audiences far and wide with his dramatic written accounts of his own enslavement.[26]

But the same ties that bound the pair together came to constrict them. Garrison's relationship with Douglass became strained when Douglass expressed a desire to edit and publish his own newspaper. The American Anti-Slavery Society and Garrison, in particular, objected. For them Douglass was much more valuable to the movement as a public speaker than he could be by publishing a newspaper.[27] In the society's view, the team was set. But it was not: Douglass insisted on his independence within the movement. "By the 1850s," the historian Stephen Kantrowitz tells us, "Douglass was heartily sick of the condescending cant of Garrison, [Wendell] Phillips, and other AAS leaders . . . Questions of autonomy, independence, and servility became intensely personal, a roiling brew of ideological, tactical, and personal differences."[28]

Douglass's break with Garrison provides important insights into the racial politics of the abolition movement. From the time Douglass began editing the *North Star* (1847–51) and *Frederick Douglass' Paper* (1851–64), he was fully aware how much the white-led movement depended on his experiences. He wrote,

It is neither a reflection on the fidelity, nor a disparagement of the ability of our friends and fellow-laborers, to assert what "common sense affirms and only folly denies," that the man who has suffered the wrong is the man to demand redress,—that the man STRUCK is the man to CRY

OUT—and that he who has endured the cruel pangs of Slavery is the man to advocate Liberty. It is evident we must be our own representatives and advocates, not exclusively, but peculiarly—not distinct from, but in connection with our white friends. In the grand struggle for liberty and equality now waging, it is meet, right and essential that there should arise in our ranks authors and editors, as well as orators, for it is in these capacities that the most permanent good can be rendered to our cause.[29]

In this statement, Douglass affirmed his dual role as a former slave—"the man who has suffered the wrong"—and as a freethinking journalist who could demand a solution for all through the end of slavery. Pointedly, Douglass's firsthand account countered southern claims that slave life was a harmonious, mutually beneficial arrangement, instead revealing it as a brutal, violent, dehumanizing practice.

The break was clear. Although Garrison shared a principal stake in the social movement against slavery, as a white man he acted from a necessarily privileged position. In 1854, he showed just *how* privileged when he committed an act that would distinguish him from Douglass forever: He burned copies of the Fugitive Slave Law and the *Constitution* in front of a large July 4 crowd. An article in the *Liberator* on July 7, 1854, described the event. It read:

> Mr. Garrison said he should now proceed to perform an action which would be the testimony of his own soul to all present, of the estimation in which he held the pro-slavery laws and deeds of the nation. Producing a copy of the Fugitive Slave Law, he set fire to it, and it burnt to ashes. Using an old and well-known phrase, he said, "And let all the people say Amen"; and a unanimous cheer and shout of "Amen" burst from the vast audience. In like manner, Mr. Garrison burned the decision of Edward G. Loring in the case of Anthony Burns, and the late charge of Judge Benjamin R. Curtis to the United States Grand Jury in reference to the "treasonable" assault upon the Court House for the rescue of the fugitive—the ultimate ratifying the fiery immolation with shouts of applause.

Here Garrison burned a copy of the Fugitive Slave Law, which was causing all sorts of problems in its inability to distinguish free Blacks from formerly enslaved escapees. The law encouraged an informal industry of white kidnappers and bounty hunters to legally seize any Black person to sell into, if not back into, slavery. If that dramatic performance went well with the mixed audience and with Douglass, in particular, Garrison's next move did not:

> Then holding up the U.S. Constitution, he branded it as the source and parent of all the other atrocities,—"a covenant with death, and an

agreement with hell"—and consumed it to ashes on the spot, exclaiming, "So perish all compromises with tyranny!" And let all the people say, "Amen!'" A tremendous shout of "Amen" went up to heaven in ratification of the deed, mingled with a few hisses and wrathful exclamations from some who were evidently in a rowdyish state of mind, but who were at once cowed by the popular feeling.[30]

Garrison's rejection of the American political system touched on the fundamental difference between him and Douglass: As a white man, Garrison could afford to burn the Constitution in public, while remaining secure in his claim on citizenship. But as a Black man, Douglass knew that he could not afford to ignore that document's promise of equality, because it remained a viable, if uncertain, promise.

Maria Stewart, the Grimké Sisters, and the Uneven Privilege of Protest

Garrison's ambitions were not dampened by his rift with Douglass as he remained on the lookout for talented writers and orators. As early as 1831, he engaged Maria Stewart (1803–79) to write a column for the newly founded *Liberator*. Stewart was the first Black woman in America to speak to mixed-race audiences, the first to speak to mixed-gender, or "promiscuous," audiences, and the first to address women's rights in public. The logo on her 1831 column, "The Ladies Department," in Garrison's *Liberator*, adapted the popular British abolitionist slogan, "Am I not a man and a brother?" to read "Am I not a woman and a sister?"

Garrison had recruited her when he recognized the power of Stewart's moral arguments about race and equality for blacks and about themes she struck that would develop in the affiliated temperance movement later in the century.

As Stewart's language in the example that follows indicates, her prime influences were religious. Stewart's explicit references to the Christian New Testament in her 1831 speech, "Religion and the Pure Principles of Morality," demonstrated the rhetoric of "moral suasion" by arguing that all people—white and black—were equal in the eyes of a common God. Moral suasion offered a way for Stewart to use the logic of positive comparisons to point out how much more similar than different were Black and white Americans. Such positive comparisons—based mainly on what seemed like a shared belief in Christian principles—made the case that slavery had no place in what should have been their shared moral system.

In her speech—one of four reprinted in the *Liberator*—she urged northern blacks to claim their full humanity by acknowledging and using their

The logo that accompanied Maria Stewart's column in *The Liberator*.

intellects. Moreover, she pointed to the opportunities for them to act through a free press. As she developed her position, she used the language of a religious crusade to elicit empathy about her life story from her audiences. Note that she had not been enslaved, but she had been an indentured servant. Effectively similar to enslavement, indentured people were held under a contract that would convert to freedom after an agreed time.

Stewart told her rather unwilling audience,

> I was born in Hartford, Connecticut, in 1803; was left an orphan at five years of age; was bound out in a clergyman's family; had the seeds of piety and virtue early sown in my mind; but was deprived of the advantages of education, though my soul thirsted for knowledge. Left them at 15 years of age; attended Sabbath Schools until I was 20; in 1826, was married to James W. Steward; was left a widow in 1829; was, as I humbly hope and trust, brought to the knowledge of the truth, as it is in Jesus, in 1830; in 1831, made a public profession of my faith in Christ.
>
> From the moment I experienced the change, I felt a strong desire, with the help and assistance of God, to devote the remainder of my days to piety and virtue, and now possess that spirit of independence, that, were I called upon, I would willingly sacrifice my life for the cause of God and my brethren.

She was using the comparative logic of moral suasion when she pointed out that Black and white Americans, as well as Black men and women, shared religious values. If they could agree to that bond, could they not see that they shared a responsibility to live against slavery, too?

In this speech, she was addressing a room full of free but hostile Black men who were angered because she was challenging them at all, and all the more by her demand that they live up to the standards of what David Walker had called "colored chosen-ness."[31] Continuing, she directly challenged the men in the room to engage in the fight against slavery, saying, "All the nations of the earth are crying out for Liberty and Equality. Away, away with tyranny and oppression! And shall Africa's sons be silent any longer? Far be it from me to recommend to you, either to kill, burn, or destroy. But I would strongly recommend to you, to improve your talents; let not one lie buried in the earth. Show forth your powers of mind. Prove to the world, that though black your skins as shades of night, Your hearts are pure, your souls are white."

As she pushed this gathering of men to see that being Black meant living up to being "chosen." She said,

> This is the land of freedom. The press is at liberty. Every man has a right to express his opinion. Many thinks, because your skins are tinged with a sable hue, that you are an inferior race of beings; but God does not consider you as such. He hath formed and fashioned you in his own glorious image, and hath bestowed upon you reason and strong powers of intellect. He hath made you to have dominion over the beasts of the field, the fowls of the air, and the fish of the sea. He hath crowned you with glory and honor; hath made you but a little lower than the angels; and, according to the Constitution of these United States, he hath made all men free and equal. Then why should one worm say to another, "Keep you down there, while I sit up yonder; for I am better than thou?" It is not the color of the skin that makes the man, but it is the principles formed within the soul.
>
> Many will suffer for pleading the cause of oppressed Africa, and I shall glory in being one of her martyrs; for I am firmly persuaded, that the God in whom I trust is able to protect me from the rage and malice of mine enemies, and from them that will rise up against me; and if there is no other way for me to escape, he is able to take me to himself, as he did the most noble, fearless, and undaunted David Walker.
>
> NEVER WILL VIRTUE, KNOWLEDGE, AND TRUE POLITENESS BEGIN TO FLOW, TILL THE PURE PRINCIPLES OF RELIGION AND MORALITY ARE PUT INTO FORCE."[32]

Although eloquent, Stewart's speech moralizing about "chosen-ness" was not well received. Historian Shirley Yee wrote of Stewart's 1831 speech hat "her audience of Black men jeered and threw rotten tomatoes . . . when she delivered an address . . . that criticized them for failing to follow basic Christian principles of thrift, sobriety, and hard work." The assault effectively ended Stewart's brief career as a public speaker, and she left Boston. Although she remained active in the movement, she retired to more socially acceptable work, including education.[33]

The Grimké sisters, Sarah Moore (1792–1873) and Angelina Emily (1805–79), were born twelve years apart in Charleston, South Carolina. Growing up in a family that owned enslaved people, they developed an uncommon, but early, disgust with slavery. They especially objected to "the routine whippings and other forms of torture administered in the nearby workhouse or right there in their own household." In many ways, they were ahead of their time: They chafed at the common restrictions on education and public speaking then commonly placed on women and girls, and they insisted on developing friendships with the slaves in their father's house, against all rules.[34]

In 1821, Sarah abandoned her southern home to live in Philadelphia away from slavery. Angelina would join her in 1829. In 1835, Garrison read a letter that Angelina had written about the terrible conditions faced by slaves in her own family's house. At once, he recognized her voice as providing the kind of eyewitness testimony that the society needed. In addition, her appeal was directed at a new audience, the kind of privileged southern white women she and her sister had been raised to be.

In her open letter, "Appeal to the Christian Women of the South," Angelina encouraged her southern sisters to act for change from the seat of power that they occupied—the home. This excerpt, which Garrison reprinted in the society's new newspaper in New York, *The Anti-slavery Examiner*, shows how she argued that gender could be women's strength. Even as she assumed that their shared Christianity bound her to her southern audiences against slavery—not a guaranteed point at all—she was mapping a strategy that gave southern women a way to change their men's minds:

> Perhaps you will be ready to query, why appeal to women on this subject? We do not make the laws which perpetuate slavery. No legislative power is vested in us; we can do nothing to overthrow the system, even if we wished to do so. To this I reply, I know you do not make the laws, but I also know that you are the wives and mothers, the sisters and daughters of those who do; and if you really suppose you can do nothing to overthrow slavery, you are greatly mistaken. You can do much in every way: four things I will name. 1st. You can read on this subject. 2d. You can pray over this subject. 3d. You can speak on this subject. 4th. You can act on this subject. I have not placed reading before praying because I regard it more important, but because, in order to pray aright, we must understand what we are praying for; it is only then we can pray with the understanding, and the spirit also.[35]

Tired of the racist patriarchy of the Quaker elders they had encountered in Philadelphia, the sisters moved in 1836 to New York before settling in

Boston, where they could work under less scrutiny. Once there, Garrison quickly put them on the speaking circuit, and Angelica continued to write essays against slavery for the society.

The historian Jacqueline Jones noted that when Angelina addressed "the Massachusetts State Legislature on February 21, 1838—she was the first woman in the U.S. to address a legislative body." Jones added, "The sisters quickly earned the disapproval—and at times outright condemnation—of New England's conservative clergy for their willingness to address "promiscuous" audiences and to provide graphic, heartrending firsthand descriptions of slavery in the South."[36]

In 1838, Angelina married abolitionist Theodore Weld (1893–95), author of the anti-slavery tome *American Slavery as It Is*. Weld's book presented a compilation of news stories and first-person accounts detailing the neglect, abuse, and dehumanization of slaves throughout the South. Each entry related a new horror, defying the myth of the benevolent slave owner over and over.[37]

Immersed in the culture of the movement, Sarah would live with Angelina and Theodore until her death in 1879. In 1868, they found that their brother had fathered three children with a slave named Nancy Weston. In a gesture that embodied the late movement's hopes for Reconstruction, Sarah and Angelina embraced their nephews, sending one to college at Harvard and a second to Howard.[38]

In one brief example, the book revealed the violence against slaves as constant and naturalized. As Weld recounted,

Mr. T. related the whipping habits of one of his uncles in Virginia. He was a wealthy man, had a splendid house and grounds. A tree in his front yard was used as a whipping post. When a slave was to be punished, he would frequently invite some of his friends, have a table, cards and wine set out under the shade; he would then flog his slave a little while, and then play cards and drink with his friends, occasionally taunting the slave, giving him the privilege of confessing such and such things, at his leisure, after a while flog him again, thus keeping it up for hours or half the day, and sometimes all day. This was his habit.[39]

Weld knew his subject well: This kind of testimony—brutal, firsthand, and immediate—was just what Garrison sought from his speakers and writers to persuade the unconvinced.

Not all abolitionists sided with Garrison. In his quest to destroy slavery, he had been willing to destroy the nation. He had made that result sound necessary. Still, between reform and revolution, lay a third option for enslaved people in the 1850s: escaping to Canada. In 1854, as the Fugitive

Slave Act made life more perilous for Blacks, Black journalist Mary Ann Shadd Cary (1823–93) moved to western Canada with her family. One of the first women admitted to the bar in Canada, she was also the first woman in Canada to own a newspaper, the *Provincial Freeman*. Cary would later join the women's suffrage movement. The *Freeman* (1854–58) put her in competition with Henry Walton Bibb (1815–54), the formerly enslaved person and self-exiled American editor of the Canada-based newspaper *Voice of a Fugitive*.[40]

The all-male world of Black newspapers was a difficult place. Bibb attacked Shadd repeatedly, although Douglass was supportive. Beyond sexism, their tensions centered on political beliefs about Blackness and its place in liberation. As Fagan explained, "*Freedom's Journal, The Colored American,* and *The North Star* had taught readers to fulfill the responsibilities of Black chosen-ness by acting appropriately, prophetically, and revolutionarily." In this millennialist outlook, where the world—or, perhaps, the *world of slavery* and its discontents—would come to an end, each of these American newspapers saw acting chosen as an available weapon in the fight for Black liberation in the United States.

But Shadd did not believe in fighting for freedom in the United States. Indeed, she did not believe in the United States as a solution to slavery, at all. Where Bibb favored a kind of Black separatism, Shadd discounted the value of "race-based communal identity." Instead, as a feminist who would become active in the American suffrage movement, she argued that Black émigrés should renounce all things American. In the *Provincial Freeman*, she made the case that "being British was more important than being Black." After all, as members of the British Commonwealth, the Canadians had ended slavery in the British colonies twenty years before.[41]

From her home in western Canada, she often traveled back to the United States to guide escaped slaves on the Underground Railroad to safety in Canada. She took great risks. Under the Fugitive Slave law, she could have been captured by bounty hunters and sold into slavery in the South. In the *Provincial Freeman* on March 7, 1857, Shadd wrote of her Canadian hometown of Chatham in present-day Ontario:

> They know how the fugitives and others, from the land of bondage arrive—where they arrive at in Canada,—and what help they receive and who they are who help them in an honest and liberal way. Let us awaken attention to the efforts of the colored people about Chatham, and we hope that British solicitude and sympathy and monied help, will also be extended to those who are and who reside on British colonial soil, and who promote the interests on the spot, of those who flee for "liberty dearer than life."[42]

By rejecting the United States as a place where slavery could be success-fully stopped, Mary Ann Shadd Cary and her competitor, Henry Bibb, invested their abolitionist work in the already successful British postslavery experience. Action mattered to Shadd. Tired of the endless conferences and meetings held by men in the movement, in 1848, she wrote to Douglass to say, "We should do more and talk less." In response, he published her letter.

Solidarity and Disagreement in the Abolition Movement

Through its emphasis on Black chosen-ness, the Black press—represented here by *Freedom's Journal* and the *Colored American*—added a distinct ele-ment to the broader, white-led abolition movement, its journalism, and its broader effort to find a slavery-free place in the American public. By making the claim on their own "American exceptionalism," especially during the national religious movement of the Second Awakening, Black Americans embraced a new kind of moral order. Further, they consciously adopted the idea that they could survive and rise above the tyranny of slavery and the lasting racism it aimed at them.

Stewart's position proved to be more radical than that taken by the nation's major white sects, the Baptists and the Methodists. Numbering a million strong each, neither group found changing from their conservative positions in favor of slavery to be attractive. The ingroup strains between southern and northern congregations of both sects ultimately drove them to split along regional lines in 1844 and 1845. "Abolitionists, some of whom had lashed out at the Constitution and even at the Bible as being pro-slavery, harshly criticized the churches for their lack of conviction and decisive action." In an important sense, the schisms that split these two denominations and their millions of congregants foreshadowed the fault lines of the Civil War.[43]

At a more personal level within the abolition movement, the tensions between Garrison and Douglass highlighted the movement's white paternal-ism that Douglass so resented. Even so, Garrison's management of writers and speakers about slavery for the society successfully generated resources, especially for the movement's press. Garrison's ability to adapt the postal system to circulate its ideals among mainstream newspapers and their hun-dreds of thousands of subscribers signaled a victory for the abolitionist movement against a pro-slavery mainstream press. Like the movement it served, the abolitionist press only needed to last until the issue of slavery was settled. The *Liberator* published its final edition on New Year's Eve, 1865.

By that point, the issue of slavery had long been a crisis that threatened the nation's future. It had been settled not with news stories, broadsides, and editorials, but on bloody battlefields in many of the former colonies. The moment of change for the movement's persuasive effort came in the mid-1850s. At the time, two large urban newspapers, in particular, showed this upward shift. In New York, Horace Greeley's (1811–72) *New York Tribune* adopted abolitionism as an editorial position. Soon afterward, the much larger *Chicago Tribune*, and its Republican owner, Joseph Medill (1823–99), also joined the movement. Symptomatic of the increasing impact of the abolition movement, as well as the limitations of the mainstream press, their endorsements helped to change the direction of the fight over slavery.

At the cost of more than a million deaths combined, the four-year Civil War was the deadliest ever for American soldiers. Even as this "second America Revolution" certified that the states would remain a Union, it led to major changes to the makeup of the "public." Most prominently, during the Civil War in 1863, President Abraham Lincoln issued the Emancipation Proclamation, declaring four million enslaved people in the Confederacy free.

That executive order was followed by three major changes to the Constitution meant to remedy the ways in which slaves had been denied full citizenship. The Thirteenth Amendment, which was ratified on December 6, 1865, ended American slavery throughout the United States. The Fourteenth Amendment, ratified on July 9, 1868, has four parts, of which two apply today. The first guarantees equal treatment for all citizens, and the second part rules that if a people are denied the right to vote, then the number of representatives in the House of Representatives will also be reduced. The Fifteenth Amendment was ratified on February 3, 1870, to guarantee the right to vote to all citizens regardless of race. None of these measures proved effective immediately or offered a real remedy to the residual racism left from slavery. The struggle for basic legal rights would remain open.

3

The Long Struggle for Women's Suffrage

In June 1840, Elizabeth Cady Stanton and her new husband, Henry Brewster Stanton, arrived in London, England. The Quaker couple had just been married in New York under unconventional terms. (They had altered the traditional wife's vow to "love, honor and obey.") Their honeymoon was equally unconventional, for the new couple had made the transatlantic journey to attend the World Anti-Slavery Convention. The meeting was well attended, impassioned, and contentious.

An early debate focused on the question of equality in an unexpected way. Many conventioneers wanted to bar women from participating on the basis that the Bible forbade it or that allowing women equality in an already radical movement would make their anti-slavery claims appear ridiculous. Eventually, the all-male conventioneers agreed to bar women from participating. They were welcome to sit in the ladies' section behind a screen, where they could hear the speeches and strategies being discussed. But they would not be allowed to speak or to vote on any resolutions.

Some men were outraged. Saying he could "take no part in a convention that strikes down the most sacred rights of all women," noted abolitionist William Lloyd Garrison (1805–79) dramatically withdrew from the convention and sat in the ladies' section of the hall in protest.

As Elizabeth Cady Stanton (1815–1902) watched all this with great interest, she began talking to a prominent activist and the leader of a contingent of American delegates, Lucretia Mott (1793–1880). Mott, a prominent American reformer, made an enormous impression on Stanton. She later remembered that "Mrs. Mott was to me an entire new revelation of womanhood . . . I had never heard a woman talk what, as a Scotch Presbyterian, I had scarcely dared to think."[1]

As the two watched the hypocritical claims of justice and equality tossed about on the convention floor, they determined to do something to address the rights of women. As Stanton later recalled, "As the convention adjourned, the remark was heard on all sides, 'It is about time some demand was made for new liberties for women.' As Mrs. Mott and I walked home, arm in arm, commenting on the incidents of the day, we resolved to hold a convention as soon as we returned home, and form a society to advocate the rights of women.[2]

Stanton, Susan B. Anthony, Mott, and other reformers aside, the majority of Americans in the mid-nineteenth century quickly dismissed the idea of women's rights, if they had ever considered it at all. But the personal, material, and social limitations women suffered were nearly absolute. For example, it was generally accepted that women were forbidden from owning or inheriting property. If a woman married, her property (including whatever wages she earned) became the property of her husband. She had no legal defense from spousal abuse or marital rape. In the event of a divorce, she had no right to the custody of her children. Women could not serve on juries, could not attend college, and could not enter a profession or make contracts. They faced ridicule if they dared to speak in public, and, of course, they were forbidden from voting. This system of patriarchy—a set of values and practices that privileges men at the expense of women—was not, however, viewed by most men and women in mid-nineteenth-century America as a pressing social problem.

The dominant view of the day was that women were the natural keepers of the home, biologically tempered to raise children and to create nurturing environments for their husbands and children. Men, on the other hand, were seen as naturally suited to the rough and tumble world of politics and business, even if they needed women to help restore them to the refinements of Christian civilization. This line of thought, known to historians as the "Cult of True Womanhood," offers an excellent example of hegemony. Hegemony results from securing broad, but implicit, consent for inequitable social and political arrangements from the very people it disadvantages. In nineteenth century America and elswhere, in return for women's unquestioning subservience, the culture of patriarchy offered them a respected, but clearly secondary, role in the maintenance of civilization: the privilege of taking care of men and children.[3]

To be sure, the origins of the early suffrage movement shared that traditional domesticity. Upon their return to the United States, the Stantons settled into a stately home in Boston, where he worked for the suffrage cause outside the home, and she oversaw the children and their servants. Their wealth afforded them this privilege.

In 1847, however, financial pressures forced the family to move to the upstate New York town of Seneca Falls. Separated from the intellectual stimulation she had enjoyed among Boston's community of reformers and freethinkers and no longer enjoying the comfortable life of a society matron, Stanton began to feel she was suffering from what she called a "mental hunger."

The following summer, Stanton was excited to learn that her old friend Lucretia Mott was coming to town. It had been many years since their promise to one another to raise the issue of women's rights, but neither had forgotten their pledge. Motivated by each other's presence, they resolved to hold a convention to discuss the problem of women's rights. Stanton, Mott, and the other organizers composed a declaration for the conventioneers to consider.[4]

The long struggle for women's suffrage in America began with this fateful decision. Between 1848 and 1920, their work for women's rights grew in alliance with other social movements of the time that addressed abolition and temperance in opposition to mainstream journalism. During those seven decades, mainstream journalism was going through its own significant changes in structure and scope but never changed its traditionally conservative position. The mainstream press consistently offered a defense of patriarchy and a dismissal of the demands of suffragists.

To counter the intractability of mainstream opinion, some suffragists eventually turned to journalism, although the doing so sometimes meant difficult choices and compromises. Eventually, the changing realities of the media system and the implacability of the mainstream press would lead activists to divergent strategies in the movement.

The "Declaration of Rights and Sentiments"

The resolution that emerged from Mott and Stanton's convention in Seneca Falls, the "Declaration of Rights and Sentiments," very closely resembled the American Declaration of Independence, which would have been familiar to most adults of the day. Employing the logic and language of Thomas Jefferson's famous document, the women revised it to direct attention to the ways in which women had been excluded from the self-evident rights of equality, liberty, and autonomy.

Their choice to revise such sacred language provoked the publicity that its authors wanted, for it scandalized mainstream observers. Fueled by that outcry, the suffragists challenged the very foundations of women's place in society, declaring in language that was familiar and sacred to all Americans that women should be equal to men:

When, in the course of human events, it becomes necessary for one portion of the family of man to assume among the people of the earth a position different from that which they have hitherto occupied, but one to which the laws of nature and of nature's God entitle them, a decent respect to the opinions of mankind requires that they should declare the causes that impel them to such a course.

We hold these truths to be self-evident: that all men and women are created equal; that they are endowed by their Creator with certain inalienable rights; that among these are life, liberty, and the pursuit of happiness; that to secure these rights governments are instituted, deriving their just powers from the consent of the governed. Whenever any form of government becomes destructive of these ends, it is the right of those who suffer from it to refuse allegiance to it, and to insist upon the institution of a new government, laying its foundation on such principles, and organizing its powers in such form, as to them shall seem most likely to affect their safety and happiness.[5]

By taking this text as their own, they made charges against the system of patriarchy that offended and enraged the mainstream. At one point, they described American men—their husbands, fathers, and brothers—in the same terms with which the colonists had demonized George III. And once more the remedy was liberty, this time in the form of votes for women.

These women made it clear that they understood what full enfranchisement—the vote—would mean, as they spelled out the definition of full citizenship and the lack of it in their lives. In one declaration, the suffragists took aim at the institution of marriage, blaming matrimony for a kind of "death" in the eyes of the law as a property owner, a citizen responsible for criminal laws, and an individual apart from marriage. In this fashion with their "Declaration of Rights and Sentiments," the women violated every social norm for speaking to and about men. In particular, they challenged the ultimate order of gender and its place in religion, going so far as to identify patriarchy more with the devil than with the saints.

In practical terms, nineteenth-century social values expected that public events like their conference be the sole domain of men. As a result, the Seneca meeting's women organizers felt unqualified to chair the convention. Instead, that job fell to Lucretia Mott's husband, James, who supported their feminist work. So, when Stanton rose to speak before him, she knew that she was violating an unwritten but cardinal rule that women should never speak in public or about politics. Here, as elsewhere, Stanton was exercising her agency to act apart from and even in opposition to the dominant rules of the day for women.

After reading the declaration to the attendees, Stanton offered a slate of resolutions for ratification by the convention. The last demanded that women be granted the right to vote. This radical suggestion directly challenged the mainstream view that politics were men's concern. Some of those closest to Stanton, including her husband, feared that asking for the vote for women would discredit the whole convention with its outrageousness. Lucretia Mott warned her, "Lizzie, thou wilt make the convention ridiculous." In spite of these warnings, Stanton pressed forward with the resolution.[6]

As debate over the topic swelled, the prominent abolitionist orator and former slave, Frederick Douglass, rose to support the resolution. He would later summarize his argument in his abolitionist newspaper, the *North Star*:

> We hold women to be justly entitled to all we claim for man. We go farther, and express our conviction that all political rights which it is expedient for man to exercise, it is equally so for women. All that distinguishes man as an intelligent and accountable being is equally true of woman," he said. "If that government only is just which governs only by the free consent of the governed, there can be no reason in the world for denying to woman the exercise of the elective franchise, or a hand in making and administering the laws of the land. Our doctrine is that 'right is of no sex.' We therefore bid the women engaged in this movement our humble Godspeed.

Douglass's comments helped carry the resolution to success as the world's first convention on women's rights adjourned.[7]

The Mainstream Press and the Cult of True Womanhood

The Seneca Falls convention was reported in the mainstream press in mocking, derisive terms. The *Lowell Courier* from Massachusetts, for example, derided the idea of women's rights as absurd. In the view of the *Courier*, threatening the "natural" order of things threatened the very basis of civilization:

> "Progress" is the grand bubble, which is now blown up to balloon bulk by the windy philosophers of the age. The women folks have just held a Convention up in New York State, and passed a sort of "bill or rights," affirming it their right to vote, to become teachers, legislators, lawyers, divines, and do all and sundries the "lords" may, and of right now do. They should have resolved at the same time, that it was obligatory upon the "lords" aforesaid, to wash dishes, scour up, be put to the tub, handle

the broom, darn stockings, patch breeches, scold the servants, dress in the latest fashion, wear trinkets, look beautiful, and be as fascinating as those blessed morsels of humanity whom God gave to preserve that rough animal man, in something like a reasonable civilization. "Progress! Progress, forever!"[8]

The *Courier's* ridicule was not unique. It echoed a widespread logic, which insisted that men and women were naturally suited to two separate spheres. In the first, men should act as natural adversaries in the public realms of industry and politics. In the second, women should act as compassionate nurturers suited to creating and maintaining the compassionate sanctuary of the home. This understanding of a natural role for women as keepers of the home in the "Cult of True Womanhood," offered respect, even reverence, for women who adhered to roles in the domestic realm. But it also policed women's ambitions for "*un*natural" rights that exceeded that sphere.

In spite of mainstream scorn for women's rights, Stanton soon found allies. One was Susan B. Anthony, a teacher turned fulltime reformer who was also active in the temperance and abolition movements. She had read newspaper accounts about the 1848 Seneca Falls Convention. The two met

Elizabeth Cady Stanton (1815–1902) and Susan B. Anthony (1820–86), photographed sometime after 1880.

in 1851 when Anthony had visited Seneca Falls to hear an anti-slavery speech by William Lloyd Garrison. They both sensed an immediate connection. "How well I remember the day," Stanton would later write. "I liked her thoroughly, and why I did not at once invite her home with me to dinner I do not know."[9]

The two women complemented each other perfectly. Stanton was an excellent writer, but the demands of her large family and her own preferences for a quiet, private life made it difficult for her to spread her message. Anthony, on the other hand, was unmarried, possessed seemingly boundless resources of energy, and was a passionate and effective organizer. "She forged the thunderbolts," Anthony remembered of Stanton decades later. "I fired them."[10]

Reconstruction Splits the Movement

In 1863, President Abraham Lincoln declared all enslaved people in the rebelling states free by signing the Emancipation Proclamation. After the war in 1865, Congress passed three amendments to the *Constitution* in order to structure the Republican-led program of Reconstruction. Intended to rehabilitate the fallen southern states as they rejoined the Union, Reconstruction saw Union troops occupy the defeated South. In 1877, the military occupation of the defeated South was ended in a backroom deal. In brief, the Republicans withdrew federal troops from the South as part of a political compromise between the two major parties that left Republican Rutherford B. Hayes president. The deal ended Reconstruction, leaving newly free Black Americans in the hands of the same white supremacist governments that had enslaved them before.

While the Emancipation Proclamation had freed all people who were enslaved in rebelling states in 1863, it did not end the slave trade in America. Effecting that change would require another federal intervention. The Thirteenth Amendment ended slavery in 1865. Three years later, in language that included every American citizen, the Fourteenth Amendment closed a significant gap by redefining formerly enslaved people as citizens instead of property. From there, it ensured all citizens access to fair legal treatment, or "due process," through the courts and "equal protection under the laws."

In 1870, the Fifteenth Amendment made it illegal to deny the vote "based on race, color or previous condition of servitude." Suddenly, Black men could vote, though white women could not. Never before had gender been officially declared as a qualification for suffrage in the United States Constitution. Revealing the frustration of this new barrier to the women's vote and the racism of their upper-middle-class white privilege, Stanton and Anthony were outraged. After all, the two causes had been linked in the fight to end slavery. Yet here, at the realization of abolition, the impact of Reconstruction was defining the vote as a male-only institution.[11]

Many of the suffragists' male supporters tried to explain the sequence of rights as a compromise with conservatives. Others framed it as the natural progression of rights, as Wendell Phillips did, when he told Stanton, "One idea for a generation, to come up in the order of their importance: First, negro suffrage, then temperance, then women's suffrage. Three generations hence, women's suffrage will be in order."[12]

In May 1869, at the annual meeting of the Equal Rights Association in New York, the former allies for abolition and women's suffrage finally reached a breaking point. There Stanton's anger over what she saw as the abandonment of women's rights revealed the classist and racist presumptions of her worldview, radically feminist though it was. As she implored the delegates to consider the vote for women, she played to racist fears, already circulating widely, that the enfranchisement of black men would imperil the sexual safety of white women.

She followed a common, but not uncontested, set of assumptions of the time. They held that, while women were deserving of the vote, neither immigrants nor Black men could be trusted with it without imperiling the Republic. These assumptions caused consternation among the delegates, not least from Frederick Douglass, who spoke against Stanton and urged the attendees to back the Fifteenth Amendment. The attendees did just that, overwhelming the women's votes.

Disillusioned by these events, Stanton and Anthony formed a new organization to continue the struggle for women's suffrage. The newly organized National Women's Suffrage Association (NWSA) struck a radical approach: It would not allow men to serve in the leadership. At the same time, Lucy Stone, a longtime ally of Stanton's and Anthony's, who had been outraged by Stanton's comments in New York, organized a more moderate alternative to Stanton and Anthony's group. Soon, her American Women's Suffrage Association (AWSA) outnumbered the NWSA and men were permitted to serve as officers in it. Unlike Stanton and Anthony's NWSA, Stone's AWSA did not oppose Black male suffrage or the Fourteenth and Fifteenth constitutional amendments.

The fracture in the movement also divided its financial and human resources, creating two distinct and competing visions of the women's movement. Stone's AWSA promoted a gradual approach to women's rights, while the NWSA was committed to a more radical timeline. To advance their views, both organizations launched newspapers. Between 1868 and 1870, Stanton and Anthony helped produce *The Revolution*, a weekly publication, to highlight women's issues and accomplishments and to provide a mouthpiece for their new organization. The journal was bankrolled by George

Francis Train, a wealthy, globetrotting—and enthusiastically racist—political activist. Working through a male financier proved almost inevitable, as women rarely controlled significant resources. Their alignment with him also signaled their commitment to white women above people of color of whatever gender. Anthony managed the business side of the venture, while Stanton edited the journal and was a frequent contributor.[13]

In the following excerpt from *The Revolution*, Stanton fairly shouts her condemnation of two entwined social issues of the day—prostitution and infanticide—as the ills of patriarchy. With her choice of words to describe the wanton destruction caused by the senseless privilege enjoyed by men in their sexual relationships with prostitution, she meant to upset her readers. Polite women in the mid-nineteenth century did not raise such vulgar topics or challenge men's behaviors so publicly. Of course, Stanton did not mean to be polite. She wanted to shock her audience into recognizing that social problems like this could be solved only by giving women the vote, educating them, and giving them the means to control their bodies and to keep their unborn children safe.

"INFANTICIDE AND PROSTITUTION" BY ELIZABETH CADY STANTON
FEBRUARY 5, 1868

Scarce a day passes but some of our daily journals take note of the fearful ravages on the race, made through the crimes of Infanticide and Prostitution.

For a quarter of a century sober, thinking women have warned this nation of these thick coming dangers and pointed to the only remedy, the education and enfranchisement of woman; but men have laughed them to scorn. Let those who have made the "strong minded" women of this generation the target for the gibes and jeers of a heedless world repent now in sackcloth and ashes, for already they suffer the retribution of their folly at their own firesides, peevish, perverse; children deformed, blind, deaf, dumb and insane; daughters silly and wayward; sons waylaid at every corner of the streets and dragged down to the gates of death, by those whom God meant to be their saviors and support.

Having described the irreversible effects of syphilis on children, Stanton calls for education on the subject to avoid its spread. As a feminist, Stanton found the other women involved in this cycle of contagion deserving of consideration as well. Noting the alarming mortality rate among prostitutes for whom there was no moral support, she wrote, "We ask our editors who pen those startling statistics to give us their views of the remedy. We believe the cause of all these abuses lies in the degradation of woman. Strike the chain from your women; for as long as they are slaves to man's lust, man will be the slave of his own passions." Making direct comparisons between prostitution and enslavement likely stuck a nerve, but blaming prostitution on "man's lust" was a bold step in a society where men acted with sexual impunity and women were expected to remain quiet. By describing the deadly cycle of prostitution and infanticide, she was indicting uncaring men for ignoring the truth: that when they had sex with prostitutes, they likely became carriers of diseases that infected, maimed, and often killed their wives and children.

In that scenario, she mused about how American women could expose themselves to the corrupt indifference of masculine culture. Describing the awful position that so many women were forced into, she sympathized with the things they had to do to survive:

> Wonder not that American women do everything in their power to avoid maternity; for from false habits, dress, food and generations of disease and abominations, it is to them a period of sickness, lassitude, disgust, agony and death.
>
> What man would walk up to the gallows, if he could avoid it? And the most hopeless aspect of this condition of things is that our Doctors of Divinity and medicine teach and believe that maternity and suffering are inseparable.

How could men remain so smug in an era when a woman's death during childbirth was a prominent risk? Stanton's comparing pregnancy to a likely death sentence targeted the supreme advantage enjoyed by men: They could never get pregnant.

Charging "every thinking man" with responsibility to his wife, she wrote,

> So long as the Bible, through the ignorance of its expounders, makes maternity a curse and women through ignorance of the science of life and health find it so, we need not wonder at the multiplication of these fearful statistics. Let us no longer weep and whine, and pray over all these abominations; but with an enlightened conscientiousness and religious earnestness bring ourselves into line with God's just, merciful and wise laws. Let every thinking man make himself today a missionary in his own house. Regulate the diet of dress, exercise, health of your wives and daughters. Send them to Mrs. Plumb's gymnasium, Dio Lewis's school, or Dr. Taylor's Swedish movement cure, to develop their muscular system and to Kuczhowski to have the rhubarb, the sulphur, the mercury and "the sins of their fathers" (Exodus xx.5) soaked out of their brains.[14]

A half-century before the introduction of penicillin or antibiotics, there were no cures for syphilis or other sexually transmitted diseases. Anthony's laundry list of useless remedies offered men twofold advice: ensuring that their "wives and daughters" lead healthy lives and, barring that, getting them a crude, unreliable, and often toxic mercury-based treatment for syphilis. Crucially, her admonition that "every thinking man make himself today a missionary in his own house" laid the responsibility for breaking the cycle of infection squarely on men.[15]

Because of its unvarnished discussion of taboos affecting women, *The Revolution* failed to attract either readers or recruits. It lasted a little more than two years before low circulation and high debts, both problems that would frequently hinder politically radical publications, forced its closure in 1870.

The fallout from that bold effort was still being felt by Anthony years later. In 1872, she was arrested for voting illegally in the presidential election, a charge, which she fought publicly, arguing that the law she was arrested for breaking violated her rights, as protected by the Fourteenth Amendment. After being forbidden from testifying on her own behalf, Anthony was informed that she was to pay a fine of $100 plus court fees. She responded defiantly:

> May it please your honor, I shall never pay a dollar of your unjust penalty. All the stock in trade I possess is a $10,000 debt, incurred by publishing my paper—*The Revolution*—four years ago, the sole object of which was to educate all women to do precisely as I have done, rebel against your manmade, unjust, unconstitutional forms of law, that tax, fine, imprison and hang women, while they deny them the right of representation in the government; and I shall work on with might and main to pay every dollar of that honest debt, but not a penny shall go to this unjust claim. And I shall earnestly and persistently continue to urge all women to the practical recognition of the old revolutionary maxim, that "Resistance to tyranny is obedience to God."[16]

With Stanton's help, Anthony drafted a proposed amendment to the US Constitution securing women the right to vote. Aaron A. Sargent, a senator from California who supported the cause of women's suffrage, introduced the amendment in 1878. Stanton was one of many women who testified before Congress, but she failed to convince the Senate, who sat on the amendment for nine years, before finally rejecting it by more than a two-to-one margin.

Stone's organization, the American Women's Suffrage Association (AWSA), launched a newspaper of their own, with a noticeably different tone. *Woman's Journal* was a journal advancing more mainstream views than those expressed in *The Revolution*. Its first issue featured work by Julia Ward

Howe, the author of the well-known Civil War anthem "The Battle Hymn of the Republic" and the "Mother's Day Proclamation." Howe's position, in contrast to Stanton and Anthony's critiques of patriarchal injustice, is optimistic and conciliatory:

> The New Year had just stepped across its threshold, and after it, clinging closely to its skirts, comes our new enterprise. We begin the year's work with the year, hoping that both may prosper. We have begun many new years with this same vision of work and of usefulness, never quite realized. But the progress of time makes our task clearer to us, and we may say that never was work more joyous to us than that which at present stands ready to our hand.
>
> The cultivation of wide and tender revelations with the beings nearest to us in nature and sympathy, the removal of a thousand barriers of passion and prejudice, the leaping out of the whole heart of womanhood towards a new future, a future of freedom and of fullness—our prospectus shows us such things as these. To see them even in a dream is blessed, but these are of the prophetic dreams that enjoin our own fulfillment.

Note the optimistic tone in contrast to the force of Stanton's writing. Of course, this does not mean that the AWSA was any less committed to the goal of women's suffrage. But Howe knew that time was running out for the original stalwarts. It was time to pass the torch to a new generation. She wrote,

> We who stand beside the cradle of this enterprise are not young in years. Our children are speedily preparing to take our place in the ranks of society. Some of us have been looking thoughtfully toward the final summons, not because of ill health or infirmity, but because, after the establishment of our families, no great object intervened between ourselves and that last consummation. But these young undertakings detain us in life. While they need so much of care and of counsel, we cannot consent to death. And this first year, at least, of our journal, we are determined to live through.

Howe concluded with a call to arms as Christian soldiers for justice, invoking a theme for which the author of the *Battle Hymn of the Republic* had become famous:

> We must not promise too much, but we may promise that the trust confided to us in the *Woman's Journal* shall be administered by us in the interests of humanity, according to our best understanding of them. As we claim admission to life in its largeness and universality, it will not

become us to raise side issues and personal griefs. Too much labor lies before us to allow us time for complaints and criminations, were such utterances congenial to us. Our endeavor, which is to bring the feminine mind to bear upon all that concerns the welfare of mankind, commands us to let the dead past bury the dead.

The wail of impotence becomes us no longer. We must work as those who have power, for we have faith, and faith is power. We implore our sisters, of whatever kind or degree, to make common cause with us, to lay down all partisan warfare and organize a peaceful Grand Army of the Republic of Women.

Having invoked the Grand Army, which had vanquished the Confederacy, she emphasized that her objective was friendly to all, men and women together against sexism:

But we do not ask them to organize against men, but as against all that is pernicious to men and women. Against superstition, whether social or priestly, against idleness, whether aesthetic or vicious, against oppression, whether manly will or feminine caprice. Ours is but a new manoeuvre, a fresh phalanx in the good fight of faith. In this contest, the armor of Paul will become us, the shield and the breastplate of strong and shining virtue. And with a Scripture precept we will close our salutation. With sisterly zeal and motherly vigilance, "Let brotherly love continue." [17]

The more moderate approach of *Woman's Journal* attracted significant financial support, allowing the magazine to publish for more than sixty years.

Alice Paul: Finishing the Fight

As Howe expected, the founders of the women's suffrage movement would not live to see it realized.[18] Stone died in 1893 at the age of seventy-five, though Stanton and Anthony both lived to see the twentieth century. Stanton died at the age of 86 in 1902. Anthony followed four years later. Their constant efforts had led to a slow transformation of laws, conventions, and attitudes that benefited many women, but, near the end of the nineteenth century, progress had been slowing. Although many states had reformed their laws, granting at least limited voting rights to women, by 1890 the movement had foundered in a state-by-state effort to gain the vote.

As resources grew scarcer, the two main suffrage movement organizations—the AWSA and the NWSA—merged just as Howe had suggested in her call for unity and action—to support state-level efforts. The result of this reorganization was the National American Woman Suffrage Association (NAWSA).

A *Woman's Journal and Suffrage News* with the headline "Parade Struggles to Victory despite Disgraceful Scenes," showing images of the women's suffrage parade in Washington, March 3, 1913.

As the movement entered its eighth decade, familiar critiques from the mainstream continued to appear as challenges to the movement. A 1910 article from *Pearson's Magazine*, which targeted the educated, middlebrow readers with political analysis and debate, focused on the many women who did not want the vote. As the editor wrote in an introductory note, "A considerable number of women in this country actively oppose votes for women. Their organizations number, perhaps, as many women as those organizations which are actively seeking votes for women. . . . Why? Women of dignity, intellectual grasp, and womanly charm make explanatory statements in the following article."[19]

To find out, a journalist for the magazine, John Barry, interviewed several women who opposed suffrage, weaving their objections into his own arguments against extending the vote to women. He began by quoting Mrs. Helen Kendrick Johnson, a New York socialite. In his report, Johnson objected to the suffragette theme comparing the cause to the American Revolution. She complained, "These women are always comparing their rebellion to the American Revolution. Think—how ridiculous that is! The Revolution was the natural result of earnest and united protest of a large majority of men and women of the American colonies against the tyranny of a monarchical government. The Women's Rebellion is the protest of a very small band of men and women made up of two parts—emotional discontents and impractical theorists—against what they claim is universal tyranny."[20]

Johnson soon got to the core of her objection to women's suffrage: it violated the traditional values of the Cult of True Womanhood, and its assertion of separate, but complementary, gender roles for men and women:

> The true environment of woman is womanliness; but making herself a distorted woman cannot make her even an imperfect man. . . . The mere act of going to the polls is not unwomanly. . . . It might be as proper as going to the post-office. But attempting to encroach upon duty that is laid upon man in her behalf is neither womanly nor manly. In fact, it seems most cowardly for women to ask for the vote, which, in itself, is nothing but a measure of political power, a symbol as it were, of physical sovereignty. She wants to vote, but she has no power to enforce what she may decree at the polls.
>
> "You can't change the laws of Nature," Johnson claimed. Suffrage for women, she said, "aims to sweep away the natural distinction between the sexes and to make humanity a mass of individuals with an indiscriminate sphere."[21]

In the same article, Mrs. Richard Watson Gilder lent support to this line of argument, asking, "If women vote everything will have to be readjusted. Will it be improved? Nature has made man the superior in strength, grasp of intellect, in nervous energy; wisdom and power and glory are his; yet without us his is a vain shadow, for we, who seem so inferior, have the one gift without which all his achievement goes for naught. We are the transmuters, the transmitters of all he has accomplished. Like a clear glass we hold it all and carry on—a frail, half unconscious 'vessel of the Lord,' spiritually the equal of man."[22]

Barry concludes by recounting an argument against women's suffrage popular among southern whites. This was the argument that the violence used to keep Black men from the ballot would be unseemly directed against women: "The negro kept the franchise only until the will of the majority of the natural male electorate in his vicinity could find a way to suppress him, despite the law. Suffrage is a sovereign power that cannot be divided. It must either be held intact, or abdicated. Man could no more permit woman to share it with him than a ship could have two captains."[23]

Against such stubborn opposition, the movement nevertheless continued. Their main objective was to keep their demands at the forefront of public attention. On one front, the struggle was taken up by the newly formed National Association for the Advancement of Colored People (NAACP), which in 1915 published a special issue of its magazine *The Crisis* dedicated to the debate over women's suffrage. Women's suffrage was a contentious issue among African Americans. As Jane Rhodes observed, "For many African Americans, women's suffrage was a direct threat to patriarchal authority, a dominant ideology that structured racial uplift and respectability norms."[24]

For others, granting the vote to women was a natural and necessary extension of African American liberation. The tension between these forces is illustrated in Coralie Franklin Cook's short entry. Cook was a member of the board of education for the District of Columbia who sought to link women's valorized role as mothers with the cause, arguing that mothers make ideal public-minded citizens:

> I wonder if anybody in all this great world ever thought to consider man's rights as an individual, by his status as a father? yet you ask me to say something about "Votes for Mothers," as if mothers were a separate and peculiar people. After all, I think you are not so far wrong. Mothers are different, or ought to be different, from other folk. The woman who smilingly goes out, willing to meet the Death Angel, that a child may be born, comes back from that journey, not only the mother of her own adored babe, but a near-mother to all other children. As she serves that little one, there grows within her a passion to serve humanity; not race, not class, not sex, but God's creatures as he has sent them to earth.[25]

Cook then argued that women's suffrage would bring motherly concerns to public attention with the benefits extending to all. Playing to the politics of respectability, Cook asserted that women voters were better prepared to curtail vice and sex crimes: "It is not strange that enlightened womanhood has so far broken its chains as to be able to know that to perform such service, woman should help both to make and to administer the laws under which she lives, should feel responsible for the conduct of educational systems, charitable and correctional institutions, public sanitation and municipal ordinances in general." Echoing Stanton's "Prostitution and Infanticide" editorial in *The Revolution* fifty years earlier, she asked,

> Who should be more competent to control the presence of bar rooms and "redlight districts" than mothers whose sons they are meant to lure to degradation and death? Who knows better than the girl's mother at what age the girl may legally barter her own body? Surely not the men who have put upon our statute books, 16, 14, 12, aye, be it to their eternal shame, even 10 and 8 years, as "the age of consent!" If men could choose their own mothers, would they choose free women or bondwomen?[26]

By linking the disenfranchisement of women with racial discrimination, and by underscoring her insistence that extending suffrage to women would ensure that motherly concerns would be better reflected in public policy, she concluded that

> disfranchisement because of sex is curiously like disfranchisement because of color. It cripples the individual, it handicaps progress, it sets a limitation upon mental and spiritual development. I grow in breadth, in vision, in the power to do, just in proportion as I use the capacities with which Nature, the All-Mother, has endowed me. I transmit to the child who is bone of my bone, flesh of my flesh and thought of my thought; somewhat of my own power or weakness. Is not the voice which is crying out for "Votes for Mothers" the Spirit of the Age crying out for the Rights of Children?[27]

As historian Linda M. Grasso notes, the themes in Cook's essay attempt to maximize support for the cause by employing "contradictory ideas about women's sameness and women's difference, thereby appealing to adherents of both convictions."[28] Women's suffrage was a big tent. Holding everyone together sometimes required broad appeals.

Harriot Stanton Blatch, a New York activist, prioritized publicity for suffragettes as part of a long-term strategy to normalize debate on the topic. As one of Blatch's allies would remember,

> They were, of course, always trying to think of ideas which would get us publicity. There were some women reporters who were very helpful to us—who tried to get us all the publicity they legitimately could. But of course, they didn't mind how ridiculous the thing was.
>
> Mrs. Blatch's whole idea was that you must keep suffrage every minute before the public so that they're used to the idea and talk about it, whether they agree or disagree. It must be something that everybody was conscious of. I think she was quite right.[29]

In 1910, Blatch would organize a march in New York City to demonstrate the centrality of women's contributions to society and their demand for the vote. It drew weeks of attention in the press.

Alice Paul studied the success of Blatch's march carefully. Paul had been radicalized for the cause of suffrage while a student in London, where she encountered Emmeline Pankhurst and the militant push for suffrage in the United Kingdom. Paul had gained notoriety for going on a hunger strike while in Britain, which led to brutal force-feedings by prison authorities.

On her return to the United States, Paul sought to grow the movement by harnessing the power of the media spectacle. She led an effort to organize a massive march in Washington, DC, to demonstrate women's contributions to society and their "Great Demand"—the vote. In 1913, when the march was scheduled, mass demonstrations in the nation's capital were almost unheard of. The only previous demonstration of note, by unemployed workers in 1894, had ended in mass arrests.

"The Great Demand": Unity and Dissent within the Movement

The Women's Suffrage Procession was planned to coincide with the inauguration of President Woodrow Wilson the following day. The timing was orchestrated to create maximum publicity and political leverage on the eve of a new administration. The march was a success in terms of publicity, but it also exposed the decades-long tensions about racism within the suffrage movement. White suffragists from the District of Columbia refused to participate in an integrated march. Paul and the organizers worried about alienating the local delegation, and other southern white women, and so agreed to racially segregate the march.

Ida B. Wells, fifty years old, married, and going by Ida Wells-Barnett, had planned to march with the Illinois delegation. She was shocked when members of her state's delegation told that, to avoid offending eastern and southern delegations, she would have to march with a segregated contingent at the rear. By now nationally famous, Wells-Barnett, whose journalism career began with her refusal to move from a whites-only train car, told the delegation, "If the Illinois women do not take a stand now in this great democratic parade, then the colored women are lost. When I was asked to come down here, I was asked to march with the other women of our state. And either I go with you, or not at all."

She and other suffragists of color watched the parade from the route, however. When the Illinois delegation passed by, Wells-Barnett defiantly joined the ranks. As the *Crisis* summarized afterward of Wells-Barnett and the other suffragists of color, "In spite of the apparent reluctance of the local suffrage committee to encourage the colored women to participate, and in spite of the conflicting rumors that were circulated and which disheartened many of the colored women from taking part, they are to be congratulated that so many of them had the courage of their convictions and that they made such an admirable showing in the first great national parade."[30]

The march was larger than its most optimistic supporters had hoped for. It was carefully organized to present a narrative of women's progress and demonstrate their contributions to society. Soon, though, the marchers encountered tens of thousands of men, some of them drunk, who heckled, jeered, and spat on the marchers. Some marchers were assaulted. Some one hundred sought treatment at area hospitals. Police offered little protection. To Alice Paul, the attacks demonstrated the urgent need for women to obtain the legal protections that only the vote can bring. The attacks also dramatized the danger of subjugation more effectively than anything the suffragists could have organized themselves. Paul pressed for a congressional investigation into the attacks on the nonviolent marchers, which kept the event on the front pages for weeks.

In addition to shaping the national conversation, Paul, together with Lucy Burns, also a veteran of the British movement, launched a new feminist newspaper. *The Suffragist* was published from 1913 to 1919 in affiliation with Paul's radical Congressional Union. Typical of nineteenth-century movement newspapers, *The Suffragist*'s circulation peaked in February 1918 at 5,599 copies. Distributed nationally, the newspaper served its purpose by reaching its audience of activists.

On its pages, articles encouraged women to publicly challenge traditional gender roles. In an era of floor-length skirts, long sleeves, and high collars for women, Paul and her colleagues wanted to jolt the faltering movement back to life. Under Paul as editor, who was known for her dictatorial style, the newspaper featured a notable staff, including journalist Rheta Childe Dorr and political cover artist Nena Allender. A year in, Lucy Burns brought some relief to the group by replacing the zealous Paul.

Paul used the newspaper to unify suffragists' demands for a constitutional amendment in place of the failed state-based effort. As they built momentum, movement journalists encouraged a new generation of radical suffragists to violate every rule of acceptable femininity by picketing the White House and President Wilson for his refusal to support the proposed amendment. While marching back and forth in front of the White House gates demanding the vote, they carried banners taunting the president. A typical banner read "Mr. President, what will you do for woman suffrage?"[31]

Alice Paul hoists a glass to victory.

Their protests drew stiff penalties. For daring to speak in public at all, much less for harassing the president, they were sometimes attacked by men in military uniform as police officers stood by. Their perceived impertinence provoked Wilson to the extreme. In November of 1918, the president had the protesters forcibly arrested and imprisoned at the notorious Occoquan workhouse prison. Only after the war would he change his mind about women and the vote, and then only as part of an effort to join the League of Nations.

After the states ratified the Nineteenth Amendment on August 18, 1920, the issue seemed settled. But for Paul it was not. Shortly after the amendment was passed into law by Congress on August 20, 1920, she wrote an editorial in *The Suffragist* calling for women to keep up the fight for equality. She wrote,

> When the women of the United States first met to consider their position in the state and in human society, they drew up a Bill of Rights which—without power of any kind, political or economic, but with inspired determination—they started out to secure.

Almost seventy-three years from the date of that first convention, the women of the United States again meet to consider where they stand. During these seventy-three years, women have won the right without which all others are insecure, the right of a full and equal voice in the government under which they live.

Armed with this power, they meet now to consider the remaining forms of the subjection of women.

At the first convention in 1848, one of the resolutions unanimously adopted had read

"RESOLVED, that the women of this country ought to be enlightened in regard to the laws under which they live, that they may no longer publish their degradation by declaring themselves satisfied with their present position, nor their ignorance by asserting that they have all the rights they want."

This resolution still applies to the women of today. They have gained much since 1848, but they have made their gains piecemeal; rights that they possess in one state, they do not possess in another.

This, added to the fact that in many states, laws are not coded, makes it very difficult to secure accurate information in regard to their legal status, but enough facts have been collected to prove that the "present position" is not "satisfactory."

Many of the laws against which the early convention protested continue to exist to the detriment and humiliation of women. Discriminations persist in the universities. Women are far from enjoying equality in the trades and professions. They are discriminated against by the Government itself in the Civil Service regulations. They do not share in all political offices, honors and emoluments; there is in one state at least a law which prohibits women from holding office at all. They have not attained complete equality in marriage or equal rights as married women over their property or even in the matter of the guardianship of their children.

In light of those remaining obstacles at home, she turned to Wilson's bid to join the League of Nations, warning that "the very representation in Government which they have won in individual countries may lose its significance by an international association of governments in which—unless they take prompt steps to secure it—they will not have an equal voice."[32]

She concluded that "there is danger that, because of a great victory, women will believe their whole struggle for independence ended. They still have far to go." Ready for the battles to come, she claimed the leadership role for her new movement organization and with it the essential resource of *The Suffragist*. She said, "It is for the Woman's Party to decide whether there is any way in which it can serve in the struggle which lies ahead to remove the remaining forms of woman's subordination."[33]

For contemporary observers in the era of #metoo, the movement to win women votes seems perfectly reasonable. Certainly, it has become common to challenge the hegemony of patriarchy in ways that reflect the drive and values of these earliest feminists. Then as now, the sexism of the Cult of True Womanhood was more than mere oppression—it was a complex system of meaning that was embraced by many women as well as men. In spite of the power of this narrative, however, some women (and some men) advocated for change. Adopting a position in opposition to the mainstream has always been a difficult task.

As the movement met a series of obstacles, from former allies as well as opponents, Stanton and Anthony adopted a radical stance, viewing compromises with the mainstream as an ill-advised mistake. The more moderate Lucy Stone, meanwhile, attempted to win rights for women by appealing to some of aspects of the dominant ideology. Stanton and Anthony would bear the cost of their refusal to compromise in the form of the debts they incurred from their failed newspaper, *The Revolution*. But their insistence on criticizing the hegemony of patriarchal power infused the movement with strategies that would inspire Paul to invest in *The Suffragist* as the way to complete the drive for women's suffrage.

4

The Haymarket Riot
and the Rights of Labor

The Chicago socialist movement boiled over on May 4, 1886, when an unknown assassin threw a homemade bomb into a protest rally at Haymarket Square. Gathered to listen to speeches by anarchist labor leader and journalist Albert Parsons (1848–87) and two others, the crowd of several hundred had gathered to protest the police's shooting of striking laborers at a labor protest the day before. The police quickly arrested eight known anarchists, including Parsons, as part of an alleged conspiracy. In the end, Parsons and three others were hanged in what has traditionally been seen as miscarriage of justice. Until recently, the accepted version of events has been that the court's attitude was fueled by the mainstream press's aggressive nativism and provoked by the dramatic language that Parsons and his peers published in the city's several anarchist newspapers.

Over time, the belief that the Haymarket affair was a tragic miscarriage of justice has become an article of faith for labor activists. The story of their false convictions and unjust trial has been enshrined as a story of cynical, anti-immigrant prosecutor driven by the mainstream press's own panicky fear of immigrants. The weight of time has given that tragic account a kind of sacred meaning for a later labor and immigrant community.

The tragedy of the Haymarket riot remains a horror for all involved, but a more recent historical investigation of trial transcripts, letters, and other original documents by scholar Timothy Messer-Kruse shows that the anarchists did, in fact, plan and carry out the attack. Still, neither the trial at the time nor Messer-Kruse's recent examination of the evidence has shown that Parsons was directly involved.

The trial's broader meaning considers the hostile positions taken by mainstream journalists to frame the anarchists as un-American because they were not native born—not Anglos. That prejudice further reflected the existing anti-immigrant stance taken by the mainstream press to limit the labor movement's political boundaries in the late nineteenth century. Violent clashes between labor and capital were common, with the owners of the stockyards, banks, and factories, on one side, and the labor unions on the other, challenging them for better pay and safer working conditions.

Anglo elites in business and in the mainstream Chicago press feared that the immigrant laborers they employed would undermine control over labor, work schedules, and wages by forming unions and using nativist ideas to justify their fears. Meanwhile, inspired by new ideas about capital and communism, the anarchists of the day had something more radical in mind: they wanted total freedom.

As we show in this chapter, journalism helped to organize labor participants in what became known as the Haymarket affair. At the same time, they sparked nativist fears of foreign-born revolution that incited the mainstream press. For a rapidly expanding city not quite in control of itself, the anarchists presented a set of threatening events that were met with violence. The Anglo leadership's related anxieties about non-native and non-Anglo citizens played a prominent role, dating at least to the Alien and Sedition Acts of 1798. What we see in the convergence of the mainstream and movement presses is what happened when absolute authority met absolute defiance.[1]

Albert Parsons: The Making of a Radical

Albert Parsons's career as the national leader of the socialist-anarchy movement had an unlikely beginning. Seeking adventure, the orphaned Parsons followed his older brother, William, into the Confederate army. The experience of seeing the end of slavery firsthand—and, by his account, his having been raised by a Black caregiver, whom he loved—turned him into an abolitionist. He would carry his early experiences with slavery and race into his life's work in the labor movement.[2] He certainly believed that one person's profit earned through the labor of another invariably produced a kind of slavery.

Before the war, he had apprenticed with his brother as a printer. While still in Texas after the war, he found his footing as a journalist and a Republican advocate for Reconstruction. When Reconstruction failed, Parsons took a position at the *Waco Spectator*. From 1869 to 1871, he was employed by the Internal Revenue Bureau in Texas.[3]

In 1873, he and his wife, Lucy Eldine González (1851–1942), a formerly enslaved person who described herself as being of African American,

Lucy Eldine Gonzalez Parsons (1851–1942), photographed in 1886.

Chicana, and Native American ancestry, moved from their home in Texas to the growing and, they hoped, more racially tolerant city of Chicago. In Texas, their interracial marriage had confounded their neighbors, associates, and local white supremacist organizations, all of whom opposed miscegenation.

By 1886, Albert Parsons had become the US leader of the leftwing labor organization the International Working People's Association (IWPA), which was founded in London in 1881. By 1885, some twenty thousand laborers belonged to the Chicago chapter. Notably, the IWPA "rejected the politic and incremental methods of its socialist predecessors and instead pledged itself to immediate revolutionary change by any means."[4]

The Parsons did not seem to embrace the extremism of the IWPA and its openness to violent revolution. Rather, through the union, both Albert and Lucy developed close associations with the movement's journalists, including the community center for the anarchist press in Chicago, the Socialists Publishing Company. The company published the German-language newspapers the *Fackel*, the *Vorbote*, and the *Arbeiter-Zeitung*, along with the *Alarm*, which Albert took over as editor in 1884. The editor of the *Arbeiter-Zeitung*, August

Spies, had himself arrived from Germany in 1872. In short, by the time of the bombing on May 4, 1886, Albert and Lucy Parsons were deeply involved in radical politics in Chicago.[5]

The booming work culture of contemporary Chicago lent itself to the movement's appeals. In 1848, the year Albert Parsons was born, Chicago's population had numbered less than thirty thousand people. But, by the 1880s, it would swell to more than half a million, a figure that would double again by 1890. Hundreds of thousands of immigrants were entering the city, many of them from Germany and impoverished regions of eastern Europe. Each came hoping to find work in one of the city's many industries.

Even by the meager standards of the day, living and working conditions for most Chicagoans were appalling. Virtually no laws protected worker safety, child labor was common, and wages kept most workers in dire poverty. On Prairie Avenue, just south of downtown, the owners and managers of Chicago's factories, department stores, and stockyards lived in opulent mansions paid for with profits that outstripped the average employee's wages by a factor of several thousand.

To many of these workers, the problem lay with the basically unfair foundations of the political and economic system in the United States. After Karl Marx (1818–83) and Friedrich Engels (1820–95) published *The Communist Manifesto* in 1848, a growing number of people in Europe and the United States had begun calling for revolutionary change. As Parsons would learn once he and Lucy had gotten settled in Chicago, the communists represented but one part of the nineteenth-century labor movement there. While not all who embraced a broad critique of capitalism might have called themselves communists, they and other radicals on the political left shared a common Marxist goal of overthrowing capitalist societies in order to replace them with what they saw as more humane and equitable conditions.

In contradicting this extremism, historian James Green has challenged the notion that Parsons advocated even the notion of violence. He explained that "Parsons and his fellow agitators devoted themselves far more to practical activity—writing, speaking, agitating and organizing—than to creating coherent revolutionary theory." Describing Parsons as a craftsman, Green allowed that the "Chicago anarchists applied Marx's axioms when they seemed to explain what was happening before their eyes," but they also made free use both of French revolutionary writers and their American peers. They "drew inspiration from Thomas Paine (1736–1809), the most influential of propagandists; Thomas Jefferson (1743–1826), who proclaimed the right and the duty to rebel against unjust authority; from Patrick Henry (1736–99), whose words, 'Give me liberty or give me death' were often quoted; and from John Brown (1800–59), the most heroic of all revolutionary martyrs." Sincere in his opposition to government, Parsons advocated a form of anarchy that would advance the "dream of a self-governing community of equal producers."[6]

The Newspapers, Anticommunism, and Nativism

The mainstream press kept the Chicago labor movement informed about the European labor movement. Known as the first International, the European-American labor movement was organized in 1881 to advance Marx's ideas about labor, capital, and equity. Bound by his widely read economic theory, comparisons of the French Commune of 1871 with Chicago's labor scene was apparent to all. So, even as the movement's leadership and members embraced Marx's critique of "wage slavery," others made more sinister comparisons. Chicago police inspector John Bonfield (1836–98) thought that the laborers used the streets of Chicago to mount running street battles just as their Parisian comrades used theirs.

While not a full-fledged French revolution, the commune mounted a terribly bloody uprising by Parisians against a corrupt national regime. In Chicago, where news of the commune was read by all parties, mainstream journalists paid close attention. They did so, first, out of support for what seemed to be a new democratic victory. Then, as quickly, they reversed field out of concern that the latest French revolutionary violence would spread to the United States.

As the fighting in France drew on and the insurrectionists appeared to be losing, the *Chicago Tribune* abandoned support for the French communards. Ignoring the apparent irony of an American failure to support a democratic insurrection, the *Tribune*'s editors joined many of the nation's newspapers in framing the Parisian rebels as "communists who confiscated property and as atheists who closed churches." In the most strident tones, the newspaper warned that the French violence could be exported to America.[7]

Making a clear distinction between American socialists and anarchists, historian Timothy Messer-Kruse referred to the socialists' own words from their 1883 Baltimore convention: "At the conclusion of their convention, the Socialist Labor Party clarified their differences with the anarchists: "We do not share the folly of the men who consider dynamite bombs as the best means of agitation. We know full well that a revolution must take place in the heads and in the industrial life of men before the working class can achieve lasting success."[8]

Even if the socialists knew the difference between themselves and anarchists, the general public did not make such distinctions. Left was left. Instead, they lumped anarchists and socialists in with the generic threat of leftist communism. If the tone of this first Red Scare felt familiar to

Chicagoans in the mid-1880s, it was: Similar fears of an exported French revolution had inspired the passage of the Alien and Sedition Acts of 1789 in John Quincy Adams's (1767–1848) administration. An original characteristic of the American political mindset, this fear of foreign influences on American political stability would become an enduring mainstream belief.

That anxious climate certainly defined the social context in 1874 when Albert Parsons secured a job with the *Chicago Times*. As he reported on the plight of working immigrants there, he became increasingly concerned with the need to improve their living and working conditions. In 1875, with that idea in mind, he moved his political allegiance once more away from the right, leaving the Republican Party for the Social Democratic Party of America. He later joined the Knights of Labor, a powerful labor organization and founded the organization's first Chicago branch.

Parsons's transition to the left continued on July 23, 1877, as the massive nationwide strike of railroad workers known as the Railroad War was growing. As he addressed a crowd of tens of thousands gathered on Market Street, expounding on the rights of labor, he urged change through democratic elections.[9] Parsons's employers at the *Chicago Times*, who strongly opposed the railroad strike, fired him immediately. The *Times* editor had Parsons taken to a secluded room where Chicago police chief Bonfield and several representatives for the city's most powerful business figures confronted him. They accused him of inciting a revolution and told him that his life would be in danger if he continued to cause trouble for them.

The stacked deck of Chicago working life, which put workers at the mercy of business elites and the police, frustrated Albert and Lucy. Still, even after the police crackdown against labor in 1877, the Parsons would remain engaged with the moderate, labor-friendly anarchism of the first International Commune of 1871. Known internationally as the "Chicago idea," the Parsonses would champion this local concept of a government-free community of interdependent artisans for the rest of their lives.[10]

In a speech to a Chicago crowd a week before Christmas in 1886, Lucy Parsons explained their position as peaceful and opposed to the violence associated with anarchism. She said, "Anarchists are peaceable, law-abiding people. What do anarchists mean when they speak of anarchy? Webster gives the term two definitions—chaos and the state of being without political rule. We cling to the latter definition. Our enemies hold that we believe only in the former." She declared her conclusion at the top of her voice: "I am an anarchist!"[11]

Like her husband, Lucy Parsons believed in a utopian and libertarian ideal that regarded government as a symptom of a society that was too morally decrepit to live free on its own terms.

Activism, Violence, and the Eight-Hour Day

The Parsonses' idealized view of the world contained two complicating flaws: Chicago actually had a government that had no sympathy for anarchism, and their fellow anarchists had bombs that they were prepared to use. Backed by a ferocious mainstream press, the city's government stood firmly against the labor movement and what it saw as labor's outrageous demands. Together with George Engel and other Chicago-area anarchists, the anarchists supported a campaign to limit normal working hours to eight hours a day. For many of Chicago's quickly growing number of factory workers, militating for the eight-hour day represented an opportunity to strike a blow for the rights of workers. The movement was asking for workers to be paid the same wage they received for a ten-hour workday and to spend a few hours each day engaged in leisure time, a new concept in that era.

For the anarchists, though, the eight-hour day represented something more. It was, many thought, a revolutionary demand, since employers would never bow to the demands of workers on this issue. In that way, the anarchists were trying to develop a catalyzing issue to bring about the collapse of the social order they hoped for. On May 1, 1886—the first-ever celebration of the movement's "May Day"—the Parsons led more than eighty thousand workers on a march through Chicago's business district. Their parade even approached the stately homes of Marshall Field (1834–1906), Potter Palmer (1826–1902), Cyrus McCormick (1809–84), Jay Gould (1836–92), and other magnates of the Chicago business establishment. As they marched, they chanted, "Eight for ten!"[12]

Two days later, at Chicago's McCormick Reaper Works, striking Irish-American ironworkers angry about plans to mechanize the plant that would endanger their jobs, were confronted by four hundred Chicago police officers armed for battle. The police fired into the crowd, killing two strikers. Several newspapers reported six fatalities, while the *New York Times* reported a dozen police deaths.[13]

August Spies (1855–87), who had earlier delivered a fiery speech in support of the strikers, witnessed the shooting. To Spies, the police protection for the strikebreakers and their willingness to fire on the striking workers provided further evidence that the so-called forces of law and order would be forever on the side of business owners and would be mobilized against the workers whenever the capitalists requested it.

Outraged, Spies returned to the offices of the *Arbeiter-Zeitung* to organize a reply and to plot revenge with a group of anarchists. He hurriedly composed the text for a poster, leaving it to his assistants to give it a title and print it. Here is what appeared on the streets of Chicago the next day:

REVENGE!

Workingmen, to Arms!!!

Your masters sent out their bloodhounds—the police—; they killed six of your brothers at McCormick[']s this afternoon. They killed the poor wretches, because they, like you, had the courage to disobey the supreme will of your bosses. They killed them, because they dared ask for the shortening of the hours of toil. They killed them to show you, "Free American Citizens," that you must be satisfied and contended [*sic*] with whatever your bosses condescend to allow you, or you will get killed!

You have for years endured the most abject humiliations; you have for years suffered unmeasurable iniquities; you have worked yourself to death; you have endured the pangs of want and hunger; your Children you have sacrificed to the factory-lords—in short: You have been miserable and obedient slave[s] all these years: Why? To satisfy the insatiable greed, to fill the coffers of your lazy thieving master? When you ask them now to lessen your burden, he sends his bloodhounds out to shoot you, kill you!

If you are men, if you are the sons of your grand sires, who have shed their blood to free you, then you will rise in your might, Hercules, and destroy the hideous monster that seeks to destroy you. To arms we call you, to arms!

Your Brothers.

The next evening, at Chicago's Haymarket Square, Parsons led a rally to protest the McCormick police violence. Though the rhetoric was fiery, Spies began the rally by stressing that it should be a peaceful demonstration. Mayor Carter Harrison (1825–93) made an appearance and, after telling Bonfield that the gathering posed no threat, he left. Bonfield then dismissed some of police, but he kept a group of more than a hundred and fifty to monitor the situation as speakers took turns denouncing the actions of the previous day from the back of a produce wagon.

As Parsons addressed the unusually thin crowd from the wagon, a light rain began to fall. After he had finished speaking, many in the crowd dispersed. Some of them followed the Parsonses to Zepf's Hall, a local meeting place where further organizing work was planned. Only a few hundred spectators remained to hear Samuel Fielden (1847–1922) speak about how the law was being used to oppress working people: "The law is . . . framed for those that are your enslavers!" he was reported to have exclaimed. "Throttle it! Kill it! Stab it! Do everything you can to wound it—to impede its progress!"[14]

Considering the speech to be a provocation, Bonfield marched his club-swinging officers toward the crowd and ordered it to disperse. Fielden, who had by then concluded his speech, objected and stepped down from the wagon. In that instant, the anarchists' violent plot played out as one of them, probably Rudolph Schnaubelt (1863–1901), threw a homemade bomb toward the police, creating panic as the explosion filled the air with deadly shrapnel. When the smoke cleared, seven Chicago police officers lay dead, while dozens of others lay wounded. In the chaos, the police had shot several dozen protesters and bystanders who were running for cover.[15]

May 5, 1886: The Day After

The day after the bombing at Haymarket Square, martial law was declared in Chicago. Hundreds of the city's labor leaders were imprisoned. The police raided the offices of the anarchist flagship newspaper, the *Arbeiter-Zeitung,* where they found bombs, dynamite, blasting caps, and fuses. They arrested "all twenty-three editors, writers, printers, typesetters, and 'devil boys'." They also arrested eight anarchists, including Parsons, Spies, Fielden, and Michael Schwab.[16]

The mainstream press howled for revenge. In its nativist outlook, it drew no distinctions between the anarchist speakers at the rally, the unknown person who had thrown the bomb, and any other immigrants. As the *New York Times* front page reported the following day, "The villainous teachings of the Anarchists bore bloody fruit in Chicago tonight." Beneath the headline "ANARCHY'S RED HAND," the account suggested sinister intent, even a plot, by Fielden, Spies, and Parsons. As evidence of his dubious nature, Parsons was described as "an Anarchist with a negro wife." The story also quoted a police officer, who insisted that the bomb "was thrown from the wagon" where the speeches had been made, a claim that other eyewitnesses could not confirm.

The newspaper's report showed its support for the police, which contrasted starkly with its nativist hostility toward the demonstrators. Because the *Times* did not have the technology in 1886 to print color graphics—Joseph Pulitzer's printers at the *New York World* would introduce that ten years later—the instant of the bombing was described in fiery detail on the paper's all-text front page:

Fielden had just uttered an incendiary sentence, when Bonfield cried:
"I command you in the name of the law to desist and, you," turning to the crowd, "to disperse."
Just as he began to speak the stars on the broad breasts of the blue coats, as they came marching down the street so quietly that they had not

An 1886 engraving of the Haymarket incident.

been heard, reflected the rays of light from the neighboring streetlamp. From a little group of men standing at the entrance to an alley opening on Des Plaines Street, opposite where Fielden was speaking, something rose up into the air, carrying with it a slender tail of fire, squarely in front of the advancing line of policemen. It struck and sputtered mildly for a moment. Then, as they were so close to it that the nearest man could have stepped upon the thing, it exploded with terrific effect.

The men in the centre of the line went down with shrieks and groans, dying together. Then from the Anarchists on every side, a deadly fire was poured in on the stricken lines of police, and more men fell to the ground. At the discharge of the bomb the bystanders on the sidewalk fled for their lives, and numbers were trampled upon in the mad haste of the crowd to get outside. The groans of those hit could be heard above the rattle of revolvers, as the police answered the fire of the rioters with deadly effect. In two minutes the ground was strewn with wounded men. Then the shots straggled, and soon after all was quiet and the police were masters of the situation.[17]

After a few days, the mainstream press's attentions turned to explaining the broader social forces that had precipitated the violent unrest at the Haymarket. Mainstream newspapers pointed to the "foreign" and, usually,

German backgrounds of many in the movement. In the press's view, the immigrant laborers believed that the socialist-anarchists did not have legitimate grievances about their working conditions. Rather, they were just of an inferior cultural background. What else could their resistance to the Anglo upper-class standards of Americanization mean?

The *Chicago Times* called the demonstrators "ragtag and bobtail cutthroats of Beelzebub from the Rhine, the Danube, and the Elbe."[18] An editorial in the *Chicago Daily Tribune* on May 7, 1886, "THE UNAMERICANIZED ELEMENT," compared Philadelphia to Chicago, noting that labor disputes in Philadelphia had not erupted in violence and had not been marked by the "insane demand" of the eight-hour day made in Chicago. Again, this difference was attributed to the comparative ethnic—read, "non-Anglo"—makeup of the working class in the two cities.

At a time when race was equated with national origin, the explicit racial and ethnic hierarchy in American culture could be seen in the mainstream press of the day. In the editorial in the *Tribune*, Philadelphia's working class was "composed mostly of Americanized Irish." Chicago's laboring classes drew heavily on "the worst elements of the Socialistic, atheistic, alcoholic European classes" from Germany and eastern Europe. The author concluded that the problem was not limited to Chicago, however: "The unreasonableness of demand, the amount of disorder, the commission of crime, the defiance of the law, and the use of brute force are in exact proportion to the numbers of this un-American, ignorant, alien class of laborers."[19]

On May 7, three days after the bombing, the *Chicago Daily Tribune* published an editorial calling for revenge against the wanton violence of the irreligious and immoral "nihilists" and their poisonous communism. Under the headline "Stamp Out Anarchy," the editor called for a purge of these foreign elements from Chicago:

> Mobbing, murder, and dynamite assassination were probably necessary to arouse the Americans and Americanized foreigners of Chicago to the danger of tolerating any longer the public teaching of imported Nihilism and Communism. For years this city has been made a hotbed for the propagation of anarchical doctrines. Under the leadership of Spies, Fielden, Parsons, and Schwab the bloody-minded anarchists congregated in this city have been urging the destruction of American ideas of government and sending out their disciples to spread seditious doctrines and encourage social and political revolution. Not an effort has been made to drive out, chain, or suppress these mad dogs, but they have been allowed to pursue their frenzied course without the slightest interference from municipal authorities.

In censuring the "foreigners," the press asserted its institutional place next to the government by helping to set the city's boundaries against "un-American" elements. Because of their supposed inferior breeding and tendency for violence, the anarchists were certain, the *Daily Tribune* continued, to commit mayhem against the people and the government of the United States again:

> In accordance with certain popular but delusive and misplaced notions about the sacredness of free speech and free print, the anarchists have been permitted to advocate murder, arson, and pillage as the means for the overthrow of American government and destruction of American society. The general idea seemed to be that the madness would run its course and that there might be a seed-sowing of anarchical doctrine without a harvest of riot and bloodshed.
>
> The events of the last week prove such expectations unfounded and demonstrate the people cannot expect to escape the effects if they tolerate the cause. They must put their heel on the Anarchists and crush them out.

Having shown how the foreigners had abused the city's good will and generous welcome, the editor called for their extermination:

> It is the old story over again of the husbandman who warmed a snake by the fire only to find it striking at him with its poisoned fangs. Driven out of Germany, Bohemia, and Poland as intolerable enemies of law and order, the Anarchists were welcomed nevertheless to the United States and invited to share all the benefits and blessings of free citizenship. The Government offered them education for their children and protection enjoyment of all property they might bring with them or acquire subsequently. For twenty-five years past they have been offered homes and farms on the public domain without cost, and the way has at all times been open to them to become independent citizens and landowners.

Perhaps worst of all, these immigrants had abused their freedom to vote as Americans, the editor complained:

> Taken into full citizenship in the course of a few years, they were invested with all the political rights of native-born Americans, with a direct voice in the government of the country and the privilege of competing on equal terms with all others for public offices, honors, and rewards. Welcomed to such opportunities and privileges, these political outlaws turned the right of free speech into license and used it to advocate dynamite, the torch, and insurrection. Now that their treasonable teachings have ripened into

actual crime, they are within grasp even of tolerant laws and subject to their severest penalties. Punishment should be visited upon them without mercy or regret.

Here the mainstream press called for a ban on any more like the anarchists. Chicago must be kept free for those who belonged:

> Let the Anarchists learn that, while the American people may be slow to wrath, they are fully able to protect themselves, their families, their institutions, and their property. While Spies, Parsons, Fielden, and Schwab are punished according to law, care should be taken that no more such social desperados are harbored in Chicago. Incendiary anarchical sheets should be suppressed by the police. Nihilistic meetings on the public parks ought to be broken up and the leaders sent home if need with broken heads. No more red flags or black flags should be flaunted in the streets of Chicago. Let the Anarchists understand that they must seek some other place to preach and practice their hellish doctrines, and while they remain here they must show at least an outward respect for American laws and institutions. The sooner dynamite conspirators understand that matters have at last reached this complexion the better for all concerned.[20]

"What Is Anarchism?"

To the end of his life, Parsons's life's work as a labor organizer depended on his skills as a writer and evangelist for anarchism as a more livable political system. Collected by Lucy Parsons as her husband's hanging drew near, Parsons's last essay, "What Is Anarchism?" appeared in his newspaper, *The Alarm*, after his death sentence in 1887. As they waited for his execution, the couple curated a collection of his work along with profiles of the other seven indicted anarchists. Lucy wrote in the foreword of that memorial collection, "This book, the reader is doubtless aware, was prepared in the gloom near the close of an eighteen-months incarceration in a lonely, narrow prison cell. . . . Should there be a tinge of sadness in these last words of a noble and courageous soul, remember they were written beneath the shadow, whose guilt fell athwart all true and loving hearts."[21]

One last time, Parsons explained the freedom he wished for and that he believed anarchy could give the country he loved:

> Anarchy is antigovernment, anti-rulers, anti-dictators, anti-bosses. Anarchy is the negation of force; the elimination of all authority in social affairs; it is the denial of the right of domination of one man over another.

It is the diffusion of rights, of power, of duties, equally and freely among all the people.

But Anarchy, like many other words, is defined in Webster's dictionary as having two meanings. In one place it is defined to mean "without rulers or governors." In another place it is defined to mean "disorder and confusion." This latter meaning is what we call "capitalistic anarchy," such as is now witnessed in all portions of the world and especially in this courtroom; the former, which means without rulers, is what we denominate communistic anarchy, which will be ushered in with the social revolution.

Socialism is a term which covers the whole range of human progress and advancement. . . . I think I have a right to speak of this matter, because I am tried here as a socialist. I am condemned as a socialist. . . . If you are going to put me to death, then let the people know what it is for.

"Socialism" is defined by Webster as "a theory of society which advocates a more precise, more orderly, and more harmonious arrangement of the social relations of mankind than has hitherto prevailed." Therefore, everything in the line of progress, in civilization in fact, is socialistic.

He took the time to explain distinctions that his captors did not care to hear:

There are two distinct phases of socialism in the labor movement throughout the world today. One is known as anarchism, without political government or authority; the other is known as state socialism or paternalism, or governmental control of everything. The state socialist seeks to ameliorate and emancipate the wage-laborers by means of law, by legislative enactments. The state socialists demand the right to choose their own rulers. Anarchists would have neither rulers nor lawmakers of any kind. The anarchists seek the same ends [the abolition of wage-slavery] by the abrogation of law, by the abolition of all government, leaving the people free to unite or disunite as fancy or interest may dictate, coercing no one.

He offered a last defense of the road to liberty that anarchy offered:

We are charged with being the enemies of "law and order," as breeders of strife and confusion. Every conceivable bad name and evil design was imputed to us by the lovers of power and haters of freedom and equality. Even the workingmen in some instances caught the infection, and many of them joined in the capitalistic hue and cry against the anarchists. Being satisfied of ourselves that our purpose was a just one, we worked on undismayed, willing to labor and to wait for time and events to justify our cause. We began to allude to ourselves as anarchists and that name, which was at first imputed to us as a dishonor, we came to cherish and defend with pride. What's in a name? But names sometimes express ideas, and ideas are everything.

In language that echoed Thomas Paine's attacks on the un-"natural" idea of government,[22] Parsons asked,

> What, then, is our offense, being anarchists? The word anarchy is derived from the two Greek words "an", signifying no, or without, and "arche" or government; hence anarchy means no government. Consequently anarchy means a condition of society which has no king, emperor, president or ruler of any kind. In other words, anarchy is the social administration of all affairs by the people themselves; that is to say, self-government, individual liberty. Such a condition of society denies the right of majorities to rule over or dictate to minorities. Though every person in the world agree upon a certain plan and only one objects thereto, the objector would, under anarchy, be respected in his natural right to go his own way.

Indicating the owners of industry here, Parsons implied that their wealth was un- "natural," a denial of basic human right:

> The great natural law of power derived alone from association and cooperation will of necessity and from selfishness be applied by the people in the production and distribution of wealth, and what the trades unions and labor organizations seek now to do, but are prevented from doing because of obstructions and coercions, will under perfect liberty—anarchy—come easiest to hand. Anarchy is the extension of the boundaries of liberty until it covers the whole range of the wants and aspirations of man.

From Parson's viewpoint, the new revolution was already underway and traveling around the globe, language that fed mainstream fears of a revolution that would strip wealth from the owners of business, whose capital gains were effectively stolen from the laborers whose work had produced it. He continued,

> The anarchists are the advance-guard in the impending social revolution. They have discovered the cause of the worldwide discontent which is felt but not yet understood by the toiling millions as a whole. The effort now being made by organized and unorganized labor in all countries to participate in the making of laws which they are forced to obey will lay bare to them the secret source of their enslavement to capital. Capital is a thing—it is property. Capital is the stored up, accumulated savings of past labor . . . the resources of life, the means of subsistence. These things are, in a natural state, the common heritage of all for the free use of all, and they were so held until their forcible seizure and

appropriation by a few. Thus, the common heritage of all, seized by violence and fraud, was afterwards made the property—capital—of the usurpers, who erected a government and enacted laws to perpetuate and maintain their special privileges. The function, the only function of capital is to confiscate the labor-product of the propertyless, non-possessing class, the wageworkers.

The charges of violence and murder may seem strong, but they matched the anarchists' understanding of their experience as laborers who had no control over their work, with the absence of any such "freedom," and the responsibility of government for making it so:

> The origin of government was in violence and murder. Government disinherits and enslaves the governed. Government is for slaves; free men govern themselves. . . . The right to live, to equality of opportunity, to liberty and the pursuit of happiness, is yet to be acquired by the producers of all wealth. . . . Legalized capital and the state stand or fall together. They are twins. The liberty of labor makes the state not only unnecessary, but impossible. When the people—the whole people—become the state, that is, participate equally in governing themselves, the state of necessity ceases to exist.
>
> Anarchy, therefore, is liberty; is the negation of force, or compulsion, or violence.
>
> It is the precise reverse of that which those who hold and love power would have their oppressed victims believe it is.

The Paris revolution of 1871 offered proof of a worldwide labor movement that the authorities and business leaders read, not without some reason, as a violent and inevitable threat to themselves and to the "American" way:

> The great class-conflict now gathering throughout the world is created by our social system of industrial slavery. Capitalists could not if they would, and would not if they could, change it. This alone is to be the work of the proletariat, the disinherited, the wage-slave, the sufferer. Nor can the wage-class avoid this conflict. Neither religion nor politics can solve it or prevent it. It comes as a human, an imperative necessity. Anarchists do not make the social revolution; they prophesy its coming. Shall we then stone the prophets?

The implicit reply was "No!" Instead, all citizens should respect the movement's advanced place in the inevitable unfolding pattern of history. The Chicago anarchists believed that as workers, they were being swept up by destiny:

In the line of evolution and historical development, anarchy—liberty—is next in order. With the destruction of the feudal system, and the birth of commercialism and manufactories in the sixteenth century, a contest long and bitter and bloody, lasting over a hundred years, was waged for mental and religious liberty. The seventeenth and eighteenth centuries, with their sanguinary conflicts, gave to man political equality and civil liberty, based on the monopolization of the resources of life.

All over the world the fact stands undisputed that the political is based upon, and is but the reflex of the economic system, and hence we find that whatever the political form of the government, whether monarchical or republican, the average social status of the wageworkers is in every country identical.

The class struggle of the past century is history repeating itself; it is the evolutionary growth preceding the revolutionary dénouement. Though liberty is a growth, it is also a birth, and while it is yet to be, it is also about to be born. Its birth will come through travail and pain, through bloodshed and violence. It cannot be prevented.

In closing, Parsons concluded that anarchism provided the only way to freedom:

An anarchist is a believer in liberty, and as I would control no man against his will, neither shall anyone rule over me with my consent. Government is compulsion; no one freely consents to be governed by another—therefore, there can be no just power of government.

Anarchy is perfect liberty, is absolute freedom of the individual. Anarchy has no schemes, no programmes, no systems to offer or to substitute for the existing order of things. Anarchy would strike from humanity every chain that binds it, and say to mankind: "Go forth! you are free! Have all, enjoy all!"[23]

Much more than just inspirational poetry for the movement, Parsons and his peers found a truth like Tom Paine's *Common Sense* or his "Crisis Essays" to believe. Of course, it read like a total threat to Chicago's community leaders. And its rhetoric was meant to be, but few in number and never well equipped, the anarchists were no match for the city and its press.

The Trial and Its Outcomes

In the turmoil after the bombing, Parsons, who had fled to Wisconsin, returned to Chicago to stand trial. Though the bomb thrower had not been identified (and remains unknown to this day), the band of leftist journalists and their peers faced charges of murder and conspiracy to murder the fallen policemen. Only three of the men—August Spies, editor of the anarchist newspaper, the *Arbeiter-Zeitung*; Albert Parsons, editor of the anarchist journal, *The Alarm*; and Samuel Fielden (1847–1922), a teamster known as "Red Sam"—had even been present in Haymarket Square at the time of the violence, and two of them, Spies and Parsons, had been on the podium, in full public view.

Others who were charged included two of Spies's assistants at the *Arbeiter-Zeitung*, Michael Schwab (1853–98), assistant editor, and Adolph Fischer (1858–87), chief compositor. Oscar Neebe (1850–1916) owned a yeast company and served as a director of the Socialist Publishing Company. George Engle (1836–77) sold toys and had once published the occasional, four-page newspaper *Der Anarchist*. Louis Lingg (1864–87) had lived in the United States less than a year.[24]

At the trial, which gripped the headlines in July and August of 1886, the state government prosecutor made the stakes clear: "Anarchy is on trial," he told the jury. "Convict these men. Make examples of them. Hang them, and you save our institutions, society."[25] Without decisive action, the prosecution warned, foreign revolutionaries would overrun the street "like a lot of rats and vermin." "You stand between the living and the dead," the prosecution concluded. "You stand between law and violated law. Do your duty courageously, even if the duty is an unpleasant and severe one."[26]

Although the prosecutors were unable demonstrate that any of the defendants had thrown the bomb, the idea that the eight men charged were complicit remained. One scholar points out that "under Illinois law, aiding and abetting a murder carried the same legal penalty as directly performing the deed."[27] In the end, the jury found the defendants guilty, sentencing seven of the eight to death. Neebe was sentenced to serve fifteen years. Henry Demarest Lloyd (1847–1903), a former editor at the *Chicago Tribune* and son-in-law of the *Tribune*'s publisher William Bross, began an international campaign to reconsider the verdict. As a result, he was fired and cut out of the family will.

Illinois governor Richard James Oglesby (1824–99) commuted two of the sentences, including Fielden's, to life imprisonment. Lingg committed suicide in prison the day before his scheduled execution. On November 11, 1887, the four remaining anarchists—Spies, Parsons, Engel, and Fischer—were hanged. Six years later, Illinois governor John Peter Altgeld (1847–1902) issued full pardons to those still imprisoned as a result of the trial, calling them victims of "hysteria, packed juries and a biased judge."[28]

To the end, Albert Parsons professed the "Chicago idea" of a utopian anarchy, even as he found working within the system for change hopeless.

He understood that the election commissions, city bureaucrats, police forces, and mainstream newspapers were not neutral forces that managed the distribution and exercise of power; they were controlled by the Anglo ruling classes, who had no interest in sharing power. For Chicago's anarchists in the mid-1880s, the response of official channels of justice and the mainstream press only confirmed Parsons's dour assessments.

In the face of that frustrated effort, however, Parsons and his colleagues' movement in Chicago also fully understood the value of a movement press. They used their press freedom to work for change from outside a system they viewed as undemocratic, unaccountable, and unjust. By contrast, the mainstream press provided an opposition that both got the story of the conspiracy right and promoted the nativist beliefs that were dominant at the time.

Perhaps the most lasting legacy of the Haymarket case was the mainstream press's active hardening of the frame of anticommunism against the Chicago anarchists. For decades later, anticommunism would serve to block leftist challenges to power. When provoked, the "American," or establishment, press would have recourse to the history of threats, real and perceived, when they sensed a threat to Anglo-hegemony. In this way, the mainstream press served not as a watchdog, but a guard dog, of the Gilded Age and its elites.

5

Reconstruction, Lynching, and Ida B. Wells's Crusade for Justice

The triumph of the Union Army in the Civil War in 1865 brought a host of dramatic changes to southern institutions that had been deeply invested in slavery. But while the institutions changed, the culture of hostility and terror that white enslavers had used to control Black people continued to shape American culture. This chapter traces the persistent arc of American racism from the end of slavery in 1863 through the failure of Reconstruction between 1865 and 1877. It offers a way to describe the emergence of a daring new Black journalism dedicated to countering lynching.

In the spirit of David Walker's self-determined "colored citizen," a few Black journalists worked at this time to create a space of identity and self-respect for Black Americans in their quest for full citizenship.[1] Of that number, Ida Wells (1862–1931) stood apart for her daring journalistic crusade against the mob violence of lynching. Born enslaved in Holly Springs, Mississippi, she fully understood the violence of the Reconstruction era. For the rest of her life, she would resist the white South's vicelike grip on the culture of slavery, which lasted a century beyond emancipation.

More than just the engine of the southern economic system, slavery structured every aspect of daily life in the South. Beginning in 1865, the program known as Reconstruction was implemented by the North. An attempt to remake the Union by enforcing the rights of newly freed black people in the former Confederacy, it failed, leaving a spectacular legacy of racist ruin to thrive in its wake.

Undermined from the start by President Andrew Johnson, the Tennessean enslaver who had become president when Abraham Lincoln was assassinated, the tenuous program of Reconstruction for racial reform only lasted until 1877, and then, only because northern Republicans had firm control of Congress. Initially, the Republicans held such a large majority in

Congress that they were able to pass—and the states were able to ratify—a trio of amendments to the US Constitution, the first in more than a half century. Each amendment offered to support formerly enslaved people's full citizenship. In 1865, the Thirteenth Amendment abolished slavery and other forms of involuntary servitude, excluding prisoners. In 1868, the Fourteenth Amendment guaranteed equal protection under the law. And in 1870, the Fifteenth Amendment prohibited the state and federal governments from denying the right to vote, including recently freed Black men.[2]

The structural changes to white power that were proposed through these amendments were met with fierce, often violent, resistance from southern whites. Antagonized by Johnson's support for former confederates over freed people, Republicans sent federal troops to reoccupy the former confederate states: In that climate of postwar polarization, Johnson so incited the Republicans that they made him the first president ever impeached. Ultimately, a divided Senate failed to convict him.[3]

A multiracial democracy glimmered briefly during this period. Under this regime, hundreds of thousands of black men voted for the first time. Several were elected to state and national offices, including the US Senate and the US House of Representatives. But just as quickly under Johnson, the former states of the Confederacy threw Blacks out of their elected offices. To reassert white racial hegemony and its effective return to slavery, southern states regained their antebellum racial dominance through a cultural and legal system known as the Black Codes. This system of laws and selective enforcement imposed criminal penalties for innocuous offenses such as vagrancy, and also kept Black people in poverty by severely restricting their ability to own property or conduct business. Once imprisoned, often for long terms, these Black convicts could be leased out to private businesses as labor, thereby returning these men to the unpaid toil from which they had recently been liberated. The historian Eric Foner explained that the most serious aspect of the Black Codes was not that they worked, but "what they showed about the determination of the South's white leadership to ensure that white supremacy and plantation agriculture survived emancipation."[4] In that context, the durability of the codes ensured that the daily culture of Jim Crow, "a 19th-century minstrel figure that would become shorthand for the violently enforced codes of the southern caste system"[5] would endure well into the next century.

If the rules of the old Confederacy ebbed during Reconstruction, they barely had time to fade. In 1874, President Rutherford B. Hayes found it politically expedient to withdraw federal troops from the state capitols of Florida, Louisiana, and South Carolina. Hayes's act did not just leave the legislators and their staffs unprotected from white supremacists; it served notice to all that "the federal government would no longer intervene to protect either the political prospects of southern Republicans or the Constitutional rights of Black citizens."[6] Black voters were purged from southern voting rolls by new regulations designed specifically to disenfranchise them. During the civil rights movement (1954–68), such restrictions would be outlawed by the Voting Rights Act of 1965. White populist voting restrictions would reappear in force under the very different Republican party led by Donald Trump, elected president in 2016.

Without the Republicans' protection in the 1870s, disaster loomed for southern Blacks. On one side were freed slaves and their descendants, determined to defend their newly won constitutional liberties. On the other side was the white establishment, which controlled every institution of power in the South. In the last decades of the nineteenth century and the first decades of the twentieth, as the white establishment reasserted its dominance through the law and violence, the US experienced what historian Rayford Logan would famously describe as "the nadir of American race relations."[7]

Lynching and the Press:
White Terrorism and Social "Order"

Of all the public violence in this painful period, lynching was the most savage. This atrocity, which captured Ida Wells's professional imagination, was defined by one historian as "an execution that is done outside the processes of established law by several or even many people in response to a perceived outrage, is motivated by a desire to vindicate the moral sense of the community, enjoys general public approval in the local community, and has as its target a specific person or persons."[8]

In the century following the Civil War, lynchings claimed thousands of lives, about three-quarters of them Black. The historian Richard Perloff reports that these acts of racial violence took on a ritual quality. He wrote, "Typically, the victims were hung [sic] or burned to death by mobs of White vigilantes, frequently in front of thousands of spectators, many of whom would take pieces of the dead person's body as souvenirs to help remember the spectacular event."[9]

Often, white people mailed photo postcards from the macabre, carnival-like scenes, smiling for friends and neighbors in front of the burned, bullet-riddled corpse hanging from a tree in the background.

These images sent through the US postal service underscored the tacit permission people felt to engage in acts of extralegal murder. So stereotyped were Black men as rapists that white families would flock to these murder scenes, proudly advertising their good citizenship. The two decades before and after the beginning of the twentieth century was a period of white terrorism that was often minimized or overlooked. But for anyone living through it, white or Black, lynching was difficult to ignore. For people of color, ignoring its risks was simply impossible.

A Racially Divided Press

At a time when the contemporary white newspaper was shifting from the partisan model to more of a consumer-driven commercial basis in the larger cities, the segregated South necessarily operated in a racially divided system of journalism. In this mix, Perloff reminds us that "crime news, particularly stories of sensational lynching of Blacks, seemed likely to attract a large audience of readers." Further, southern white newspapers were typically staffed by white men who automatically enforced norms of how a decent society should operate. Though this understanding was mostly accepted as simply common sense by whites, it was, as always, profoundly shaped by the power relations of the day.[10]

This dual news system worked at the national level, as well, where the *New York Times* voiced a mainstream point of view and a small, but potent, cadre of Black newspapers in cities nationwide, led by the *Chicago Defender*, worked against it. In every case, the role of the newspaper in perpetuating social norms about lynching was clear. From the late nineteenth century through the mid-twentieth century, most white newspapers shared a view-point that unquestioningly accepted a racist, patriarchal understanding of the social order.

A central aspect of the patriarchal worldview was the idea of white men as women's protectors against rapacious Black men. That toxic myth, which was reproduced as fact in the naïve scientific studies of the day, led many, including many white journalists, to be constantly on the lookout for alleged Black rapists. As a license for vigilante social control, it also justified whites' violence, even if the evidence supporting such acts was questionable or nonexistent. In that way, mainstream journalism during this period did not merely ignore the lives and concerns of Black people; it also criminalized and dehumanized them as a group, marking each individual as a threat to moral decency and social order. As we shall see, mainstream white journalists often played an important role in the perpetuation of race ideology as a deadly political weapon.

Unlike white newspapers, which typically banned Black perspectives from their pages, Black newspapers served as forums where the needs of their communities could be debated and asserted. Black newspapers were routinely ignored by white readers, but they gave Black readers a place to challenge the racist logic of the mainstream white social order. And they regularly interrogated the purported facts used to justify lynching and persistently attempted to discredit the practice. The newspapers attempted to dismantle the myths used to justify acts of violence by turning the lens of white manhood's own sense of propriety and honor back on itself. In an authentic voice, they asked how a civilized and well-ordered society could require or tolerate routine acts of gruesome, public, and extralegal murder.

The most prominent Black newspaper was the *Defender*. Founded in 1905 by Robert S. Abbott, the weekly lived by its name. The historian Ethan Michaeli described how the *Defender* supported Wells's reporting of a lynching during the winter of 1909–10. Blamed for the murder of a white woman, the victim, Will "Frog" James, had been murdered by a mob of some ten thousand in Cairo, Illinois. He was "dragged from his cell, hanged . . . in the town square, and subjected . . . to gunfire until the rope around his neck snapped. The lynchers then dragged the body to the site where James had allegedly killed the young white woman and burned his mutilated corpse." When Wells challenged the white sheriff for letting the mob have James and demanded action from the governor, the *Defender* supported her. Their editorial read "If only we had a few men with the backbone of Mrs. (Wells) Barnett, lynching would soon come to a halt in America."[11]

The African-American press remained far more financially vulnerable than its mainstream counterpart, because it relied largely on the revenues of the tenuous Black middle class. Although Black businesses sometimes did well, they had significantly less access to financial resources and were always in danger of targeted violence by white competitors. In attacks by white mobs on Black communities in 1866 in Memphis, Tennessee; in Wilmington, North Carolina, in 1898; and in Tulsa, Oklahoma, in 1920, nascent Black financial and political power was crushed by what can only be described as pogroms or campaigns of racial cleansing. In each of these cities, white mobs attacked Blacks, leaving many injured, dead, and homeless.

The single most important role played by the weekly *Defender* in the face or rampant racist violence in the South was to trumpet the virtues of Black people moving north to find jobs, safety, and the prospect of citizenship in a public that they could not find at home. The *Defender* was carried on trains running north and south by Pullman porters and other regional commuters, advertising a life otherwise unknown. From the end of World War I through the 1970s, Black Americans fed up with low pay, disenfranchisement, and the trauma of random but constant violence by whites found any way they could to leave the South. By its end, the population movement called the Great Migration saw some six million people strike out for northern and western cities.[12]

In some cases, as we shall see, activist Black journalists were forced to relocate to access the resources necessary for their work and to protect their own lives. But their early work helped to establish the Black press as an enduring institution, one that would play a significant role in the long struggle for political and economic equality in the century after slavery.

Miscegenation: Fake News as Race Theory

What fueled such the threat of such constant mayhem? By far, the most frequent reason given was that a Black man had raped a white woman. This obsession combined two beliefs that were ultimately powerful among southern whites of the period—white men's patriarchal duty to protect women from harm and a general revulsion against interracial sex. Mixed-race sexual relationships—consensual ones—were regarded by white America as corrupt "amalgamations."

The meaning of interracial sex changed markedly during the presidential campaign of 1864, when two Republican journalists working for the pro-slavery *New York World* created the term, "miscegenation." Prior to that moment, interracial sex had represented a threat not just to the "virtue" of the woman in question but now threatened the ideal of Anglo-Saxon "racial purity," itself a myth created by nineteenth-century pseudoscientists.

With the presidential campaign of 1864 underway, the nature of the threat perceived by whites changed markedly. The "draft riots" in New York in 1863 saw Irish immigrants who had been drafted into the Union army rioting against the idea of going to war to free Black slaves. The recent immigrants, who saw themselves as competitors with freed northern Blacks for menial jobs, rebelled. Among other sites, they attacked the offices of the pro-Union *New York Herald*, which is depicted on the cover image of this book. After the draft riots, anti-abolitionists in the North upped the ante by broadening the threat of Blacks to white racial purity into a hypersexualized image of Black men as uncontrollable sexual monsters.

The source of this lie was a fake news story produced by two reporters for the *New York World* as a way to undermine Lincoln's re-election bid. As part of this hoax, Democratic partisan journalists David Goodman Crowly and George Wakeman of the *World* weaponized "amalgamation" with the look of scientific fact. Projecting life for whites among a nation of freed slaves, they used their new term, *miscegenation*, to project the terror of a rape-ridden, half-caste future. Rehabbing a cultural notion that sold easily to whites, Stabile explained, "Blacks . . . threatened the sexual order of the world and, in so doing, were more threatening than any civil war."[13]

The fictitious report by Crowly and Wakeman, *Miscegenation: The Theory of the Blending of the Races Applied to the American White Man and Negro,* was presented as a top-secret Republican document that had been leaked to the public. Taking a position that Lincoln endorsed, the document professed the benefits of "blending" the "races" through intermarriage, offering this "scientific knowledge" as an argument for abolition. The document was meant to enrage and mobilize New York voters against abolition and Lincoln.[14]

An excerpt from the pamphlet follows, and it makes for strange reading. *Miscegenation* is presented as a scientific term. The pamphlet presents itself as an argument by Lincoln and his supporters in favor of race-mixing. Note that there is even a glossary of terms at the beginning of the pamphlet with an argument for why they should be used. Throughout the pamphlet, false scientific claims are made about the relation between the races. These claims, despite their apparent science-based presentation, did not represent the scientific consensus of the day, which held that there were unbridgeable biological gaps between the races within a clear hierarchy.

Rather, in seeking to outrage their audience, the authors ended up asserting something very close to our own twenty-first century consensus that the idea of "race" is a fiction promoted in the service one group, usually whites, at the expense of another. The comparison of fair-skinned whites and dark-skinned Africans highlighted physical differences that only fed this myth. Today the actual explanation for the different appearances among humans holds that people of different "races" are often genetically indistinguishable, and that longtime adaptation to regional climate is primarily responsible for any differences in appearance.[15] It is important to remember however, that even the leading scientific minds of this period would have dismissed such notions as nonsense. The text read:

> The author is aware that this book will call down upon itself a storm of contumely and abuse. He has withheld his name from the title page, not because he regrets any word in it, or is afraid to meet any argument against it; but because he prefers that a great truth should spread by the force of its own momentum against the heart of the world. He is patient, he is confident. He appeals from the imperfect American of today, to the more perfect race that is yet to appear upon this continent. "If God," said the great German Astronomer, "could wait six thousand years before he revealed to me the laws which govern the heavenly bodies, I too can wait until men accept them as true."

> NEW WORDS USED IN THIS BOOK.
> Miscegenation—from the Latin Miscere, to mix, and Genus, race, is used to denote the abstract idea of the mixture of two or more races.

Miscegen—is used to denote an offspring of persons of different races, with the plural form, Miscegens.

Miscegenate—is used as the verbal form of the first mentioned word, e.g.[,] to miscegenate, i.e.[,] to mingle persons of different races.

Miscegenetic—The adjective form.

Reasons for coining these words—(1) There is, as yet, no word in the language which expresses exactly the idea they embody. (2) Amalgamation is a poor word, since it properly refers to the union of metals with quicksilver, and was, in fact, only borrowed for an emergency, and should now be returned to its proper signification. (3) The words used above are just the ones wanted, for they express the ideas with which we are dealing, and, what is quite as important, they express nothing else. . . .

If any fact is well established in history, it is that the miscegenetic or mixed races are superior, mentally, physically, and morally, to those pure or unmixed. Wherever on the earth's surface we find a community which has intermarried for generations, we also find evidences of decay both in the physical and mental powers. On the other hand, wherever, through conquest, colonization, or commerce, different nationalities are blended, a superior human product invariably results . . .

Whatever of power and vitality there is in the American race is derived, not from its Anglo-Saxon progenitors, but from all the different nationalities which go to make up this people. All that is needed to make us the finest race on earth is to engraft upon our stock the negro element which providence has placed by our side on this continent. Of all the rich treasures of blood vouchsafed to us, that of the negro is the most precious, because it is the most unlike any other that enters into the composition of our national life.[16]

The document was intended to look like a secret shared among scholarly experts. Its conclusions were scripted to enrage an audience of average citizens. It advanced a theory that would have sounded somewhat familiar to many readers during the 1860s, promoting eugenicist ideas of selectively breeding humans to create a racial hierarchy with "powerful" and "vital" races at the top with those below subject to mental and physical decay. Some of the most respected scientific experts of the day made just this claim. The point of the pamphlet's argument, however, would have been difficult for most white people to accept: that mixed-race people, not whites, were the superior race. That suggestion flew in the face of what most scientists were claiming at the time. It was also carefully designed to elicit an outraged response from white readers, many of whom would have been shocked and appalled by the suggestion that whites were not superior and that only reproducing with other, presumably Black, races would make them so.

The text continued thus:

> The people do not yet understand; but the old prejudices are being swept away. They say we must free the negroes. To free them is to recognize their equality with the white man. They are to compete with the white man in all spheres of labor. They are to receive wages. They are to provide for themselves. Therefore, they will have the opportunity to rise to wealth and high position. Said a speaker at a Republican meeting at the Cooper Institute, in New York: "If the time ever comes when a majority of the people of this State desire a negro Governor, and elect him as such, I believe he ought to be Governor." It was a statement that commended itself to the common sense of the audience, and they did well to applaud. And the argument goes further. If a white woman shall prefer this black Governor, or any black man of wealth or distinction, for her husband, rather than an ignorant or drunken white man, she certainly ought to have him.[17]

The timing and pitch of the *Miscegenation* hoax suggests that the secret goal of the Republican party was to encourage the intermarriage of freed African Americans with whites. That menacing idea would also circulate in visual propaganda for the Democrats in the leadup to the 1864 election. Consider, for example, the image below, which appeared in the *World* on September 23, 1864 (before Pulitzer had bought the paper). Like the pamphlet, it pretends to be authentic. The text reads as follows:

> The Miscegenation Ball at the Headquarters of the Lincoln Central Campaign Club, Corner of Broadway and Twenty Third Street New York Sept. 22d. 1864 being a perfect facsimile of the room &c. &c. (From the New York World Sept. 23d. 1864). No sooner were the formal proceedings and speeches hurried through with, then the room was cleared for a "negro ball," which then and there took place! Some members of the "Central Lincoln Club" left the room before the mystical and circling rites of languishing glance and mazy dance commenced. But that Many remained is also true. This fact We Certify, that on the floor during the progress of the ball were many of the accredited leaders of the Black Republican party, thus testifying their faith by works in the hall and headquarters of their political gathering. There were Republican Office-Holders, and prominent men of various degrees, and at least one Presidential Elector On The Republican Ticket.[18]

POLITICAL CARICATURE. No 4.

UNIVERSAL FREEDOM
ONE CONSTITUTION
ONE DESTINY
ABRAHAM LINCOLN PRES.

THE MISCEGENATION BALL

A depiction of an imagined "Miscegenation Ball" produced by enemies of Lincoln in the September 23, 1864, edition of the *New York World*.

Lincoln would win reelection in 1864 despite this kind of disinformation, but the legacy of miscegenation would last much longer. After the war, miscegenation became the dominant theme in a continuing moral panic about sex between whites and African Americans. The fear would become a potent force in public life, especially in the southern states. Most southern states would pass antimiscegenation laws forbidding intermarriage between Blacks and whites in the decades immediately after the Civil War. These laws would stay on the books until 1968, when the Supreme Court finally declared them unconstitutional.

Fear of sex between whites and blacks would also become a strong justification for segregated schools, where integration was typically conflated with the specter of intermarriage. Even in mutually consenting relationships, interracial sex quickly became a taboo punished by the community violence we know as lynching.

Ida B. Wells: Documenting the Horror of Lynching

Amid the fake news of nineteenth-century American racism, one journalist, Ida B. Wells, stands out for her willingness to strike back. Just one year before the publication of the *Miscegenation* pamphlet and months before Lincoln signed the Emancipation Proclamation on September 22, 1862, Wells was born into slavery in Mississippi. The first twenty-one years of her life were marked by personal tragedy. In 1878, both of her parents and a younger sibling died during an outbreak of yellow fever. Only sixteen years old, Wells faced the daunting prospect of caring for her three remaining younger siblings. After teaching in schools in northern Mississippi and Arkansas to support the family, she moved to Memphis in 1883.

But Wells did not accept her plight quietly. Her parents had been politically active, and she showed a similar conviction for justice. In 1884, she sued the Chesapeake and Ohio Railroad for removing her from a railroad car against her will in order to enforce segregation in their carriages. Though Wells would win a verdict that would ultimately be overturned by the Tennessee Supreme Court, she gained notoriety for writing about her ordeal for *The Living Way*, a newspaper sponsored by a local Black church.

This foray into journalism led to several more articles by Wells and, eventually, to her becoming editor and co-owner of the *Free Speech and Headlight* in 1892, a newspaper that advocated Black civil rights. Wells's work with the *Free Speech and Headlight* included criticisms of the poor conditions in the schools that Black students attended. The newspaper's complaints attracted the attention of the Memphis Board of Education, which fired her from her job as a teacher.

The incidents that finally led to Wells's leaving Memphis began in March 1892, when three of her close friends were murdered by a white mob. These friends were part of a community of African Americans who had created a successful store called the People's Grocery. Their business was providing unwelcome competition for the white-owned competitor across the street, and, predictably, tensions escalated to violence. A group of six armed white men, including plainclothes law officers, invaded the grocery, prompting the proprietors to defend themselves. Three of the white invaders were shot in the ensuing scuffle, leading to a retreat, the deputizing of several other white men, and the eventual arrest of the three proprietors of the People's Grocery. While jailed and awaiting trial, as so often happened, the accused were released by the authorities to an angry mob of white men and lynched.

Wells was out of town at the time of the murders. When she returned, she wrote about the incident as evidence that the institutions and laws of the city were turned against its Black citizens. Seeing no other recourse, Wells urged Black people to leave the city:

> The city of Memphis has demonstrated that neither character nor standing avails the Negro if he dares to protect himself against the white man or become his rival. There is nothing we can do about lynching now, as

we are outnumbered and without arms. The white mob could help itself to ammunition without pay, but the order was rigidly enforced against the selling of guns to Negroes. There is therefore only one thing left that we can do, save our money and leave a town which will neither protect our lives and property, nor give us a fair trial in the courts when accused by white people, but takes us out and murders us in cold blood when accused by white persons.[19]

In May, Wells went further. Because most lynchings were justified by whites' accusations that Black men had raped white women, she felt it was crucial to discredit them. She announced her intentions defiantly: "Eight negroes lynched since last issue of the Free Speech one at Little Rock, Ark., last Saturday morning where the citizens broke into the penitentiary and got their man; three near Anniston, Ala., one near New Orleans; and three at Clarksville, Ga., the last three for killing a white man, and five on the same old racket—the new alarm about raping white women. The same programme of hanging, then shooting bullets into the lifeless bodies was carried out to the letter."[20]

Mainstream newspapers in Memphis were furious, issuing threats at Wells's nerve for questioning this central tenet of white supremacy. As Wells herself would later document, the *Daily Commercial* responded to Wells on May 25 with the following:

Those negroes who are attempting to make the lynching of individuals of their race a means for arousing the worst passions of their kind are playing with a dangerous sentiment. The negroes may as well understand that there is no mercy for the negro rapist and little patience with his defenders. A negro organ printed in this city, in a recent issue publishes the following atrocious paragraph: "Nobody in this section of the country believes the old threadbare lie that negro men rape white women. If Southern white men are not careful they will overreach themselves, and public sentiment will have a reaction; and a conclusion will be reached which will be very damaging to the moral reputation of their women.

The fact that a black scoundrel is allowed to live and utter such loathsome and repulsive calumnies is a volume of evidence as to the wonderful patience of Southern whites. But we have had enough of it.

There are some things that the Southern white man will not tolerate, and the obscene intimations of the foregoing have brought the writer to the very outermost limit of public patience. We hope we have said enough.[21]

They had. A group of what Wells describes as "committee of leading citizens" descended on the offices of the *Free Speech and Headlight* and "destroyed the

MISS IDA B. WELLS.   Ida B. Wells, circa 1893.

type and furnishings of the office, and left a note saying that anyone trying to publish the paper again would be punished with death."[22] Wells was in New York at the time and was offered the opportunity to stay on with the *New York Age*. With her livelihood destroyed and her life threatened, Wells accepted the offer to stay in New York, where she would be encouraged to continue her journalistic investigations into lynching.

She compiled her results in a pamphlet with the title "Southern Horrors: Lynch Law in All Its Phases." The report examined individual incidents and also criticized the institutions that perpetuated lynching. Among those institutions, Wells asserted, was the mainstream white press, which gave cover to mob violence and, occasionally, instigated it. In the following section of the pamphlet, Wells described the role of the press in encouraging the vigilantism, and further describes the murder of her friends:

"The Malicious and Untruthful White Press"

The *Daily Commercial* and *Evening Scimitar* of Memphis, Tenn., are owned by leading business men of that city, and yet, in spite of the fact that there had been no white woman in Memphis outraged by an Afro-American, and that Memphis possessed a thrifty law-abiding, property-owning class of Afro-Americans the *Commercial* of May 17, under the head of "More Rapes, More Lynchings" gave utterance to the following:

The lynching of three Negro scoundrels reported in our dispatches from Anniston, Ala., for a brutal outrage committed upon a white woman will be a text for much comment on "Southern barbarism" by Northern newspapers; but we fancy it will hardly prove effective for campaign purposes among intelligent people. The frequency of these lynchings calls attention to the frequency of the crimes which causes lynching. The "Southern barbarism," which deserves the serious attention of all people North and South, is the barbarism which preys upon weak and defenseless women. Nothing but the most prompt, speedy and extreme punishment can hold in check the horrible and bestial propensities of the Negro race. There is a strange similarity about a number of cases of this character which have lately occurred.[23]

In this passage quoted by Wells, the *Memphis Evening Scimitar* issued a staunch defense of vigilante justice to defend the city and the region against the claim that lynching was a form of "Southern barbarism." The newspaper argued, as Wells would have predicted, that such measures were necessary to protect white womanhood from the threat posed by Black men. The newspaper would go on to elaborate on the nature of this threat, which, according to the racist logic of the *Evening Scimitar*, was the result of "the Negro's lustful imagination":

In each case the crime was deliberately planned and perpetrated by several Negroes. They watched for an opportunity when the women were left without a protector. It was not a sudden yielding to a fit of passion, but the consummation of a devilish purpose which has been seeking and waiting for the opportunity. . . . No man can leave his family at night without the dread that some roving Negro ruffian is watching and waiting for this opportunity. The swift punishment which invariably follows these horrible crimes doubtless acts as a deterring effect upon the Negroes in that immediate neighborhood for a short time. But the lesson is not widely learned nor long remembered. . . . The facts of the crime appear to appeal more to the Negro's lustful imagination than the facts of the punishment do to his fears. He sets aside all fear of death in any form when opportunity is found for the gratification of his bestial desires.[24]

In its June 4, 1892, issue, the *Memphis Evening Scimitar* further explained that the danger posed by Black men to white women was especially urgent now that slavery had ended. The slave system, the editors argued, had helped to keep Black people docile. But, since emancipation, they had increasingly lost control of themselves, endangering the white population. Lynching, they argued, was the unseemly but necessary social remedy:

Aside from the violation of white women by Negroes, which is the outcropping of a bestial perversion of instinct, the chief cause of trouble between the races in the South is the Negro's lack of manners. In the state of slavery, he learned politeness from association with white people, who took pains to teach him. Since the emancipation came and the tie of mutual interest and regard between master and servant was broken, the Negro has drifted away into a state which is neither freedom nor bondage. Lacking the proper inspiration of the one and the restraining force of the other he has taken up the idea that boorish insolence is independence, and the exercise of a decent degree of breeding toward white people is identical with servile submission. In consequence of the prevalence of this notion there are many Negroes who use every opportunity to make themselves offensive, particularly when they think it can be done with impunity. . . . The white people won't stand this sort of thing, and whether they be insulted as individuals are as a race, the response will be prompt and effectual.[25]

Referring to an assault by white mobs on Black Memphians, Wells wrote that

the bloody riot of 1866, in which so many Negroes perished, was brought on principally by the outrageous conduct of the blacks toward the whites on the streets. It is also a remarkable and discouraging fact that the majority of such scoundrels are Negroes who have received educational advantages at the hands of the white taxpayers. They have got just enough of learning to make them realize how hopelessly their race is behind the other in everything that makes a great people, and they attempt to "get even" by insolence, which is ever the resentment of inferiors. There are well-bred Negroes among us, and it is truly unfortunate that they should have to pay, even in part, the penalty of the offenses committed by the baser sort, but this is the way of the world. The innocent must suffer for the guilty.[26]

Here she echoed the often-class-conscious values of the "colored chosen nation" and its concern with propriety as a point of access to a white alliance and to freedom.[27]

She continued,

If the Negroes as a people possessed a hundredth part of the self-respect which is evidenced by the courteous bearing of some that the Scimitar could name, the friction between the races would be reduced to a minimum. It will not do to beg the question by pleading that many white men are also stirring up strife. The Caucasian blackguard simply obeys the promptings of a depraved disposition, and he is seldom deliberately rough or offensive toward strangers or unprotected women.

The Negro tough, on the contrary, is given to just that kind of offending, and he almost invariably singles out white people as his victims.[28]

Reporting the Facts of Lynching

Wells reprinted these claims to make clear that these acts of mob violence against Black people were commonly, but falsely, justified by the white press. But she did not stop there. Her investigation backed her impassioned outrage with a veritable mountain of evidence to refute the justifications she had laid before the reader. Using statistical information from the *Chicago Tribune*, Wells first took the total number of lynching deaths recorded in 1892: 241. She then showed that 160 of the 241 victims were Black people and that almost all of them had been murdered in southern states.

Wells carefully documented the charges victims faced. She found that rape, attempted rape, and murder were the most common allegations, but there were many other infractions listed as well. She then investigated the alleged incidents of assault in order to determine the likelihood that they occurred. As she summarized in the passage that follows, Wells found that a great many of these alleged crimes were not supported by evidence. She did not deny that women regularly suffered assaults from men, but she noted how outrage only seemed to emerge when white women were its victims. She wrote,

> Indeed, the record for the last twenty years shows exactly the same or a smaller proportion who have been charged with this horrible crime. Quite a number of the one-third alleged cases of assault that have been personally investigated by the writer have shown that there was no foundation in fact for the charges; yet the claim is not made that there were no real culprits among them. The negro has been too long associated with the white man not to have copied his vices as well as his virtues. But the negro resents and utterly repudiates the efforts to blacken his good name by asserting that assaults upon women are peculiar to his race. The negro has suffered far more from the commission of this crime against the women of his race by white men than the white race has ever suffered through his crimes. Very scant notice is taken of the matter when this is the condition of affairs. What becomes a crime deserving capital punishment when the tables are turned is a matter of small moment when the negro woman is the accusing party.[29]

In addition to her demolition of the justifications for lynching, Wells argued that the practice hurt local and national economies. She said that its violence and brutality made a mockery of the "Anglo-Saxon civilization" then touted as the apex of the human condition.[30] Still, her lonely campaign against lynching did not immediately capture the attention of policymakers or even of other journalists. Indeed, northern papers, as well as southern outlets, usually framed reports on lynchings in ways that tacitly or explicitly supported the claims of the murderers and assigned guilt to the victims.

Nor did her efforts yield decisive government action. In fact, racial violence arguably got worse in both the North and South. Lynchings continued as repeated attempts at federal legislation that would criminalize, if not prevent, the violence languished in Congress. Lynching would not be made a federal crime until 1969.

After white terrorists led a deadly rampage through Black neighborhoods in Springfield, Illinois, in 1908, a group of activists founded the National Association for the Advancement of Colored People. Wells-Barnett (as she was known after her marriage) was one of the organizers. The NAACP would also use journalism to push back against racist domination, launching its own magazine, *The Crisis*, in 1910. Wells later left the NAACP, frustrated with their lack of action, but the organization she helped to found and its magazine would inspire new generations of writers, thinkers, and activists opposed to the racism that saturated US society. Both would play a significant role in the Harlem Renaissance, the Double V Campaign of the 1940s, and the early days of the civil rights movement.

From 1920 to 1938, a simple flag was from the NAACP's headquarters on Fifth Avenue in New York City. Against a black background, in white block letters, it read, "A Man Was Lynched Yesterday." The flag first appeared regularly, but not every day. Even as the frequency of lynching declined in the 1920s, the flag gave a stark reminder that such murders were continuing. The landlords hated it and threatened the organization with eviction.

In her crusade against lynching, Wells struck at the dark heart of southern racial hegemony by attacking its violence and feeding it back the insanity of its own logic. Like journalists of other eras, Wells did not solve the problem she addressed, but she publicized it in ways that lent Blacks Americans a social space of respite from the constant assault of Jim Crow. In that action, she and other Black journalists of the day worked to force the wider, white public to see racism not as a norm to uphold but as a national disgrace.

The election of Barack Obama to the presidency in 2008 and 2012 made it possible to believe that the United States had achieved what was commonly called a "postrace America." But that isn't true today and it wasn't in 1865 either. Rather, the "fear and terror that were the vehicle and tenor of Jim Crow's metaphors of white supremacy" continue to hold on. But Wells' work also shows that one individual journalist can make her mark in a way that defines the threat for others to avoid and act on in the future.[31]

6

Dreams and Nightmares of Empire

The early American ambition to global power ascended on the lofty rhetoric of "manifest destiny." Coined by journalist John L. O'Sullivan (1813–95) in an editorial in the *New York Morning News* on February 27, 1845, during the Mexican-American War, the term reflected much of the competing politics of 1840s America at once.[1] Perhaps the most common theme was the idea of a divinely ordained territorial expansion. Some in the Polk administration (1845–49) wanted the United States to annex all the land between the Mississippi River and the Pacific Ocean. Others wanted all of North America.

The victory over Mexico was decisive, but it nevertheless posed a set of problems. For many in the North and the South, the prospect of offering citizenship to the Black and brown citizens of Mexico violated acceptable racial beliefs. South Carolina senator John Calhoun (1782–1850), the leading advocate for slavery of the day, doubted that the US Constitution could apply or even be appreciated by nonwhites. In Calhoun's popular formulation of white supremacy, race served as the criterion for judging what kinds of people could *not* be admitted to the Union.

Although today we think of race as being based on skin color, recent scholarship shows that the concept of race has been constructed around the mythical assumption that white is normal. In that sense, white is neither a color nor a race, but the invisible standard against which all other races are defined as *less than* white. Definitions of physical beauty, the capacity for citizenship, and the admission to otherwise normal aspects of cultural life were then, as now, based on these idealized norms.

From her research on the British Empire, historian Caroline Elkins identifies the initial period of American imperialism in Africa as the moment when "the marker of race became skin color" in America. By that measure,

Black Africans were seen as the opposite of white. Thinking of the often violent backlash against two million mostly Catholic Irish immigrants who came to the United States in the 1830s and 1840s during the potato famine, Painter observes that "hatred of Black people did not preclude hatred of other white people."[2]

The Commercial Press and Empire

In the election campaign of 1844, James K. Polk (1795–1849) campaigned on the promise to annex Texas from Mexico and to expropriate the Oregon Territories from Britain. Although he suggested purchasing these vast tracts as was the case with the Louisiana Purchase from France, force remained his preference for resolving a dispute over the borderline between the two nations. After the Mexican army had been baited into firing first, Congress authorized the military to attack on May 11, 1844. The annexation of Texas the next year threatened the balance between slave and free states in ways that contributed to the oncoming Civil War. By the time the Treaty of Guadalupe was signed by Mexico in 1848 to end the Mexican-American War, the United States had taken a third of Mexico's territory.

At a time when most wars lasted a year or less, this two-year-long conflict became unpopular well before its end. The war was a boon to the penny press, however, which churned out dramatic accounts of war and conquest. The historian Frederick Merk asked, "Is it conceivable that the *New York Herald* and their equivalents everywhere were read on account of their freshness and coverage of news, on account of their sensationalism; or even because they satisfied their readers' earthy tastes, and not at all because their editorial views had deep-seated popular support?"[3] Merk's answer was yes. If the *Herald*'s James Gordon Bennett Sr. (1841–1918) and Moses Yale Beach (1800–68) of the *New York Sun* thought that they were opinion leaders about a military takeover of all of Mexico, they were wrong. In Merk's view, their interests lay in selling newspapers, not in making national policy.

Nevertheless, in the late nineteenth and early twentieth centuries, the United States was usually described as a nation that had deliberately *not* pursued imperial ambitions. This alternate way of imagining the United States—based on the false notion of American-Saxon exceptionalism—set it apart from the major European powers of the day. England, France, Germany, and Belgium were each openly pursuing imperial projects around the globe. But where their empires were explicitly built to extract raw materials for colonial gain, US designs were pitched as offering the benefits of Americanism to the lesser peoples of foreign lands.[4]

Driven as much to preserve their idealized white, Protestant nation, American popular opinion changed to favor a new empire. In particular,

American-Saxons believed that it was their "duty to regenerate backward peoples of the continent." In this version of chosen-ness, the doctrine of Manifest Destiny offered a moral license for white Americans to conquer brown and Black peoples. Moreover, it provided an excuse to "liberate" their land.[5] Securing territory as imperial possessions, they argued, would announce the nation's arrival on the world stage. It would add vast resources to the already copious natural American wealth and its growing industrial appetite. To the satisfaction of some and the horror of others, by the beginning of the twentieth century, the United States had gone from defeating an empire to gain its freedom to becoming one.

Many sought to justify the US road to empire as a kind of crusade, a way to extend the blessings of white civilization and its version of democracy to those who were not yet ready to govern themselves. But not everyone agreed with this race-based logic. Though their position would not triumph, US newspapers and magazines included scathing critiques of imperial ambitions.

The Rise of the Commercial Press: Pulitzer and Hearst

As detailed in the previous chapter, the post–Civil War era saw a shift in the institutional affiliations in the mainstream press from direct political party sponsorships to a barely viable, advertising-driven enterprise. By the 1870s, newspapers in New York City were becoming increasingly profitable with advertising dollars chasing audiences numbering in the six figures. In 1883, Joseph Pulitzer (1847–1911) bought the *New York World* and immediately transformed it by focusing on popular interests, scandal, crime, and other objects of public fascination. Within five years, he had taken the *World's* circulation to more than a million and opened new possibilities for a newspaper's wealth and influence.

In 1895, William Randolph Hearst (1863–1951), the successful managing editor of the *San Francisco Examiner*, with the help of his family's fortune bought the *New York Morning Journal*. He immediately sought to rival Pulitzer's *World*. These two papers were soon battling each other for dominance of the New York market, each seeking to fill their paper with the most alluring content. They utilized the newest printing techniques available, including dazzling color illustrations. They also designed new kinds of content to attract and retain new readers, bringing readers sports news, human interest stories, and, for the imperial imagination, travelogues.

The two publishers also competed to hire and retain the most popular journalists and cartoonists of the day. One of these was Richard Outcault, the creator of the popular comic strip "Hogan's Alley," which featured a main character known as the Yellow Kid. The character wore a yellow smock, because the *World* had first experimented with color printing by applying yellow printer's ink to the cartoon. A significant pay raise lured Outcault—and the Yellow Kid—from Pulitzer's *World* to Hearst's *Journal*. Although the strip lasted only a few more years, the inking episode inspired an enduring putdown of the sensationalist tactics that news organizations sometimes employ to gain readers—"yellow journalism."

As the century neared its end, the largest and most powerful media outlets began to see that their interests aligned with those of other capitalists. Supporting the general expansion of markets (as illustrated in the previous chapter) meant siding with management over labor in most disputes. Such attitudes prevailed at many of the most profitable newspapers, but not at all of them. The politics of some publishers and influential editors could and did alter the shape of some newspapers, journals, and the emerging medium of illustrated magazines. At the same time, as shown in the last chapter, an oppositional, grassroots press continued to challenge the power elite. Opinion remained divided on the question of American imperial expansion, even among elites.

As we shall see, the national division over the issue of imperialism was reflected in the struggle that unfolded in the pages of the nation's newspapers. While prestigious journals like the *New York Times* catered to a small, educated elite, its massive competitors sought the vastly larger readership of the "commoner." Across these media and their publics, the imperialistic assumption that whites' dominance could not be matched was casually aired and sometimes contested. Despite the fierce debate that journalism produced in this period, some things seem clear about the changing nature of the press and how these changes influenced the outcome of the debate over imperialism.

Mainly, the daily newspaper provided a new kind of outlet for storytelling about the nation. In Benedict Anderson's evocative term, it provided the medium for a daily "national bestseller." According to Anderson's argument, national news in US newspapers became more than just a daily record of events. It became a relatively coherent, nonfiction story about the United States. This story helped to consolidate the sense of the nation, which the Civil War had almost ended just years earlier. The newspapers provided the essential storylines for rebuilding a coherent sense of the nation—what Anderson called the imagined community.

In the last three decades of the nineteenth century, that storytelling included a regular set of narratives that, themselves, included a new topic: what the US responsibilities were to the rest of the world, especially to those lands near and south of the equator. Notions of white supremacy informed much of the writing on this question, but so did the (not unrelated) notion of American exceptionalism. As discussed in chapter 2, exceptionalism was the belief that the United States was—unlike the despotic nations of Europe—the last, best hope for humankind. The notion that the United States was God's "chosen" land often came up. Flush with possibilities, some even argued for the idea that an American empire could promote what would later be called "human rights," but these notions proved to be too easily set aside.

As important as newspapers and periodicals were in scripting ideas of the new frontier, they were not telling the story alone. Alongside the editorials, speeches, reports, and exposés that journalists reported about the expanding colonial enterprise, a number of fictionalized accounts shaped public ideas. As Americans debated whom to "liberate" and how, thousands filled arenas to watch Buffalo Bill's Wild West Show reenact the defeat of the Native American. Countless more read serialized fictions about "how the West was won." These stories told of how the American "civilization's" conquest of "savages" had been both a thrilling adventure and the way to a better future. But other accounts would vie for attention as well.

In 1899, Joseph Conrad's novel, *Heart of Darkness*, based on the horrors of the Belgian colonization of the Congo, offered a more complicated and less heroic imagining of imperial ambitions. What Andrew Griffiths noted of the British context was also true of the United States: Nonfictional and fictional accounts of colonialism influenced one another in style, as well as content. He explained, "The popular press was able to appeal to a mass readership by adopting features of the novel, while novelists adopted features more closely associated with newspapers for the same purpose."[6] In this sense, the influence of journalism about colonialism shaped more than the debate about colonialism. It shaped (and was shaped by) the wider popular culture in which that debate was engaged.

"Dr. Livingstone, I Presume?"

In the years after the Civil War, industrial capitalism and immigration expanded American cities and transformed everyday life. The white domination of the continent now extended to the Pacific Ocean. The European powers France, Germany, and Great Britain were already competing for colonies in Asia and Africa, as was Belgium. For many Americans, this convergence of global powers made overseas expansion an attractive prospect. Imperial ambitions were seen as a way to escape the drudgery of industrial life. They offered a way to continue the taming of "savage" places and people that had for long been romanticized in literature and political culture. By the 1870s, the exploits of missionaries and adventurers were circulating widely in newspapers, promoting a vision of unknown, mysterious places, supposedly untouched by civilized (that is, white) men.

Around this same time, some newspaper editors were experimenting with a new model of journalism. Rather than the typical content about politics and commerce, publishers such as James Gordon Bennett Jr. of the *New York Herald* sought content that would seize the attention of average readers and keep them returning to the paper day after day for updates. When David Livingstone (1813–73), a Scottish missionary, doctor, and explorer working in central Africa lost contact with European explorers, Bennett assigned Henry Morton Stanley to find him and to send back periodic reports of his exploits from the farthest recesses of the "dark continent."

British by birth, Stanley had come to the United States in 1859 and found work after the Civil War as a journalist for the *Herald*. He specialized in news from distant lands and dangerous missions from the western United States, the Middle East, and elsewhere. As a reporter, he was an unreliable, self-serving (and longwinded) narrator of his own experiences. He followed each exploration with a multivolume set of his adventures. By his own account, he had a dismissive, patronizing attitude toward the people of Africa, and he treated his workers brutally.

In November 1871 in present-day Tanzania, Stanley found Livingstone living in a village near Lake Tanganyika. Like much of Stanley's reporting, his famous greeting, "Dr. Livingstone, I presume?" may have been fabricated. The story he constructed excited Americans and Europeans, who were eager to imagine "uncivilized" and "primitive" locales as ideal settings for white masculine heroism. This publicity stunt provided *Herald* readers with absorbing accounts of exotic peoples. It also familiarized them with the often-brutal measures Stanley took to subdue them.

In the following passage, he describes his arrival in Unyanyembe, in modern Tanzania. He recounts how, upon receiving word that the regional ruler would not let them pass, he attacked them with the aid of Arab allies. Notice how he featured himself in the action against mostly incompetent natives:

> I gave assistance on the first day, in concert with the Arabs; attacked two villages, and captured, killed and drove away the inhabitants. On the second day I caught a fever. On the third day the Arabs were ambushed and routed with terrific slaughter. On the fourth day there was a general desertion of the Arabs and my own men; all but six Mirambo threatened Unyanyembe. I fortified the houses, collected 150 fugitives, with five days provisions, and hoisted the American flag. Mirambo retired without attacking. I then started for Ujiji on another road. The Arabs endeavored to dissuade me, and said that death was certain, and frightened my followers. Shaw deserted, but I nevertheless pushed forward over untrodden desert for 400 miles, and reached the suburbs of Ujiri, which I entered firing guns and carrying the American flag at the head of the procession.

The astonished natives flocked out in crowds, with deafening shouts. I noticed in the center of a group of Arabs, strongly contrasting their sun-burned faces, a hale-looking, grey-bearded white man, wearing a naval cap, with a faded gold band, and red woolen shirt, preserving a demeanor of calmness before the Arabs. I inquired, "Dr. Livingstone, I presume?"[7]

Every line of this story *by* Stanley *about* Stanley reflects the author's self-serving arrogance. Surrounded by hapless and overwhelmed "natives," he extends the superprotection of colonial whiteness to Livingstone. The story then turns to the "discovery" of a continent and its rivers that, for lack of white men, was treated as uninhabited. He went on:

He, smiling, answered yes. He informed me that he started in March, 1866, with twelve Sepoys, nine Johanna men, and seven liberated slaves. He travelled up the bank of the Rouuma; his men got freightened [*sic*], deserted and reported Livingstone dead, as an excuse for desertion. He crossed the Chambezi, and found it not the Portuguese Zambese, but a wholly separate river. He traced it and found that it was called further on Lualaba. He explored 700 miles, and found that the Chambezi is doubtless the source of the Nile, and that the length on the Nile is 2,600 miles. It is not supplied by the Taugauyika. He reached within 180 miles of the explored ground when he was obliged to return to Ujiji destitute. He here met me. We both left on the 16th of October, and arrived at Unyanyembe at the end of November. We spent twenty-eight days exploring the district together.

We spent Christmas in Ujiji. I arrived on the coast March 14, leaving Livingstone at the Unyanyembe, to explore the north of Tanjanyika Lake, and the remaining 180 miles of the Lualoba River. This will occupy the next two years.[8]

Stanley would go on to aid Belgian king Leopold's colonization of the Congo, which was so bloody and ruthless even by the standards of the day, that it would elicit worldwide condemnation. The Belgians' extreme violence would appear in Conrad's novel *Heart of Darkness*.

Like many colonial enterprises of the time, the colonization of the Congo was framed for readers in the United States as an opportunity to show primitive cultures the way to economic, political, and cultural development. Still, there were critics. African American George Washington Williams (1849–91) would expose the abuses of the colonial regime in a document with the lengthy title of "An Open Letter to His Serene Majesty Leopold II, King of the Belgians and Sovereign of the Independent State of Congo." The following selection from the *New York Daily Tribune* relates a portion of Williams's critique:

The agents of your Majesty's Government have misrepresented the Congo country and the Congo railway. Mr. H. M. Stanley, the man who was your chief agent in setting up your authority in the country, has grossly misrepresented the character of the country. Instead of it being fertile and productive, it is sterile and unproductive. The natives can scarcely subsist upon the vegetable life produced in some parts of the country. Not will this condition of affairs change until the native shall have been taught by the European the dignity, utility and blessing of labour. There is no improvement among the natives, because there is an impassable gulf between them and your Majesty's Government, a gulf which can never be bridged. Henry M. Stanley's name produces a shudder among this simple folk when mentioned; they remember his broken promises, his copious profanity, his hot temper, his heavy blows, his severe and rigorous measures, by which they were mulcted of their lands. His last appearance in the Congo produced a profound sensation among them, when he led 500 Zanzibar soldiers with 300 campfollowers on his way to relieve Emin Pasha. They thought it meant complete subjugation, and they fled in confusion. But the only thing they found in the wake of his march was misery. No white man commanded his rear column, and his troops were allowed to straggle, sicken and die; and their bones were scattered over more than two hundred miles of territory.[9]

Stanley later told the *Tribune* that he "regarded the letter or pamphlet as a deliberate attempt at blackmail," but subsequent historical work has confirmed the brutal treatment Williams described.

The casual disregard for Black lives in the Congo reflected the dominance of white supremacist attitudes, which prevailed both in Belgium and in the United States. Indeed, a key argument for imperial expansion rested on racist assumptions that were already well developed at home. The people inhabiting these countries could not, it was argued, simply be freed and left to rule themselves. After all, the thinking went, they were members of inferior races, who had not evolved to the extent of the white races. Even within the United States, Black people, Chicanos, and indigenous people were treated as populations to be managed, not treated as full and equal participants in American democracy.

An August 1893 cartoon in the popular British magazine *Puck* demonstrates how racism at home made the subjugation of dark-skinned people abroad seem natural and desirable. The cartoon anticipates the "Colored People's Day" at the World Columbian Exposition, which would take place later that same month. It shows the inhabitants of African village displays (who were exhibited at the fair to demonstrate the savagery of the "lower races") mixing easily with the African Americans visiting the fair. Both are depicted with demeaning racial caricatures.

The previous month at the fair, historian Frederick Jackson Turner had delivered the paper "The Significance of the Frontier in American History." His thesis emphasized the central role of settlement and westward expansion in forging the "American character." It quickly became influential with intellectuals and politicians. Among them, Theodore Roosevelt (1858–1919) saw an end to westward expansion on the North American continent and began advocating for imperial expansion overseas.

Roosevelt envisioned overseas empires as a testing ground for national manliness. He believed that such virility was essential for the realization of American greatness. "No nation," he wrote, "can achieve real greatness, if its people are not both essentially moral and essentially manly."[10] The military conflicts that would accompany the taking and maintaining of overseas possessions, Roosevelt thought, would sharpen and harden young men for the demanding, but necessary, task of subjugating inferior peoples. As he wrote in 1895, "I should welcome almost any war, for I think this country needs one." But nothing in Roosevelt's vivid imagination brought together essential manliness and essential morality like wars of racial conquest. "The most ultimately righteous of all wars is a war with savages. . . . The rude, fierce settler who drives the savage from the land lays all civilized mankind under a debt to him."[11]

"Take Up the White Man's Burden"

By 1896, proimperialist enthusiasts believed they had found an opportunity to realize their goals of an overseas empire. Guerillas in the Spanish possession of Cuba were agitating for independence, and publishers like the *New York Journal*'s William Randolph Hearst had been publishing heroic accounts of the Cuban resistance against the Spanish.

In the example that follows, Hearst's star reporter, Richard Harding Davis (1864–1916), meticulously detailed the execution of a Cuban revolutionary named Rodríguez by the Spanish. Davis's account presents Rodríguez as a noble patriot and the Spanish troops as clumsy, thoughtless, and cruel. As we join Davis's narrative, the prisoner is about to be executed by a Spanish firing squad:

> The officer had given the order, the men had raised their pieces, and the condemned man had heard the clicks of the triggers as they were pulled back, and he had not moved. And then happened one of the most cruelly refined, though unintentional, acts of torture that one can very well imagine. As the officer slowly raised his sword, preparatory to giving

the signal, one of the mounted officers rode up to him and pointed out silently what I had already observed with some satisfaction, that the firing squad were so placed that when they fired they would shoot several of the soldiers stationed on the extreme end of the square.

Like a racist joke, the members of the Spanish firing squad, who were not white according to the race science of the day, were too dimwitted to avoid shooting each other.

> Their captain motioned his men to lower their pieces, and then walked across the grass and laid his hand on the shoulder of the waiting prisoner.
>
> It is not pleasant to think what that shock must have been. The man had steeled himself to receive a volley of bullets in his back. He believed that in the next instant he would be in another world; he had heard the command given, had heard the click of the Mausers as the locks caught—and then, at that supreme moment, a human hand had been laid upon his shoulder and a voice spoke in his ear.

Having shown the Spanish to be clumsy and cruel, Davis offers a contrasting portrait of Rodríguez, who is portrayed as dignified and almost superhuman in his composure:

> You would expect that any man who had been snatched back to life in such a fashion would start and tremble at the reprieve, or would break down altogether, but this boy turned his head steadily, and followed with his eyes the direction of the officer's sword, then nodded his head gravely, and, with his shoulders squared, took up a new position, straightened his back again, and once more held himself erect.
>
> As an exhibition of self-control, this should surely rank above feats of heroism performed in battle, where there are thousands of comrades to give inspiration. This man was alone, in the sight of the hills he knew, with only enemies about him, with no source to draw on for strength but that which lay within himself.
>
> The officer of the firing squad, mortified by his blunder, hastily whipped up his sword, the men once more leveled their rifles, the sword rose, dropped, and the men fired. At the report the Cuban's head snapped back almost between his shoulders, but his body fell slowly, as though some one had pushed him gently forward from behind and he had stumbled.
>
> He sank on his side in the wet grass without a struggle or sound and did not move again.

A final dramatic flourish again contrasts the clumsy and callous Spanish troops with the nobility of the rebel.

Each soldier as he passed turned and looked down on [the rebel's corpse], some craning their necks curiously, others giving a careless glance, and some without any interest at all, as they would have looked at a house by the roadside or a passing cart or a hole in the road.

One young soldier caught his foot in a trailing vine and fell forward just opposite to it. He grew very red when his comrades giggled at him for his awkwardness. The crowd of sleepy spectators fell in on either side of the band. They had forgotten it, too, and the priests put their vestments back in the bag and wrapped their heavy cloaks about them, and hurried off after the others.

At that moment the sun, which had shown some promise of its coming in the glow above the hills, shot up suddenly from behind them in all the splendor of the tropics, a fierce, red disc of heat, and filled the air with warmth and light.

But as I fell in at the rear of the procession and looked back the figure of the young Cuban, who was no longer a part of the world of Santa Clara, was asleep in the wet grass, with his motionless arms still tightly bound behind him, with the scapula twisted awry across his face and the blood from his breast sinking into the soil he had tried to free.[12]

In his next piece, he wrote a dramatic story about the strip search of a young Cuban woman suspected of aiding the Cuban rebels. The suggestive tone of the story crossed all limits of propriety, and Hearst knew it would sell. Though Davis had reported that the search had been conducted by women, Hearst had omitted this redeeming detail. Further, he added an illustration of Spanish men conducting the search of the woman's naked body.

Hearst's edits were calculated to provoke maximum offense to American readers—and no doubt, not a little yellow journalism–like titillation—for whom such violations of women demanded violent responses from noble men. As discussed in chapter 5, this same logic supported the lynching of Black men accused of violating the honor of white women. But for Davis, Hearst's misuse of the story was too much to bear, and he resigned in protest.

The USS *Maine*: Gateway to Empire

On February 15, 1898, the USS *Maine*, a US naval vessel, exploded under mysterious circumstances and sank in Havana harbor. Without evidence, the *Journal* strongly suggested foul play by the Spanish. By early March, war with Spain was imminent. Victory would mean the liberation of Cuba and the Philippines, something that appealed to millions of Americans. Others saw in Spain's potential demise an opportunity for expanding American influence overseas. Many advocates of an American imperial policy saw it as an opening to the moral duty owed to the "lower orders" in the name of American-Saxon exceptionalism.

Not only was such a view popular in the United States, but it was a tried-and-true justification for imperialism across the Atlantic, as well. English poet and novelist Rudyard Kipling (1865–1936) memorialized the view in a poem that was published in newspapers across the United States on February 5, 1899. It began with a stanza that perfectly captured the spirit of this imagined benevolent imperialism.

Take up the White Man's burden—
Send forth the best ye breed—
Go bind your sons to exile
To serve your captives' need;
To wait in heavy harness,
On fluttered folk and wild—
You new-caught sullen peoples,
Half-devil and half-child.[13]

Defenses of the policy continued. The argument for American imperialism that follows is by Whitelaw Reid (1837–1912), editor-in-chief of the *New York Tribune*, who had earned a role as an imperial administrator. In this speech on October 21, 1899, at a Princeton University commencement, Reid explained the virtues of US colonization in the recently acquired property of the Philippines. At the time of this speech, the colonization effort was under siege at home, where opponents of colonial policies had made public their objections, and abroad, where Emilio Aguinaldo was leading a Filipino rebellion against American forces. Reid presented objections to US imperialism and dismisses each, framing the imperial project as a benevolent rule that would lead the subject of US colonization toward civilization and (eventually) to self-government:

Is it said that this is imperialism? That implies usurpation of power, and there is absolutely no ground for such a charge against this Administration, at any one stage in these whole transactions. If any complaint on this score is to lie, it must relate to the critical period when we were accepting responsibility for order at Manila, and must be for the exercise of too little power, not too much. It is not imperialism to take up honestly the responsibility for order we incurred before the world, and continue under it, even if that should lead us to extend the civil rights of the American Constitution over new regions and strange peoples. It is not imperialism when duty keeps us among these chaotic, warring, distracted tribes, civilized, semicivilized and barbarous, to help them, as far as their several capacities will permit, towards self-government on the basis of these civil rights.

Here, Reid refers to the maturation process of lesser nations as an evolutionary process, one that casts the United States atop the world order and offers little hope for the lesser tribes. He continued:

But you cannot fit people for freedom—they must fit themselves, just as we must do our own crawling and stumbling in order to learn to walk. The illustration is unfortunate. Must the crawling baby, then, be abandoned by its natural or accidental guardian, and left to itself to grow strong by struggling, or to perish, as may happen?

"Governments derive their just powers from the consent of the governed." "No man is good enough to govern another against his will." Great truths, from men whose greatness and moral elevation of the world admires. But there is a higher authority than Jefferson or Lincoln, who said: "If a man smite thee on thy right cheek, turn to him the other also." Yet he who acted literally on even that divine injunction toward the Malays that attacked our own army in Manila would be a congenital idiot to begin with, and his corpse, while it lasted, would remain the object lesson of how not to deal with the present stage of Malay civilization and Christianity.

Having argued that force would be the only sensible response to an attack by, in this case, the Filipino-Malay army that attacked the US Army in Manila, Reid argued for a very British response through an equally violent reply. The certitude of this outlook owed much to the Americans' adoption of Anglo-Saxon exceptionalism from the British. Reid argued that Americans should accept what he saw as an accomplished fact: The United States had an empire that had been building for decades, if not longer. He said,

Why mourn over the present course as a departure from the policy of the Fathers? For over a hundred years, the uniform policy which they began and their sons continued has been acquisition, expansion, annexation, reaching out to the remote wilderness far more distant than the Philippines are now,—to disconnected regions like Alaska,—to island regions like Midway, the Guano Islands, the Aleutians, the Sandwich Islands,—and even to the quasi-protectorates like Liberia and Samoa. Why mourn because of the precedent we are establishing? The precedent was established before we were born.[14]

Other proimperial sentiments drew an implicit comparison between the people of color already in the United States, who were deemed unable

"Holding His End Up," cartoon appearing in the August 9, 1898, edition of the *Philadelphia Inquirer*.

to properly govern themselves, with the inhabitants of the nation's new colonial possessions. This cartoon from the *Philadelphia Inquirer*, shows the United States mastering its imperial possessions to the admiration of European onlookers. Note the depiction of the colonized nations as children, indistinguishable from hyperracialized Africans.

The Anti-Imperialist League: Questioning "the Blessings of Civilization"

But not everyone saw the conflict in this way. Many Americans hoped their country would steer clear of the foreign entanglements of Europe, just as George Washington (1732–99) had famously warned in his Farewell

Address. Some of the nation's most prominent citizens, despite differences on other matters, came together to oppose the establishment of a US overseas empire. The Anti-Imperialist League was founded in Boston in November 1898. Its activities would be bankrolled by the steel magnate Andrew Carnegie (1835–1919) and would come to include a diverse array of prominent Americans, including the social worker Jane Addams (1860–1935), the civil rights leader Booker T. Washington(1856–1915), the former presidents Grover Cleveland (1837–1908) and Benjamin Harrison (1833–1901), and the labor organizer Samuel Gompers (1850–1924).

The league rooted its opposition to empire in an understanding of American history, which stressed its essential difference from the powers of Europe. The United States, they pointed out, had been formed by liberating itself from the world's largest empire and should remain a force for liberation, not domination. Even some who strongly supported war with Spain as a liberating mission now opposed the notion that US officials and troops should remain in the far-flung parts of the world now freed from Spanish rule. They called, instead, for democratic elections and a withdrawal of US forces.[15]

The Treaty of Paris, which ended the fighting with Spain in 1898, designated the Philippines as a colony of the United States. Knowing that the treaty required ratification from two-thirds of the US Senate, the Anti-Imperialist League turned its efforts toward securing the necessary votes to defeat it. The anti-imperialists were disappointed however, when the treaty secured ratification by a single vote in February 1899.

Opponents of the emerging imperial consensus continued their efforts. Some attempted to emphasize what they saw as the absurdities of the paternalistic suggestion that the newly freed peoples of the Philippines required indefinite guidance by the United States in order to climb some kind of civilizational ladder. Although not many of the anti-imperialists were antiracist by our modern definition, there were many who objected to the notion that imperialism was some kind of benevolent duty to the benighted people of the Earth—Kipling's "white man's burden."

The Anti-Imperialist League would find their most barbed and effective spokesperson in Samuel Clemens (1835–1910), the famous author better known as Mark Twain. Just before sailing for home from London in the fall of 1900, Twain gave an interview to the *New York World* in which he announced his opposition to the US conflict in the Philippines.

By the time he arrived in New York, his words had caused an uproar. Greeted by reporters at the dock, Twain was harangued. "You've been quoted here as an anti-imperialist!" one exclaimed. "Well, I am," Twain admitted.

In an interview with the *New York Herald*, he elaborated:

I left these shores a red-hot imperialist. I wanted the American eagle to go screaming into the Pacific. It seemed tiresome and tame for it to content itself with the Rockies. Why not spread its wings over the Philippines, I asked myself? And I thought it would be a real good thing to do. I said to myself, "Here are a people who have suffered for three centuries. We can make them as free as ourselves, give them a government and country of their own, put a miniature of the American constitution afloat on the Pacific, start a brand new republic to take its place among the free nations of the world!" It seemed to me a great task to which we had addressed ourselves. But I have thought some more since then, and I have read carefully the Treaty of Paris, and I have seen that we do not intend to free, but to subjugate the people of the Philippines. We have gone to conquer, not to redeem. . . . And so I am an anti-imperialist. I am opposed to having the eagle put its talons on any other land.[16]

Twain's late entry into the fray was greeted warmly by the now well-organized and well-financed anti-imperialists, who encouraged him to continue his attacks.

He made his next intervention in late December, when he wrote one of several "salutations to the twentieth century" published in the *Minneapolis Journal*. Twain's blistering entry skewers imperialist pieties undertaken in the name of Christian charity. In the following brief passage, he condemns the imperial ambitions of the Germans, Russians, British, and Americans for exploiting people, while proclaiming a desire to help them:

A SALUTATION SPEECH FROM THE NINETEENTH CENTURY TO THE
TWENTIETH TAKEN DOWN IN SHORTHAND BY MARK TWAIN

I bring you the state matron called—CHRISTENDOM—Returning bedraggled, besmirched and dishonored from pirate raids in Kiaochow, Manchuria, South Africa and the Philippines; with her soul full of meanness, her pocket full of boodle and her mouth full of pious hypocrisies. Giver her soap and a towel, but hide the looking glass."

Twain's words scandalized many readers, but the New England Anti-Imperialist League liked it so much they had it printed as a New Year's card, with the following addendum: "Give her the glass; it may from error free her / When she shall see herself as others see her."

Twain followed this statement with a commentary in the *North American Review* in February of the following year. In the following excerpt, Twain suggested that the justification of a "civilizing mission" cloaks a more exploitative arrangement. He lampooned what he called "The Blessings-of-Civilization Trust" by carrying their arguments to an absurdist conclusion. In the process, he revealed the "person sitting in the darkness" to be the colonizer himself, blinded to that fact by his own arrogance and shortsightedness:

> Extending the Blessings of Civilization to our Brother who sits in Darkness has been a good trade and has paid well, on the whole; and there is money in it yet, if carefully worked—but not enough, in my judgment, to make any considerable risk advisable. The People that Sit in Darkness are getting to be too scarce—too scarce and too shy. And such darkness as is now left is really of but an indifferent quality, and not dark enough for the game. The most of those People that Sit in Darkness have been furnished with more light than was good for them or profitable for us. We have become injudicious.

As he continued, he said that the American experience as an empire was wearing thin, that the people they claimed to help were well aware of being taken advantage of.

> The Blessings-of-Civilization Trust, wisely and cautiously administered, is a Daisy. There is more money in it, more territory, more sovereignty, and other kinds of emolument, than there is in any other game that is played. But Christendom has been playing it badly of late years, and must certainly suffer by it, in my opinion. She has been so eager to get every stake that appeared on the green cloth, that the People who Sit in Darkness have noticed it—they have noticed it, and they have begun to show alarm. They have become suspicious of the Blessings of Civilization. More—they have begun to examine them. This is not well. The Blessings of Civilization are all right, and a good commercial property; there could not be a better, in a dim light. In the right kind of a light, and at a proper distance, with the goods a little out of focus, they furnish this desirable exhibit to the Gentlemen who Sit in Darkness:

LOVE,	LAW AND ORDER,
JUSTICE,	LIBERTY,
GENTLENESS,	EQUALITY,
CHRISTIANITY,	HONORABLE DEALING,
PROTECTION TO THE WEAK,	MERCY,
TEMPERANCE,	EDUCATION,

> —and so on.
> There. Is it good? Sir, it is pie. . . .

Having now laid all the historical facts before the Person Sitting in Darkness, we should bring him to again, and explain them to him. We should say to him:

"They look doubtful, but in reality they are not. There have been lies; yes, but they were told in good cause. We have been treacherous; but that was only in order that real good might come out of the apparent evil. True, we have crushed a deceived and confiding people; we have turned against the weak and the friendless who trusted us; we have stamped out a just and intelligent and well-ordered republic; we have stabbed an ally in the back and slapped the face of a guest; we have bought a Shadow from an enemy that hadn't it to sell; we have robbed a trusting friend of his land and his liberty; we have invited our clean young men to shoulder a discredited musket and do bandit's work under a flag which bandits have been accustomed to fear, not to follow; we have debauched America's honor and blackened her face before the world; but each detail was for the best. We know this. The Head of every State and Sovereignty in Christendom and ninety per cent of every legislative body in Christendom, including our Congress and our fifty State Legislatures, are members not only of the church, but also of the Blessings-of-Civilization Trust. This world-girdling accumulation of trained morals, high principles, and justice, cannot do an unright thing, an unfair thing, an ungenerous thing, an unclean thing. It knows what it is about. Give yourself no uneasiness; it is all right."

Twain had no love left for American imperialism, but he had a sharp tongue and a sharper pen:

And as for the flag for the Philippine Province, it is easily managed. We can have a special one—our States do it; we can have just our usual flag, with the white stripes painted black and the stars replaced by the skull and crossbones.[17]

William Walker's cartoon for *Life* magazine took a similarly skeptical view, presenting a simple but devastating critique of racist exploitation masquerading as altruism.[18]

The hopes of anti-imperialists like Twain and Walker rested in large measure with the continuing struggle of Filipino revolutionaries, who represented an alternative leadership to American rule. But in March 1901, Aguinaldo was captured by US forces. Months later, President William McKinley was assassinated in Buffalo, New York, and Theodore Roosevelt assumed the presidency. With a staunch proponent of American imperialism in the White House and the leader of the Filipino resistance in custody, the anti-imperialist movement gradually lost steam. Although both Filipino resistance and the Anti-Imperialist League would continue

William Walker's 1899 cartoon: "The White (?) Man's Burden" from March 18, 1899.

for years afterward, imperialism and its arguments would continue to work their way into the mainstream, even as the strategies of resistance informed future movements.

Looking back, the racialized sensibilities that had informed the inward-looking "manifest destiny" were also used to justify the Mexican-American war from 1846 to 1848. In its turn, the polarization they promoted, especially around the slavery issue, contributed directly to the Civil War from 1861 to 1865. And at the end of the century, these same racial mores would shape the outward-looking, imperialist doctrine of the "white man's burden" as part of the nation's foreign policy that led to the Spanish-American war in 1896. In this pattern, we can see how Americans' racialized beliefs fueled the nation's appetite for war and conquest from the late antebellum period to the imperialism of the beginning of the twentieth century.

7

La Raza and the Rangers

Competing Narratives of Citizenship and Policing on the Borderlands

Questions of race and citizenship have long simmered and often boiled over along the southern US border with Mexico. Tensions between the United States and Mexico can be traced back to at least the 1820s and 1830s, when that two-thousand-mile border was anything but fixed. As American expansionists eyed the massive Mexican territory, they increasingly asserted their right to open the new state of Texas to cotton farming and slavery. By 1845, when Texas joined the Union, the question of admitting new slave states would begin to look inward to the verging crisis of the Civil War. Throughout, journalists and media workers would play a key role in contesting the basic questions of citizenship, belonging, and justice.

Slavery was outlawed in Mexico in 1829, but the importation of enslaved people continued. By 1836, there were more than five thousand enslaved people in Texas in defiance of Mexican law. The Mexican government tolerated these transgressions, but soon relations worsened. The new Mexican president Antonio López de Santa Anna sought to secure the border with the United States and to centralize the control of the Mexican national government. He also sought to bring "Texians," as the white settlers called themselves, under Mexican control. Many had refused to pay taxes. Some had gone as far as murdering tax officials.

Santa Anna's strategy was unpopular, not only among the Texians, but also among many of the ethnic Mexican Tejanos in the region, who favored local control and resented the incursions of the central government. Rebels in Texas, both Anglo and Tejano, began to turn their efforts toward separating Texas from Mexico. The Texas Declaration of Independence was signed on March 2, 1836. Among the Anglo signatories were also names such as

Lorenzo de Zavala, José Francisco Ruiz, and José Antonio Navarro, a close friend of Stephen F. Austin.

"Remember the Alamo": Myth-Making and the Press

The most famous (and the most widely misunderstood) incident of this rebellion took place at a Catholic mission in San Antonio. The Alamo had originally been set up to convert the native locals to Catholicism, but, like many places in Texas in 1836, it had been converted into a makeshift fortification. The large army led by Santa Anna overwhelmed the small Texian force holding the mission, killing all but a handful. Among the dead were Davy Crockett and Jim Bowie, both well-known frontiersmen.

Accounts of the attack at the Alamo quickly worked their way into mythology. The complex, multiracial dynamics of the Texas revolution were erased as tales of "Mexican barbarity" were recounted in newspapers and contrasted with tales of heroic white rebels.[1] Some papers included a report from Sam Houston, which read:

> Sir—Upon my arrival here, the following intelligence was received through a Mexican supposed to be friendly, which however was contradicted in some parts by another who arrived with him: it is therefore only given to you as rumor, though I fear a melancholy portion of it will be found true. Ansilma Burgura states that he left Alamo on Sunday the 6th and now is three days from Aroachea Rancha; that the Alamo was attacked on Sunday morning at the dawn of day, by about 5,300 Mexicans and was carried a short time before sunrise, with a loss of 520 Mexicans killed and as many wounded. Col. Travis had only 150 effective men out of his whole force of 187. After the fort was carried, seven men surrendered and called for Gen. Santa Anna and for quarter—they were murdered by his order. Col. Bowie was sick in bed and instantly murdered.
>
> The enemy expect a reinforcement of 1,500 men under Gen. Condilla and 1,500 reserve to follow them. He also informs that Ugatrechear had arrived with two millions of dollars for the payment of the troops. The bodies of the Americans were burned after the massacre—an alternative layer of bodies and wood, underlain and set fire. Lieut. Dickinson, who had a wife and child in the fort, and having fought with desperate courage, tied his child to his back, and leaped from the top of a two story building—both were killed in the fall. I have little doubt that the Alamo has fallen.[2]

The battle cry "Remember the Alamo" spurred both American soldiers and sympathizers in the battles and skirmishes that followed. But their remembrance was selective, assuming that anyone of Spanish or Mexican descent was an enemy. This frame took hold among many whites, even though several Tejanos had supported Texas independence and had fought Santa Anna at great personal risk. In the wake of the battle of the Alamo, Texas Declaration of Independence signer José Antonio Navarro's own brother was murdered under suspicion of being loyal to Mexico.[3]

In 1836, the "Texians" prevailed, establishing the independent Republic of Texas and overturned the prohibition on slavery. Nine years later, citizens of the republic would vote to join the United States, prompting a war between the United States and Mexico. The subsequent US victory brought with it a huge swath of territory, including what is now western Texas, California, Arizona, New Mexico, Nevada, Utah, and parts of Colorado and Wyoming. Though the Treaty of Guadalupe Hidalgo, which ended the Mexican-American War, excluded those of African and Indian descent from American citizenship, it formally ensured full civil rights to the thousands of Tejanos living within the new borders of Texas. In the actual practice of governance and the culture of daily life, however, "Texans," as they were coming to be known, were understood as white. Tejano citizens were treated with neglect in the best circumstances and with outright hostility and violence in the worst.

La Crónica: Championing La Raza

Caught in this complex dynamic, Tejanos struggled for recognition of their basic rights. They protested the violence and neglect with which they were often treated. Their fight for recognition and belonging was captured in an activist slogan that persists to this day: "We didn't cross the border, the border crossed us." For decades after the end of the Mexican-American War, that crossing would have important consequences for communities of color in the state—especially near the border.

Nicasio Idár, born in 1855 (d. 1914) in what was by then south Texas, would become a prominent member of the Spanish-speaking, Mexican-descended communities along the US-Mexico border. He became committed to the ideal of uplifting these communities through institution-building, starting several organizations, including La Crónica, a weekly Spanish-language newspaper published in Laredo. Idár imagined La Crónica as a voice for Tejanos in Texas and Mexicans living on the either side of the shared border. His vision of one people divided by a border would come to be called "La Raza." This unifying idea shaped the community and constituency that Idár saw himself fighting for. The newspaper became part of a network of institutions that were built to protect the human rights of La Raza.

As Nicasio's children took up his political commitments, his sons Eduardo and Clemente became journalists for La Crónica. They committed themselves to a concept of community uplift they called "gente decente." Described by historian Gabriella González as a movement for "cultural redemption, the movement was organized around a philosophy of moral, cultural, and material uplift that developed into the political strategy of respectability."[4] *Gente decente* cast a wide net, encompassing "people from wealthy merchants, to low-salaried teachers, to skilled workers, and perhaps even the very poor." In that sense, Eduardo and Clemente supported this class-based movement guided by "middle class moral standards."[5]

Jovita Idár: Leading the Fight for Racial Preservation

Eduardo and Clemente's younger sister, Jovita (1885–1946), soon joined them. She had first pursued a career as a teacher but had quickly found herself frustrated by the barriers Tejano children typically faced to receive an education. Eventually, her frustration would lead her to pursue a diverse career in journalism, health care, and the law. As a writer, she shared her thoughts on the importance of education, and particularly, an education that could connect students to their culture and history. She insisted on the right of people to speak and learn the language of their communities, proposing that attempts to deny this were part of an effort to erase Tejano identity.

In the article, "For Our Race Preservation of Nationalism We Should Work," she explained her position:

> In our previous article we stated that "most regrettably, we have seen Mexican teachers teaching students of their race English without taking into consideration, at all, their mother tongue." With that we did not intend to imply—not in the least—that the language of the land they inhabit should not be taught, as it is the medium available for direct contact with their neighbors, and that which will allow them to ensure that their rights are respected. What we wanted to suggest, simply, is that the national language should not be ignored, because it is the stamp that characterizes races and nations. Nations disappear and races sink when they forget their national language. For that reason, nations, like the Aztecs, no longer exist. Rome, through her language, profoundly influenced the people she had conquered. If the Jews today do not comprise a nation, it is because each one speaks the language of the land they inhabit.
>
> We are not saying that English should not be taught to Mexican Texan children, but, whether appropriate or not, we are saying you should not forget to teach them Spanish. In the same way that arithmetic and grammar are useful to them, English is useful to those people who live among English speakers.

Jovita Idár sought an education that was respectful of Tejano families and their traditions. Beyond language issues, for her this included substantial changes to the curriculum. Today, such allowances are recognized by most educators as key facets of effective pedagogy, but in the early twentieth century, when *assimilation* was widely understood to mean complete conformity with Anglo norms and traditions, this was a radical position. She continued:

> We are all creatures of our environment: we love things that we have seen since our infancy, and we believe in that which has permeated our souls since the first years of our lives. Therefore, if in the American school our children attend they teach Washington's biography and not Hidalgo's, and instead of the glorious accomplishments of Juárez they refer to the exploits of Lincoln, no matter how noble and fair these men were, that child will not know the glories of his homeland. He will not love his homeland, and will even view his parents' compatriots with indifference.

Jovita Idár's goal of securing a better, more holistic, and respectful educational opportunities for Tejano children was shared by her brother, Clemente, whose writing touched on similar themes. He viewed the disparities in Tejano education as symptomatic of a wider denial of rights to Mexican-descended people. As the Idárs knew well, however, these guarantees had been violated repeatedly by law enforcement and the courts. The following was written by one or more of them, but the article's author is not identified.

> A complete clarification of the facts will prove on the one hand that we, the Mexicans born in this country, even though we have American citizenship, do not fully enjoy the privileges and guarantees that the Federal Constitution offers. On the other hand, it will prove that those individuals who are fully Mexican have also been denied privileges and prerogatives that the Treaty of Guadalupe Hidalgo between Mexico and the United States mutually conceded. This results in the fact that Mexicans and Mexican-Americans are in the same situation. . . . We simply reclaim a right.[6]

The Texas Rangers

This unequal treatment under Texas law extended well beyond the public schools. Law enforcement routinely disregarded the civil rights of Tejanos, often murdering them for the flimsiest of reasons. The Texas Rangers, the state's law enforcement agency, were originally created in the 1820s to protect whites, who had begun claiming land in what was then Mexican territory.

In the decades that followed, the Rangers continued to view people of color as a persistent threat to be contained. Effectively a state-sponsored militia, much of what they did in the name of law enforcement was outside the law. The Rangers participated in murderous raids in Black neighborhoods and facilitated or participated in lynchings. Many Rangers proudly described themselves as "Indian killers." Tejanos were also viewed as an enemy within, especially after political instability in Mexico erupted in a civil war between 1910 and 1920, with belligerents spilling across the border into Texas. The political tensions of that civil war, which overlapped with World War I between 1914 and 1918, exacerbated deep racial hostilities that had existed for decades. A political and cultural system of exclusion targeting Mexican-descended Texans, sometimes called "Juan Crow," served the same purpose as Jim Crow in the former Confederate states.[7] Both systems communicated through the racialized rules of everyday interaction who enjoyed the privileges of citizenship and who did not.

This racialized view of citizenship was widespread in national conversations far beyond Texas. By the early 1900s, concerns about immigration from Mexico, Asia, and eastern and southern Europe and the effect these newcomers might have on the "national character" were widespread. A 1903 cartoon from *Judge*, a popular satirical magazine, declared such immigration a "danger to American ideas and institutions" and viewed the "high tide of immigration" as a "national menace." The immigrants in this image, labeled criminal, outlaw, degenerate, illiterate," and so on, are meant to represent newcomers from many places, but all bear a striking resemblance to the depiction of Tejano bandits.

Such depictions indicate the peculiar place of the Tejano in the eyes of many turn-of-the-century white Americans. They were not, in most cases, recent arrivals to the territories in which they lived. In fact, their families preceded those of the vast majority of whites who now claimed dominion over Texas. They were also deemed to be of a different and inferior racial background—one that disqualified them from the full benefits of citizenship, if not always in the language of the law.

As with Jim Crow regimes elsewhere, publicly sanctioned violence conveyed who enjoyed the full protection of the law and whose lives and safety were contingent on their conformity not to the law, but to the more potent norms and expectations of white supremacy. These expectations were enforced by everyday citizens as well as the police, but especially after violence relating to the Mexican Revolution spread into Texas, the response

THE HIGH TIDE OF IMMIGRATION—A NATIONAL MENACE.

Immigration statistics for the past year show that the influx of foreigners was the greatest in our history, and also that the hard-working peasants are now being supplanted by the criminals and outlaws of all Europe.

This 1903 cartoon from *Judge* typified anti-immigrant sentiment among white readers.

was brutal and disproportionate. As Doug J. Swanson put it in his history of the Rangers, the force pursued "bandits, suspected bandits, or men who might possibly become bandits if allowed to keep breathing."[8] The Rangers compiled a blacklist of such figures and, over time, summarily executed as many as two hundred of them.

The Mexican Revolution Intensifies the Struggle

In 1910, political developments in Mexico upset the already volatile cultural climate. The young country's president, Porfirio Díaz, who had held his post since 1876, had sought partnerships with US corporate leaders to modernize the economy. In the process, they had dispossessed thousands of Mexicans of their land, transforming them into wage laborers.

As a result of these and other initiatives, many Mexicans began to organize in opposition to them.

Among the leading voices of this rebellion were the Flores Magón brothers, Jesús, Ricardo, and Enrique, who worked together as journalists. Their rebel newspaper *Regeneración,* frequently criticized Díaz's policies to articulate an alternative vision of Mexico's future.[9] Consequently, Díaz had the brothers imprisoned repeatedly. In 1910, the brothers fled to the United States, where they continued their agitation with the help of sympathizers on the US side of the border.

Jesús Flores Magón (1871–1930), photographed in 1914.

Regeneración also regularly published a section in English to help build support for their movement in the United States. In the following example, the authors defended their commitments to socialism and anarchism against those in both the American and Mexican governments who advocated a more moderate—and, in their view, useless—course. Charging the Americans with hypocrisy, the Flores Magón brothers wrote,

> You admit that the millions have been deprived of their lands. You admit that the deprivation means wholesale misery and the reduction to slavery. You admit that the Mexicans are fighting like tigers to get back those lands, thus putting an end of their misery and redeeming themselves from that slavery into which they have been plunged. You sympathize with that heroic struggle. You have at the entrance to your great harbor a colossal figure of Liberty illuminating the world. On your coinage you stamp the figure of despotism pierced to death by the lance of freedom, and you append to it a Latin motto which, translated into your own tongue reads—"Thus may it always be with tyrants!" All this you approve and brag about a thousand times a day. But when Mexicans propose to follow that heroic lead; when they propose to slay the tyranny that to them spells death, and to declare void all the rotten title deeds by which an autocrat gave away his country to the bargain-hunters who scented the opportunity as the vulture scents the carrion, you say: "No, not that way. Property must not be touched, for property is sacred. Title deeds must be

enforced at any price. We agree that there must be social reorganization, but it must be wrought without trespassing on vested rights."

Where logic had failed, the editorial resorted to ridicule aimed at both governments:

Was there ever position more absurd? Did you never hear of the idiotic councilmen who passed three resolutions: the first being that the old school house should be torn down immediately, the second that a new school house should be built immediately with the materials of the old one, and that the third that, until completed, the old one should still be occupied? That is the course gravely recommended in Mexico; a country with fifteen million inhabitants, ninety-nine percent of them suffering frightfully. That is the course to which statesmen and publicists and all sorts of supposedly wise men of government stand committed, and it is to be noticed that, while even the capitalist papers have been forced to admit from time to time that the trouble in Mexico is purely economic, they are now writing as though it were exclusively a problem of politics. Things come to a crucial point and one hears no more of the people's pitiable plight, but—"Will not this embarrass the Democrats?" Not—"How is the position of the masses to be improved by all this?" but "How are we going to stand with England and Germany?" No discussion of human rights; only an anxious, unspeakably abject solicitude as to the wishes of the Money Power.

Well; at least the Mexican Revolution is contributing its share to the education of the race by showing it, if it would stop to look, what ALL governments actually are—the watchdogs of monopoly and nothing more.[10]

The Mexican Revolution galvanized activism on the border. The Idár brothers used *La Crónica* to express support for the Mexican Revolution and protest the abuses of the Texas Rangers. Jovita Idár left journalism for a time to help form La Cruz Blanca, a neutral infirmary service similar to the Red Cross, to provide medical care for those wounded in the conflict. When she returned to Laredo in 1914, she joined the staff of *El Progreso*, another Laredo-based Spanish-language newspaper that formed in 1912.

Both newspapers sharply criticized efforts by the US government to interfere in the Mexican Revolution on the side of Porfirio Díaz. One article in *El Progreso* criticized President Woodrow Wilson's decision to send troops to (and across) the Mexican border in 1916. The author, Manuel García Vigil, viewed this intervention as a pattern of interference in the affairs of its Spanish-speaking neighbors in the region. Vigil was a Mexican revolutionary who had sought asylum on the US side of the border.

In the heightened political tensions during the Mexican Civil War and the beginning of World War I, it was unsurprising that the editorial received the sanction of the English-speaking press. The very notion that Mexicans, wherever they lived, should be influencing public policy was usually viewed with derision. In 1915, a Loyalty Corps of Texas Rangers was established to restrict the Tejano vote in the state. In the following editorial, the English-language *Laredo Weekly Times*, produced and read by white people in the region, depicted Vigil's pro-revolutionary opinions as illegitimate and urged action by the press:

> For many months past a Mexican newspaper published in Laredo has taken occasion from time to time to publish articles reflecting upon the honor and dignity of the United States. Not content with the permission to wage its propaganda for Mexican revolution within the confines of a neutral nation, it takes advantage of every possible opportunity to cast opprobrium upon the people who grant asylum to the various writers who have left their country for their country's good.
>
> The latest specimen of abuse of hospitality was contained in yesterday's issue of El Progreso, the newspaper in question. . . .
>
> It is bad enough that they should be permitted to continue their political campaign against their adversaries from the vantage ground of a neutral country. But when they attack the government of that country, while ungratefully acepting [*sic*] the shelter it offers, they are transcending the limits of decency.
>
> We have not at hand the means of repressing sedition which other countries use without scruple. But so long as an alien receives the protection of our flag and our government, he should refrain from publicly throwing dirt upon that flag. Or if he so continues, there should be a method of punishing such an abuse of hospitality.[11]

The tone of this article is telling. It frames essential rights as courtesies and threatens that they may be withdrawn, if the tone and content of their speech offends the "hospitality" of the government. The authors of some articles in *El Progreso* were Mexicans who had crossed the border, including the author who had written the editorial in question. *El Progreso* itself, however, was run by US citizens. In principle, it enjoyed the full protections of the First Amendment, no matter how harsh its criticisms of US foreign policy might have been. Nevertheless, the "method of punishing" that the *Laredo Weekly Times* sought was encouraged by the governor, who instructed the Texas Rangers to destroy the presses of *El Progreso*.

When the Rangers arrived in Laredo, they found Jovita Idár barring the entrance. She refused to move and insisted that *El Progreso*'s right to publish criticisms of the US government was protected by the First Amendment. A crowd gathered and, after an hour or so, the Rangers left Laredo. Very early the next morning, however, they returned. With no one barring their way this time, they used sledgehammers to force open the door and then destroyed the presses of *El Progreso*. They also arrested the staff, hunted down Manuel García Vigil, beat him severely, and imprisoned him. Nicasio Idár, with the help of a friendly local judge, succeeded in winning Vigil's release, allowing him to seek life-saving medical treatment at a hospital.[12]

Devastating though it was, the Rangers' blow to *El Progreso* did not destroy the movement for Tejano rights. Thanks to the work of the Idárs and others in south Texas, several institutions persisted as vehicles for civil rights advocacy and defense. In 1911, the Idárs organized the First Mexican Congress (El Primer Congreso Mexicanista) in Laredo. The weeklong meeting brought together leaders of the local Tejano community with the aim of improving the living and working conditions for Mexican-descended people.

As Gabriella González observed, *La Crónica's* anonymous editorial calling for the congress expressed the urgent need to protect Mexican life in south Texas. After lambasting the "laziness of Mexicans in Texas regarding the matter of associations," the editorial then urged readers to explore cross-class coalitions. Further, it scolded the snobbery that was getting in the way of solidarity. "It is not possible," the anonymous author wrote, "to attain respectability, trust, and protection within the American nation, if we ourselves do not have this with our co-nationals; if we believe that the Mexicans are unworthy of our association with them, of us joining their associations, we should not expect that the Americans would gladly receive us in theirs. If we do not have trust in the men of our own race how can we expect other races to have trust in us."[13]

The language and logic of race are frequent and central in the concept of La Raza. It marks an interesting repurposing of race by a group of people treated openly as racially inferior. The concept of race had been used to justify the oppression of Mexican-descended people, but here it was in the service of uplift, celebrating the essential dignity and virtuosity of Mexican people. "To be Mexican means to be loyal, noble, generous, magnanimous, honorable, patriotic, virile, because these qualities are in our blood, they are innate, they are the inheritance of our race."

The editorial concluded with a call for a cooperative, communal effort directed toward "respectability," a concept that held significant sway in civil rights organizations of the time. It was the notion "to elevate the current condition of the Mexican who resides in the United States, by means of fraternal bonds; but by practical, generous, ample means, helping each other mutually, as brothers, all the members of the order, for the goal of

Jovita Idár (1885–1946), photographed circa 1905.

attaining respectability, NOT BY BRUTAL FORCE nor by violating the rights of others, but by intellectual, moral, and pecuniary superiority."[14]

The congress was open to both men and women and included several organizations, including the Liga Femenil Mexicanista (League of Mexican Women). Jovita Idár was elected as the Liga's first president. She advanced a vision that closely tied community uplift to women's liberation. "When you educate a woman, you educate a family," was an aphorism that she repeated frequently. It was a notion that *La Crónica* echoed when quoting the comments of activist Leonor Villegas de Magnon: "'The hand that rocks the cradle is the one which governs the world.' The intelligence, know-how, and riches that the small citizens whom God has entrusted to us . . . will provide for the nation later depends on us. With how much longing should we guard the moral and physical education of so precious a cargo!"[15]

Under Idár's leadership, the Liga encouraged women's financial independence and the opening of work outside the home. In addition, the organization celebrated Tejano and Mexican culture by helping to create free bilingual schools. The goals of Liga Femenil Mexicanista also built on and extended those of the First Mexican Congress—to provide community aid and uplift for the poorest residents.

An anonymous column in *La Crónica* explained, "One of the ends for which this society labors will also be to provide some help to the poor of Laredo. Some have been visited who find themselves in the most complete misery and abandonment, for whom clothes have been provided by some of the young women and food by the respectable Señora Doña Tomasita de Mendoza."[16] By heralding the work of those like Señora Doña Tomasita de Mendoza, *La Crónica* hoped to provide an inspiring model of virtue for others to follow.

Memory, Power, and Media: Reckoning with La Raza and the Rangers

The Idárs and other Tejano activists in southern Texas built a lasting legacy. The institutions they helped to create did not endure, but others would emerge in their places. The Tejano community would maintain various institutions committed to mutual aid and civil rights. These organizations would continue the long and ongoing struggle for civil rights along the southern border, but, with very few exceptions, most are unknown outside the region.

On the other hand, the Texas Rangers, one of the Idárs' most prominent adversaries, have enjoyed a much different profile. Unlike the hostility that Tejanos frequently encountered in the pages of the white press, the exploits of the Rangers have frequently been justified by journalists both in and beyond Texas. The glorification of the Rangers began early with their exploits in the Mexican-American War, garnering praise far beyond its place of origin. Readers who would never visit Texas were nevertheless encouraged to sympathize with the by-then normalized sense of white vengeance that the Rangers embodied. The *New York Herald*, for example, had praised the "tiger-like ferocity" of the force in the mid-nineteenth century. "God have mercy on them [the Mexican army] if the Rangers in an open field pounce down upon them with the war cry of 'The Alamo.' Very few prisoners will be taken, you may rest assured."[17]

After the Mexican Revolution ended in 1920, most journalists continued to frame Tejanos as outside the political community, usually justifying the Rangers' frequent abuses of them. On the other hand, acts of violence by Tejanos and Mexicans were usually viewed as intolerable as evidence of their savage nature. In their coverage of the Rangers' exploits, white journalists frequently transformed Tejanos into what Miguel Antonio Levario describes as an "enemy other."[18] By referring to them as Mexicans or describing them using racial epithets (which was not uncommon), white journalists helped to justify government practices that reinforced the idea of Tejanos as outsiders beyond the protection of the law.

The consequences of such journalistic frames were starkly and brutally demonstrated in 1918, when an attempted coverup failed and the massacre of fifteen men and boys in a Tejano village in west Texas became public knowledge. The Rangers did not report the incident for weeks, and when a report was finally issued, it claimed that the Rangers had been ambushed. An investigation discovered the truth of the matter, however, and the impunity of the Rangers seemed finally to be effectively challenged. State Representative J. T. Canales, a Tejano himself, led an effort to rein in the abusive power of the Rangers. His efforts detailed several incidents of rogue behavior and unjustified violence by the Rangers—a point underscored when one drunken Ranger shot and killed a colleague mere miles from where the hearings were happening. Nevertheless, Canales's Anglo colleagues gutted his efforts at reform, instead opting to scale back the size of the force while raising their pay and foregoing any meaningful reforms. When faced with this version of the bill, Canales mourned that "I do not recognize my own child."[19]

"Hi-Ho, Silver!" The Lone Ranger Enters American Popular Culture

By the 1930s, as tales of criminals and law enforcement captured Americans' interest in newspapers, novels, films, and radio dramas, the Texas Rangers became the focus of popular narratives. The Rangers appeared in dozens of tales that typically cast them not merely as heroes but as the very embodiment of wholesome, manly justice.

In 1933, *The Lone Ranger* made its debut as a radio program. The hero was said to have been the sole survivor of an ambush by a band of outlaws, nursed back to health from the edge of death by Tonto, a Comanche who becomes the Lone Ranger's loyal companion. The figure of Tonto provided someone for the Lone Ranger to talk to in what was an aural medium. (After all, Silver was a horse.)

The racial tensions of the day were normalized in this master-servant pairing. The origins of their names for each other—"Kemosabe" and "Tonto," are unclear, but one critic has pointed out that *Kemosabe*, sounds a lot like the Spanish phrase "*quien no sabe*," "he who doesn't understand," and "Tonto" means "stupid" or "crazy" in Spanish. The suggestion is that beneath their solid, master-helper relationship lay unspoken racial antagonism.

Certainly, the popular media naturalized Tonto's Indian race to make him the Lone Ranger's logical helper for an American audience of mostly white children.[20] In the way that popular media reinforce dominant cultural ideas of race, the show also served to depict the Lone Ranger (and, perhaps, the Texas Rangers more generally) as servants to all.

In 1949, the series became the basis for a television program that ran for eight years. "Nowhere in the pages of history can one find a greater champion of justice," claimed the show's famous introduction. In 1954, the five-part miniseries *Davey Crockett* began, producing a similarly sanitized version of the life of one of the martyrs of the Alamo. In 1960, the actor, John Wayne, who was in his day the icon of rugged American masculinity, produced and directed a lavish film called *The Alamo*. Wayne played the role of Davey Crockett. The film reimagined Crockett as a defender of individual liberty. In one pivotal scene, he declares, "Republic. I like the sound of the word. It means people can live free, talk free, go or come, buy or sell, be drunk or sober, however they choose. Some words give you a feeling. Republic is one of those words that makes me tight in the throat— the same tightness a man gets when his baby takes his first step or his first baby shaves and makes his first sound as a man. Some words can give you a feeling that makes your heart warm. Republic is one of those words."[21]

In these ways, the favored narratives of white Texans—that Texas stood for freedom and that the Rangers did only what was necessary to ensure justice—became familiar to millions of people. Of course, the history of both Texas and the Rangers is far more complicated and ambivalent. Certainly Tejano, Native, and Black voices might tell a very different story about the history of both. Yet even in the twenty-first century, new films and television programs about the force continue to burnish this image, and the Rangers' enduring positive reputation is evident in the fact that at least two major league sports franchises carry their name.

The struggles over meaning and justice on the borderlands—like other such cases presented in this book—took shape on the pages of *El Progreso*, *La Crónica*, and *Regeneración*. These minority newspapers opened space for Tejano voices that would not have been heard. It is true that as much as Jovita Idár rejected the racism of her time, it persists. That does not mean that her work or that of her family and other contemporaries was in vain. It was not. Rather, we must recognize that, by challenging inequalities past and present, minority journalism can hold the questions of equality and equity open to making change possible in the future.

8

What Is Democracy?

Lippmann, Bernays, and Public Opinion

Between 1880 and 1920, nearly 20 million people immigrated to the United States, most of them to the cities on the East Coast. Coming largely from southern and eastern Europe, these new Americans provided labor for American industry, started businesses, and joined the burgeoning nation. Among the diverse "huddled masses" came middle- and upper-middle-class Europeans who brought the outlook and resources of their class-based experience with them. Like their poorer countrymen, they worked hard, saw education as a way up the social ladder, and watched as their children became Americans. But, unlike their less fortunate fellow immigrants, they also enjoyed travel to and from Europe, enrolled in elite schools and universities, and had access to administrative power. These new generations of cosmopolitan citizens, thinkers, and climbers saw across national boundaries and pursued big ideas in a troubled time.[1]

That elite group, located mainly in New York, included Walter Lippman (1889–1974) and Edward L. Bernays (1891–1995). At a glance, they had a lot in common. Both were secular Jews and both embodied urban aspects of the urban-rural culture war of the twenties. Both attended college before the war, Lippmann at Harvard College and Bernays at Cornell University. In some things they differed: Lippmann's parents were born in America, Bernays's family had moved from Vienna when he was a child. Lippmann became known as the brightest student on campus, whereas Bernays studied agricultural science without much focus. Unlike Lippmann, who was a scholar of politics, essayist, and editor, Bernays was a businessman and a media entrepreneur. Their paths crossed, but they probably did not meet. Indeed, Lippmann seems to have been unaware of either Bernays or his work.[2] But it is certain that he would have disapproved.

Both were interested in the new art of propaganda, but for very different reasons. The media scholar Robert McChesney explained: "Lippmann emphasized the way government propaganda altered the traditional democratic equation. He found the emergence of such propaganda nothing short of frightening—it created an existential crisis for the notion of a free press, and therefore for self-government."[3] Lippmann warned that "Government tends to operate by the impact of controlled opinion upon administration. This shift in the locus of sovereignty has placed a premium upon the manufacture of consent. . . . Without protection against propaganda, without standards of evidence, without criteria of emphasis, the living substance of all popular decision is exposed to every prejudice and to infinite exploitation."[4]

In line with his developing ideal of an evidence-based theory, Lippmann believed that only an evidence- and fact-based journalism could connect average Americans to the issues of the day. He saw two main threats to American democracy—the imposition of propaganda between the government and the people, and the low quality of commercial journalism in his time.

In complete contrast to Lippmann's critique, Bernays's interests lay with the business of "private propaganda," which he renamed "public relations" to hide its toxic wartime roots. Rather than rejecting the commercial press, he embraced its uncritical, even pliable, nature as an opportunity to build a new industry to reinforce the power of the powerful, first in the war and from then on at home.

An Opportunity to Define Solutions

World War I lasted from 1914 to 1918. The United States joined the fight against Germany's Kaiser Wilhelm reluctantly in 1917, tipping the balance toward victory. That outcome turned over to the already imperially minded United States the Herculean task of reconsidering what a democracy in America would be like. A new mass society needed a new kind of government that could cope with crises while remaking itself for the century to come. In 1919, the smoke of mortars and the stench of death had barely cleared from the battlefield trenches. The global Spanish flu pandemic had killed millions worldwide not two years before. A Red Scare was still terrorizing Americans with the threat of a foreign insurgency of Bolsheviks from the Russian Revolution. And the Great Strike of 1919 had sent millions of laborers to picket lines over wages and job security, paralyzing the national economy, and fueling the anti-immigrant Red Scare. Not since the Civil War had the nation seen so much strife.

While both Lippmann and Bernays focused on the role of mass media in democracy, their contributions were very different. Indeed, as is shown later in this chapter, Bernays's ambition to be recognized as a major figure in the "Reconstruction" of post–World War I America led him to present Lippmann's ideas as his own.[5]

A further comparison of their biographies shows how each addressed questions of science and the power of the recently formed social sciences to analyze social and political meanings. Both admired Sigmund Freud. Lippmann read Freud's still new scientific theory of psychology early on, integrating it into his developing understanding of politics, media, and the individual. Bernays, who frequently reminded others that he was Freud's nephew, made dubious claims for the use of propaganda. In the early 1920s, Lippmann's definition of sources of propaganda included advertising, public relations, and the disinformation and misinformation of politics and wartime. What Lippmann saw as a danger, Bernays saw as a business opportunity.

Lippmann scholar Sue Curry Jansen is blunt about the effects of Bernays' self-promoting habits. She writes, "Bernays's interpretation of Lippmann grossly misrepresents and misuses the original in ways that invert and betray Lippmann's intent."[6] Not only did Bernays steal Lippmann's ideas, but he got them wrong, as well.

So, why do social and political theories matter? According to Lippmann, who was the only one of these two who could answer this question meaningfully, theories matter because their underlying concepts can be scientifically tested. In that way, they offer tools for understanding how and why people do what they do. In Lippmann's view, instead of leaving us to rely on unmeasurable traditions and beliefs, theories offer us formal ways to think, evaluate, and update our understanding of the world. For legal and policy leaders, as well as social critics like Lippmann, theories defined the conflicting boundaries and rules within the most meaningful democratic arena, debate.[7]

If Lippmann and Bernays differed over how to apply Freud's theory to the study of mass society, it was because each of them was committed to shaping a very different version of America and the role of the public in it. In their opposing views, Bernays claimed Freudian psychology should be interpreted as the basis for aggregating, or herding, the "maladjusted," but persuadable, individual in mass society to the consumer society it has become. To achieve that goal, he built the public relations industry to create new consumer needs that only his clients and their products could satisfy.

During the war, both men had experiences that would launch them in opposing directions. Bernays served enthusiastically under the Committee on Public Information (CPI), working for the Creel Commission. The CPI was charged with the task of managing public opinion about the war, through manipulation if it was deemed necessary (and it often was).

From his staff-level position, Bernays embraced former journalist George Creel's (1876–1953) massive national propaganda campaign to persuade an isolationist American public to enter the war.[8]

In his essays at the time in the *New Republic*, the New York-based magazine of public policy and politics that Lippmann had cofounded in 1914, Lippmann had been an advocate for US entry into the war. Earlier, however, he had also been a harsh critic of Creel's reporting on the 1903–4 Colorado Labor Wars. Because Lippmann thought Creel had engaged in dishonest tactics, he remained an even harsher critic of Creel and the CPI.

In 1918 as the war was coming to an end, Lippmann was sent to England by President Woodrow Wilson's chief adviser "Colonel" Edward M. House (1858–1938) to report back on a meeting of allies about the British propaganda effort. Lippmann asked for and received a commission as a captain in the army, working for Secretary of War Newton Baker in the Military Intelligence Branch (MIB). The MIB offered Lippmann several advantages. Independence of Creel's far-reaching bureaucracy helped Lippmann avoid

A propaganda poster produced by the Committee on Public Information (CPI).

working with Creel. Creel was a journalist-turned-propagandist. Lippmann saw him as tainted by his willingness to mask the truth to the American public in order to get them to support the war.

In the MIB, Lippmann was able to pursue strategies that favored persuasion over manipulation. He wrote of "getting away from propaganda in the sinister sense, and substituting for it a frank campaign of education addressed to the German and Austrian troops, explaining as simply and persuasively as possible the unselfish character of the war, the generosity of our aims, and the great hope of mankind which we are trying to realize."[9]

Working for the MIB also gave Lippmann the chance to study propaganda in the field. While on duty in France in September and October of 1918, he wrote leaflets for the Allies to drop where German and Austrian troops could find them. Troops carried them behind enemy lines, lofted them beneath balloons, and, finally, dropped them from their bi-planes. In all, "Lippmann's miniscule subunit" in Paris distributed some five million leaflets as the Germans retreated.[10]

Lippmann would finish his wartime service as a member of the Inquiry, a top-secret intelligence unit charged with developing the Fourteen Points plan, the roadmap used by Wilson to script the Treaty of Versailles. In addition to ending the war on November 11, 1918, the treaty also served as the basis for governing the postwar world.[11]

Although both men attended the Paris Peace Conference in official capacities, they brought home different views on propaganda. Where Bernays saw propaganda as a useful and efficient device for "manufacturing the consent" of the mass public, Lippmann considered that individuals— including himself—deserved to be recognized on their own, limited terms.

Lippmann's *Public Opinion*, 1922

As he thought about how journalism could bridge the gap between the individual and society, Lippmann knew that without a professionalized, scientifically based press, individuals would be left to rely on their own false stereotypes of reality. Describing the limitations of individual perceptions, he wrote, "Each of us lives and works on a small part of the earth's surface, moves in a small circle, and of these acquaintances knows only a few intimately."[12] How could we know about events that necessarily happened beyond our immediate lives? Would we always be limited by misperceptions, or would we find and share a meaningful, even democratic, reality?

Individuals, he reasoned, are not "omni-competent" to understand a world that happens almost entirely out of view; they need help to make sense of the outside world. Otherwise, Lippmann reasoned, individuals would remain limited by their own perspectives, which he called "pseudo-environments."

Because individually held notions interfered with the shared social truth he expected from a working process of public opinion, he concluded, the isolation of the individual amounted to a kind of reflexive, or self-imposed, propaganda.[13]

As a result, when Lippmann reflected on his wartime experiences, he came to see a professionalized journalism as the essential, but missing, basis of a new American political culture. He asked, "How then, is any practical relationship established between what is in people's heads and what is out there beyond their ken in the environment? How, in the language of democratic theory, do great numbers of people feeling so privately about so abstract a picture develop any common will? How does a simple and constant idea emerge from this complex of variables? How are those things known as the Will of the People, or the National Purpose, or Public Opinion crystallized out of such fleeting and casual imagery?"[14]

In teasing out the elements of this problem, Lippmann was able to blend his understanding of the psychology and the sociology of the individual in postwar society. If stereotypes inhibited individual perceptions, government-sponsored propaganda threatened any meaningful postwar system of public opinion, especially journalism. According to the journalism scholar Robert McChesney, "Lippmann emphasized the way government propaganda altered the traditional democratic equation. He found the emergence of such propaganda nothing short of frightening—it created an existential crisis for the notion of a free press, and therefore for self-government."[15]

A democratic nation needed the kind of truth that was available only from evidence-based journalism. Lippmann described the challenge to truth posed here, writing, "Government tends to operate by the impact of controlled opinion upon administration. This shift in the locus of sovereignty has placed a premium upon the manufacture of consent. . . . Without protection against propaganda, without standards of evidence, without criteria of emphasis, the living substance of all popular decision is exposed to every prejudice and to infinite exploitation."[16]

In the passage that follows, Lippmann considered the origins of the news, both within the journalistic "system of record" and as a result of wartime press agents' framing facts to suit their own interests. After seeing how badly the Paris Peace conference had gone, he remained concerned about the viability of the postwar American press in the face of propagandists now called "public relations" agents. He worried about what their culture of lying would mean to the newly professionalizing practice of journalism at home. He wrote,

> It will be found, I think, that there will be a very direct relation between the certainty of news and the system of record. If you call to mind the

topics which form the principal indictment by reformers against the press, you find they are subjects in which the newspaper occupies the position of umpire in the unscored baseball game. All news about states of mind is of this character: so are all descriptions of personality, of sincerity, aspiration, motive, intention, of mass feeling, of national feeling, of public opinion, the policies of foreign governments. So much news is about what is going to happen. So are questions turning on private profit, private income, wages, working conditions, the efficiency of labor, educational opportunity, unemployment, monotony, health, discrimination, unfairness, restraint of trade, waste, 'backward' peoples, conservatism, imperialism, radicalism, liberty, honor, righteousness. All involve data that are at best spasmodically recorded. The data may be hidden because of censorship or a tradition of privacy, they may not exist because nobody thinks [the] record important, because he thinks it red tape, or because nobody has yet invented an objective system of measurement. Then the news on these subjects which are not scored is bound to be debatable, when it is not wholly neglected. The events which are not scored are reported either as personal and conventional opinions, or they are not news. They do not take shape until somebody protests, or somebody investigates, or somebody publicly, in the etymological meaning of the word, makes an issue of them.

This is the underlying reason for the existence of the press agent. The enormous discretion as to what facts and what impressions shall be reported is steadily convincing every organized group of people that, whether it wishes to secure publicity or to avoid it, the exercise of discretion cannot be left to the reporter. It is safer to hire a press agent who stands between the group and the newspapers. Having hired him, the temptation to exploit his strategic position is very great. "Shortly before the war," says Mr. Frank Cobb, "the newspapers of New York took a census of the press agents who were regularly employed and regularly accredited and found that there were about 1,200 of them.

How many there are I do not pretend to know, but what I do know is that many of the direct channels to news have been closed and the information for the public is first filtered through publicity agents.

The great corporations have them, the banks have them, all the organizations of business and social and political activity have them and they are the media through which news comes. Even statesmen have them.

Were reporting the simple recovery of obvious facts, the press agent would be little more than a clerk. But since, in respect to most of the big topics of news, the facts are not simple, and not at all obvious, but subject to choice and opinion, it is natural that everyone should wish to make his own choice of facts for the newspapers to print. The publicity man does that. And in doing it, he certainly saves the reporter much trouble by presenting him a clear picture of a situation out of which he otherwise might make neither head nor tail. But it follows that the picture which the publicity man makes for the reporter is the one he wishes the public to see. He is censor and propagandist, responsible only to his employers, and to the whole truth responsible only as it accords with the employers' conception of his own interests.

The development of the publicity man is a clear sign that the facts of modern life do not spontaneously take a shape in which they can be known. They must be given shape by somebody, and, since in the daily routine reporters cannot give shape to facts, and since there is little disinterested organization of intelligence, the need for that is being met by the interested parties.[17]

Seeking Solutions: "A Test of the News" and *Liberty and the News*

Lippmann addressed journalism's problems more directly in two pieces published in 1920. A slender book titled *Liberty and the News* defined the failings of wartime journalism and called for their reform. In "A Test of the News," he and coauthor Charles Merz criticized the *New York Times*'s failed coverage of the Russian Revolution. Their research appeared as a forty-four-page supplement to the *New Republic*. He and Merz analyzed a thousand news headlines published during the *New York Times*'s thirty-six months of coverage between March 1917 and March 1920, and the authors' analysis exposed the *Times*'s erroneous reports that the Bolsheviks were losing in the Russian Revolution. The forty-four-page supplement to the *New Republic* assessed *Times* journalists' participation in the propaganda effort of the Red Scare. Instead of accurate and verifiable news from that war, they concluded that "The news as a whole is dominated by the *hopes* of the men who composed the news organization."[18]

Upon uncovering the *Times*'s blind support for the Wilson administration's anticommunist propaganda, Lippmann and Merz charged that "From the point of view of professional journalism the reporting of the Russian Revolution is nothing short of a disaster. On the essential questions the net effect was almost always misleading, and misleading news is worse than none at all. Yet, on the face of the evidence there is no reason to charge a conspiracy by Americans. They can fairly be charged with boundless credulity, an untiring readiness to be gulled, and on many occasions, with a downright lack of common sense."[19]

In their analysis, biased and false sources had been a key problem for outmatched reporters at the Paris Conference. Specifically, Lippmann and

Walter Lippmann
(1889–1974).

Merz concluded that the *Times* had been seriously misled by its reliance on official press agents, a deficit that left their uncritical American readers open to any passing lie. Clearly, the commercial press remained a significant part of the problem, because their often slipshod or even false reporting left readers' stereotypes of the world intact.

Writing in *Liberty and the News*, Lippmann detailed the challenges to an evidence-based truth that the undependable commercial press presented to readers:

> The news of the day as it reaches the newspaper office is an incredible medley of fact, propaganda, rumor, suspicion, hopes, and fears, and the task of selecting and ordering that news is one of the truly sacred and priestly offices in a democracy. For the newspaper is in all literalness the bible of democracy, the book out of which a people determines its conduct. It is the only serious book most people read. It is the only book they read every day. Now the power to determine each day what will seem important and what shall be neglected is a power unlike any that has been exercised since the Pope lost his hold on the secular mind.[20]

Lippmann proposed a range of remedies for the system he imagined. To cope better with the need for more effective reporting, Lippmann and Merz called for better-educated reporters. They wrote, "Reporting is one of the most difficult professions, requiring much expert knowledge and serious education. . . . It is habit, rather than preference, which makes readers accept news from a correspondent, whose usefulness is about that of an astrologer or an alchemist."[21]

In *Liberty and the News*, Lippmann argued for "political observatories" staffed by professional experts at universities that could house midlevel intermediaries—experts, including policy managers, professionals, and, ultimately, reporters in a modernized, professional press—to act as unbiased possible mediators between individual Americans and their government. In this idealized fashion, he also believed that the democratic process could be improved through the press's support for a consensus between individual citizens and government officials and other elites.[22]

At a time when journalism was undergoing professionalization—the American Society of Newspaper Editors would form and produce a professional code of ethics by 1926—Lippmann expected the recent appearance of journalism schools on American university campuses to raise reporters' standards. To illustrate his point, he told this story:

> I remember one reporter who was detailed to the Peace Conference by a leading news agency. He came around every day for "news." It was a time when Central Europe seemed to be disintegrating, and great doubt existed as to whether governments would be found with which to sign a peace. But all this "reporter" wanted to know was whether the German fleet, then safely interned at Scapa Flow, was going to be sunk in the North Sea. He insisted every day on knowing that. For him it was the German fleet or nothing. Finally, he could endure it no longer. So, he anticipated Admiral Reuther and announced, in a dispatch to his home newspapers, that the fleet would be sunk. And when I say that a million Americans learned all they ever learned from the Peace Conference through this reporter, I am stating a very moderate figure.
>
> He suggests the delicate question raised by the schools of journalism: how far can we go in turning journalism from a haphazard trade into a disciplined profession? Quite far, I imagine, for it is unthinkable that a society like ours should remain forever dependent upon untrained accidental witnesses. It is no answer to say that there have been in the past, and that there are now, first rate correspondents. Of course, there are. . . . But they are eminences on a rather flat plateau. The run of the news is handled by a much smaller caliber. It is handled by such men because reporting is not a dignified profession for which men will invest the time and cost of an education, but an underpaid, insecure, anonymous form of drudgery, conducted on catch-as-catch-can principles. Merely to talk about the reporter in terms of civilization will

make newspapermen laugh. Yet reporting is a post of peculiar honor. Observation must precede every other activity, and the public observer (that is, the reporter) is a man of critical value. No amount of money or effort spent in fitting the right men for this work could possibly be wasted, for the health of society depends upon the information it receives.

Do our schools of journalism, the few we have, make this kind of training their object, or are they trade-schools designed to fit men for higher salaries in the existing structure? I do not presume to answer the question, nor is the answer of great moment when we remember how small a part these schools now play in actual journalism. But it is important to know whether it would be worthwhile to endow large numbers of these schools on the model of those existing, and make their diplomas a necessary condition for the practice of reporting. It is worth considering. Against the idea lies the fact that it is difficult to decide just what reporting is—where in the whole mass of printed matter it begins and ends. No one would wish to set up a closed guild of reporters and exclude invaluable casual reporting and writing. If there is anything in the idea at all, it would apply only to the routine service of the news through large organizations.[23]

Lippmann saw that better-educated and better-paid reporters represented the most important aspect of an improved profession of journalism. The advantage, he thought, would come from reporters' developing a healthy skepticism of the evidence, no matter the source. In addition, this new breed of reporters should be able to show a "rigorous discipline in the use of words, while a general sense of what the world is doing." Defining the concept of the disinterested journalist, he aimed a barb at public relations men. He wrote, "Emphatically, he ought not to be serving a cause, no matter how good. In his professional activity it is no business of his to care whose ox is gored." In sum, he believed that "Only the discipline of a modern logic can open the door to reality."[24]

"Reality": The Public Relations Counsel, the Reporter, and the "Herd"

Lippmann and Bernays both worked to define reality, just not the same one. While Lippmann worked to identify the role of journalism in the individual's self-understanding in society—the creation of an empowering sense of reality. Bernays saw propaganda as a means of controlling the same people and sought to create a sense of reality that could be manipulated to serve the needs of those creating it. At a practical level, Bernays is best remembered for staging media events designed to garner free media coverage for his clients. Perhaps the best known of these "pseudo-events"—Lippmann's term criticizing the use of propaganda to create false realities[25]—was the media spectacle Bernays staged in New York for the American Tobacco Company on April 1, 1929. By getting a small group of young women to light up cigarettes while marching in the New York City Easter Parade, he aimed to change consumers' behaviors by associating cigarette smoking with women's liberation.

As Bernays re-named cigarettes as "Torches of Freedom," his goal of doubling the number of women cigarette consumers became possible. By offering the one thing his uncle "Siggy" said men could enjoy that women wished for—the liberty of owning a phallus—for the price of a Lucky Strike, he demonstrated how pliable people's desires and associations could be. The idea may not have been wholly original,[26] but it showed Bernays's canny sense of opportunism. The ability of public relations operatives to co-opt the news with staged spectacles pitted a weak press corps against opportunistic public relations men, a mismatch that favored the powerful.

At a more catastrophic level, Bernays's theory attracted the admiration of Hitler's propaganda minister Joseph Goebbels, who used Bernays's ideas "to control the opinions of the masses and deploy them in service of the power of the state." The Jewish Bernays declined an offer of employment in the Third Reich, but the Germans found other American public relations firms to step in to generate "fake news" reports that were distributed worldwide "to sow division in the United States."[27]

Because Bernays adhered to the theory of "herd instinct,"[28] he saw the emergence of the professional public relations "counsel" as a means of gathering and directing otherwise disorganized individuals. The power of the media, he thought, lay in its ability to present modern consumers with new needs and to sell them the means to satisfy their newfound appetites. The mass society concept of the herd was not unique to Bernays's outlook; Lippmann was familiar with it, too. But, according to one historian, "At the most extreme, Lippmann is seen as a proponent of having experts guide the 'bewildered herd' and use the media to 'manufacture consent' for political positions that serve elite interests."[29]

The fundamental link between the two lay in their opposite definitions of the role of the media professional: Lippmann's ideal journalist would practice a pragmatic, trial-and-error-based examination of evidence in search of the science-based approach to government that Lippmann believed was necessary to sustain the government and the public. By contrast, Bernays's public relations man sought to commodify the masses in order to sell them back reflections of themselves.

Bernays Co-opts Lippmann's Theory

In 1923, the year after Lippmann's *Public Opinion* appeared, Bernays published his own book, *Crystallizing Public Opinion*. As the title suggested, he was announcing his "new and improved" version of Lippmann's theory. In the book, he promoted his ideas as like, but more practical than, Lippmann's "purely theoretical" approach.[30] Indeed, Bernays claimed that Lippmann's work supported his own concept of public relations.[31]

But the comparison was false. Instead of adapting Lippmann's conceptual framework, Bernays reworded, selectively attended to, and, in some cases, falsified Lippmann's work. He did so in order to claim the theorist's support for the new business of public relations as a solution to the undependable journalism of the day. In a comparison of the pair's respective definitions of the public, for example, Lippmann scholar Sue Curry Jansen identified an extensive set of false claims Bernays made in *Crystallizing Public Opinion* by based on Lippmann's *Public Opinion*.

In an analysis that "demonstrates that Bernays is familiar with and actually does understand Lippmann's critique of PR, but consciously chooses to excise it," Jansen showed Bernays's intentional appropriation of Lippmann's ideas. She reported examples where Bernays reversed Lippmann's position against public relations, made up quotes that endorsed his own positions, oversimplified ideas, and ignored meaningful contexts in order to promote his idea of public relations. In some cases, he plagiarized texts.[32]

In the face of that self-serving wordplay, which she called "semantic tyranny: a form of communication that censors critical thought at the source," Jansen concluded that Bernays had "looted" *Public Opinion* for its concepts. Lippmann remained unaware of Bernays's misdeeds.[33]

Recasting the Public in *Crystallizing Public Opinion*

The effect of Bernays's interpretation of *Public Opinion* was to mangle Lippmann's theory of public opinion in the name of the newly renamed profession of public relations. In the first chapter of *Crystallizing Public Opinion*, Bernays outlined his psychological argument for public relations and the public relations counsel as the bases of managing, even controlling, public opinion. In place of journalism as the only evidence-based way for enabling individuals to know more than the "pictures in their heads," Bernays inserted his "public relations counsel." He wrote,

> The character and origins of public opinion, the factors that make up the individual mind and the group mind must be understood, if the

profession of public relations counsel is to be intelligently practiced and its functions and possibilities accurately estimated. Society must understand the fundamental character of the work he is doing, if for no other reason than its own welfare.

The public relations counsel works with that vague, little understood, indefinite material called public opinion. Public opinion is a term describing an ill-defined, mercurial and changeable group of individual judgments. Public opinion is the aggregate result of individual opinions—now uniform, now conflicting—of the men and women who make up society or any group of society. In order to understand public opinion, one must go back to the individual who makes up the group. . . .

The mental equipment of the average individual consists of a mass of judgments on most of the subjects that touch his daily physical or mental life. These judgments are the tools of his daily being and yet they are his judgments, not on a basis of research or logical deduction, but for the most part dogmatic expressions accepted on the authority of his parents, his church, and of his social, his economic and other leaders.

The public-relations counsel must understand the social implications of an individual's thoughts and actions. Is it, for example, purely an accident that a man belongs to one church rather than another or to any church at all? What are the factors that work in the conversion of a man from one political party to another or from one type of food to another?[34]

Without the guidance of public relations from one brand to the next, Bernays reasoned, the otherwise witless individual would be lost to the illogic of the "herd."

"Organizing Chaos": Bernays's *Propaganda, 1928*

By 1928, when he published, *Propaganda*, Bernays was decided about his revision, even inversion, of Lippmann's work. Within the first few pages of chapter 1, "Organizing Chaos," he managed to, at once, co-opt and invert Lippmann's theory of public opinion and treat it as his own. As is shown in the following passage, he again turned Lippmann's concept of the stereotype from a condition of isolation to be remedied through reading competent journalism into the modern individuals' need for propaganda. In the same fashion, Bernays turned Lippmann's concept of the individual's inability to cope with mass society, or "omni-competence," from a disabling psychological effect into a call for more top-down direction.

Above all, he reemphasized the publicity or public relations agent as a necessary guide for the citizen-consumer in an overwhelming world of advertising. Conflating capitalism and democracy, Bernays presented the

Edward Bernays (second from right) with a delegation from the Committee on Public Information, photographed 1919.

"new" private propaganda of public relations and advertising as the voice of "special pleaders," advocates who are needed to connect consumers to the products, services, and goods that consumers did not yet know that they needed.[35]

Here is what Bernays wrote in *Propaganda*, to describe the practice of public relations as the basis of a democracy:

> The conscious and intelligent manipulation of the organized habits and opinions of the masses is an important element in democratic society. Those who manipulate this unseen mechanism of society constitute an invisible government which is the true ruling power of our country.
>
> We are governed, our minds are molded, our tastes formed, our ideas suggested, largely by men we have never heard of. This is a logical result of the way in which our democratic society is organized. Vast numbers of human beings must cooperate in this manner, if they are to live together as a smoothly functioning society.
>
> Our invisible governors are, in many cases, unaware of the identity of their fellow members in the inner cabinet.
>
> They govern us by their qualities of natural leadership, their ability to supply needed ideas and by their key position in the social structure. Whatever attitude one chooses to take toward this condition, it remains

a fact that in almost every act of our daily lives, whether in the sphere of politics or business, in our social conduct or our ethical thinking, we are dominated by the relatively small number of persons—a trifling fraction of our hundred and twenty million—who understand the mental processes and social patterns of the masses. It is they who pull the wires which control the public mind, who harness old social forces and contrive new ways to bind and guide the world.

It is not usually realized how necessary these invisible governors are to the orderly functioning of our group life. In theory, every citizen may vote for whom he pleases. Our Constitution does not envisage political parties as part of the mechanism of government, and its framers seem not to have pictured to themselves the existence in our national politics of anything like the modern political machine. But the American voters soon found that without organization and direction their individual votes, cast, perhaps, for dozens or hundreds of candidates, would produce nothing but confusion. Invisible government, in the shape of rudimentary political parties, arose almost overnight. Ever since then we have agreed, for the sake of simplicity and practicality, that party machines should narrow down the field of choice to two candidates, or at most three or four.

In theory, every citizen makes up his mind on public questions and matters of private conduct. In practice, if all men had to study for themselves the abstruse economics, political, and ethical data involved in every question, they would find it impossible to come to a conclusion about anything. We have voluntarily agreed to let an invisible government sift the data and high-spot the outstanding issues so that our field of choice shall be narrowed to practical proportions. From our leaders and the media they use to reach the public, we accept the evidence and the demarcation of issues bearing upon public questions; from some ethical teacher, be it a minister, a favorite essayist, or merely prevailing opinion, we accept a standardized code of social conduct to which we conform most of the time.

Here he makes the case that without propaganda—mainly advertising—the public would be unable to decide which soap brand to buy:

In theory, everybody buys the best and cheapest commodities offered him on the market. In practice, if everyone went around pricing, and chemically testing before purchasing, the dozens of soaps or fabrics or brands of bread which are for sale, economic life would become hopelessly jammed. To avoid such confusion, society consents to have its choice narrowed to ideas and objects brought to its attention through propaganda of all kinds. There is consequently a vast and continuous effort going on to capture our minds in the interest of some policy or commodity or idea.[36]

Here Bernays describes a paradox wherein the individual must gain his freedom by giving it up:

> It might be better to have, instead of propaganda and special pleading, committees of wise men who would choose our rulers, dictate our conduct, private and public, and decide upon the best types of clothes for us to wear and the best kinds of food for us to eat. But we have chosen the opposite method, that of open competition. We must find a way to make free competition function with reasonable smoothness. To achieve this society has consented to permit free competition to be organized by leadership and propaganda.[37]

Bernays defends the "misuse" of "the instruments by which public opinion is organized," including, notably, journalism. He says that the messiness of life makes the oversight of public relations and advertising necessary so that we may live in a democracy:

> Some of the phenomena of this process are criticized—the manipulation of news, the inflation of personality, and the general ballyhoo by which politicians and commercial products and social ideas are brought to the consciousness of the masses. The instruments by which public opinion is organized and focused may be misused. But such organization and focusing are necessary to orderly life.
>
> As civilization has become more complex, and as the need for invisible government has been increasingly demonstrated, the technical means have been invented and developed by which opinions may be regimented.
>
> With the printing press and the newspaper, the railroad, the telephone, telegraph, radio and airplanes, ideas can be spread rapidly and even instantaneously over the whole of America. . . .
>
> It is the purpose of this book to explain the structure of the mechanism which controls the public mind, and to tell how it is manipulated by the special pleader who seeks to create public acceptance for a particular idea or commodity. It will attempt at the same time to find the due place in the modern democratic scheme for this new propaganda and to suggest its gradually evolving code of ethics and practice.[38]

In making the case for propaganda as "a mechanism which controls the public mind," Bernays suggested that in this new book he would, eventually, twin his vision of a kind of totalitarian "democracy" with a yet to be developed "code of ethics and practice."

What's a Democracy For?

While Bernays gathered himself to promote the profession of public relations for the rest of the century, by 1925 Lippmann had become discouraged. That year in *The Phantom Public*, which he offered as a late conclusion to *Public Opinion*, he wrote that "The private citizen today has become to feel rather like a deaf spectator in the back row, who ought to keep his mind on the mystery off there, but cannot manage to keep awake. He knows that he is somehow affected by what is going on. Rules and regulations continually, taxes annually, and wars occasionally remind him that he is continually being swept along by great drifts of circumstance."[39]

Lippmann thought that individual Americans were all too likely to be overwhelmed by mass society and, thus, unavailable to process the working truth of journalism. In the *Phantom Public*, he wrote, "Modern society is not visible to *anybody*, nor intelligible continuously and as a whole."[40] Because of his equally low expectations of the press's ability to overcome its own limitations, Lippmann came to see his theory of public opinion as impracticable, but not invalid.

Unlike Bernays, for whom the individual was never more than a piece to be "manufactured" into a commodifiable version of the "public,"[41] Lippmann thought of the liberal democratic public as alive and conscious. He saw in its members a constantly reforming assortment of newly—and temporarily—forming public opinions, usually in response to government crises. That ever-shifting process explains why he called the public a "phantom:" They appeared only occasionally in response to particular moments.[42]

Public relations—"private propaganda"—remained a daily threat to Lippmann's ideal of a participatory democracy supported by journalism. Without such support from a professional press, he understood that public relations counselors would be free to manipulate the general public in the service of their own commercial, rather than democratic, interests.[43]

Although Bernays insisted that his theory of propaganda matched Lippmann's, the two versions were complete opposites: where Lippmann had imagined a bottom-up world where the individual was, at least potentially, capable of reading the daily news in order to join the world of participatory public opinion, Bernays's top-down theory of propaganda offered only strategies for managing the public. Further, Bernays used his concept of the public to build a media industry based on the wartime practice of propaganda that Lippmann reviled.

This conflict would build over the next hundred years as journalists increasingly came to feel compromised by the need to work with public relations professionals whose values differed so much from their own. Where Lippmann saw the need for a new way to convene democratic meaning for self-governance, Bernays saw "herding" the masses as a market opportunity. And where Bernays left us the insidious roots of "alternative realities" and "alternative facts," Lippmann's bulletins from the war should stand as documented warnings about how quickly journalism—and democracy with it—can fail in the face of a propaganda state.

9

What Is "Americanism"?

The Second Red Scare

The period after World War II saw a major realignment of world powers. With most of Europe devastated by the conflict, the United States emerged as a global superpower. After suffering 25 million dead in the war, the Union of Soviet Socialist Republics, the world's first communist state, nevertheless emerged as the United States' main global rival. Like the First Red Scare, the Second Red Scare (1947–57) saw Congress try to root out political radicals whose commitments were deemed disloyal by the establishment. The push to eradicate alleged spies in government and positions of cultural influence quickly morphed into a national crisis that threatened anyone with leftist views, disloyal or not. The resulting reign of terror by US senator Joseph McCarthy, the junior senator from Wisconsin, took aim at the American people, rather than actual communists. The propaganda tactics used to marginalize accused radicals included disinformation and lies about the threat of communism in the US government—even the White House—and the military.

Journalism and other forms of media provided the major battleground in this struggle, in part because of the rapid growth of networks and new media technologies during the period. The Associated Press, a wire service that contracted reporting and news distribution to local, regional, and national newspapers expanded to radio in 1941. By 1950, more than two thousand radio stations were broadcasting, and 83 million radios were in American homes. Television, first introduced in 1939, on the eve of war, grew quickly in the war's aftermath. By the end of 1950, Americans had purchased 10 million sets for the 106 stations in 65 cities. By late 1954, television ownership had risen to 35 million sets with 413 stations in 65 cities.[1]

Opening (Dis)credits: The Hollywood Blacklist

Cinema was still a major force and a target of those wishing to target the influence of leftists in American culture. In 1947, after Republicans made gains in Congress, the House Un-American Activities Committee (HUAC), with encouragement from right-wingers in Hollywood, began investigating suspected communists in the entertainment industry. Like many artists and intellectuals, some in Hollywood had indeed been attracted to communism in response to the economic devastation of the Great Depression and the spread of fascism in the 1930s. Most were not revolutionaries who wished to see the overthrow of the US system, but rather saw communism as a means of reforming class and racial conflict.

For some in congress, that was a sign of their "un-American" views. John Rankin, a Democratic representative from Mississippi who was one of the leaders of the committee, opened an investigation of alleged communists in the government. Rankin nevertheless protected the Ku Klux Klan from being targeted, calling the Klan "an old American institution."[2] Congressional committees have no power to find people guilty or sentence them to prison. Having communist sympathies or even belonging to the party was not illegal. Instead, the goal of Rankin's hearings was primarily to harass and to defame political enemies. In this, it succeeded brilliantly.

Some Hollywood personalities cooperated with the committee, even naming people they suspected of being communists. Others, however, refused to answer the committee's questions, viewing the queries as an unconstitutional infringement on holding political views without government interference. A group of ten directors and screenwriters agreed to defy the committee's attempts to uncover their political backgrounds by refusing to answer their questions. Many read statements condemning the investigation. In the aftermath, calls to ban "the Ten" from working in Hollywood grew, especially from newspaper magnate William Randolph Hearst, whose vast network of papers published front-page editorials calling for action against them. But studios initially resisted, in part because of a California law that prevented employment discrimination on the grounds of one's political views.

Meanwhile, a group of Hollywood stars organized a campaign to oppose the hearings. The "Committee for the First Amendment" was led by megastars John Huston, Humphrey Bogart, Lauren Bacall, Judy Garland, and Katharine Hepburn. The group traveled to Washington to protest the hearings and recorded two radio programs to explain their position. As Judy Garland intoned with her distinctive diction:

This is Judy Garland. Have you been to a movie this week? Are you going to a movie tonight or maybe tomorrow? Look around the room. Are there any newspapers lying on the floor? Any magazines on your table? Any books on your shelves? It's always been your right to read or see anything you wanted to. But now it seems to be getting kind of complicated. For the past week, in Washington, the House Committee on Un-American Activities has been investigating the film industry. Now I have never been a member of any political organization, but I've been following this investigation and I don't like it. There are a lot of stars here to speak to you. We're show business, yes. But we're also American citizens. It's one thing if someone says we're not good actors—that hurts, but we can take that. It's something else again to say we're not good Americans. We resent that![3]

Others added their voices to the chorus of protest. Just a few years earlier, Hollywood had dutifully helped to promote the war effort with propaganda films. Surely, these stars thought, their patriotism was above suspicion and their defense of the Constitution would win the day.

But they had misjudged the mood of the public, or at least, that of the mainstream press. The reaction was swift and severe. Although the entertainers' committee had been careful to say that they were defending the Constitution, not communism, the distinction was erased in the coverage. Some prominent members began to publicly back away. Others, like Bogart, claimed to have been unaware that the Hollywood Ten included many who actually were communists. He issued a public apology, which was published in the Hearst papers. "I am not a Communist sympathizer," it read. "I went to Washington because I thought fellow Americans were being deprived of their Constitutional Rights, and for that that reason alone. That the trip was ill-advised, even foolish, I am very ready to admit. At the time it seemed the thing to do. I have absolutely no use for Communism nor for anyone who serves that philosophy. I am an American."[4]

One of the many dangers of speaking out against the anticommunist tactics was to become a target of suspicion yourself, as Bogart was learning. He followed up this statement with a fuller *mea culpa*, this one published in *Photoplay* magazine. "As the guy said to the warden, just before he was hanged: 'This will teach me a lesson I'll never forget.'

"No sir, I'll never forget the lesson that was taught to me in the year 1947, at Washington, D.C. When I got back to Hollywood, some friends sent me a mounted fish and underneath it was written, "If I hadn't opened my big mouth, I wouldn't be here." After this self-deprecating opening, delivered with his trademark humor, Bogart explained his good intentions to defend American values. As he related in the following excerpt, he was shocked to learn how his actions had played.

I first learned how wrong I was in my reasoning through a newspaper pal of mine, Ed Sullivan. He and I have been friends for close to twenty years and when we met, at Madison Square Garden during a big charity show, he called me aside and bawled the life out of me. "Stop it, Ed," I told him. "Suppose I have lost a few Republicans, likely as not, I've picked up a few Democrats." Sullivan looked at me as if I had two heads. "Look, Bogie," he said, "this is not a question of alienating Republicans or Democrats—this is a question of alienating the Americans. I know you're okay. So do your close friends. But the public is beginning to think you're a Red! Get that through your skull, Bogie."

Me a Red! That was the first inkling I had of what was happening. Impossible though it was to comprehend that anyone could think of me as a Communist, here was an old friend telling me just that. If it had begun and ended there, okay. But it didn't. Letters began to arrive. There were local newspaper stories and word of mouth spreading rumors across the country. Something had to be done quickly. But what?

I was in the position of the witness who suddenly is asked, "Have you stopped beating your wife?" If he answers "Yes" or "No" he is a dead pigeon.[5]

Bogart concluded by insisting that what had really been demonstrated by the hearings is that the number of Communists working in Hollywood was, in fact, very small:

In the final analysis, this House Committee probe has had a salutary effect. It cleared the air by indicating what a minute number of Commies there really are in the film industry. Though headlines may have screamed of the Red menace in movies, all the wind and fury actually proved that there's been no Communism injected on American movie screens.

As I said, I'm no Communist. If you thought so, you were dead wrong. But, brother, in this democracy, no one's going to shoot you for having thought so![6]

The pressure was building to charge the Hollywood Ten with contempt of Congress for their refusal to cooperate with HUAC. Hedda Hopper, whose gossip column "Hedda Hopper's Hollywood" was read by more than 30 million people, led the charge. In her weekly, Hopper profiled the left-wing politics of screenwriters, directors, and actors, and public and political events began to turn against the Hollywood Ten. In November, they were cited with contempt of Congress in a 346–17 vote in the House of Representatives. The heads of the major studios issued a joint statement, which said, in part, "We will forthwith discharge or suspend without compensation those in our employ, and we will not re-employ any of the Ten until such time as he is acquitted or has purged himself of contempt and declares under oath that he is not a Communist." They had been blacklisted and would remain so for the next thirteen years. The Ten still held out hope that their fortunes could change if their convictions were overturned by the Supreme Court, but the court declined to hear the case and the Ten were sentenced to prison terms.

Red Channels: Attacking Radio and Television

In 1950, a damning pamphlet was published by the right-wing journal *Counterattack*. *Red Channels: The Report of Communist Influence in Radio and Television* claimed to uncover the otherwise unknown communist plot to overthrow the American government by using American television and radio networks to push anti-American propaganda out to almost every home in America. The alleged goal was to turn the American public against their own country in favor of communism.

The pamphlet listed 151 names of people who were actually working in radio or television, but it alleged that they had ties to communism. The report named some established figures in US popular culture, including conductor Leonard Bernstein, author Arthur Miller, filmmaker Orson Welles, musician Pete Seeger, and journalist William L. Shirer. For most of those named in the pamphlet, the accusations were enough to effectively end their careers in broadcasting.

The cover of *Red Channels*.

The man claiming responsibility for the list, J. B. Matthews, would soon work closely with Senator Joe McCarthy. Matthews's exploits are detailed in the next section. The pamphlet's introduction (which follows) explains why American broadcasting networks were considered to be an important front in the Cold War. The report began by invoking the authority of J. Edgar Hoover and announcing the Communist Party's strategic shift from print to electronic media:

> Testifying before a US Congressional committee on March 26, 1947, J. Edgar Hoover, Director of the Federal Bureau of Investigation, stated: "The (Communist) party has departed from depending upon the printed word as its medium of propaganda and has taken to the air. Its members and sympathizers have not only infiltrated the airways, but they are now persistently seeking radio channels."
>
> Director Hoover's concise summary of Communist activities in the radio-TV field will be expanded in the following report to the broadcasting industry and to those who are both its client and its judge—the American public. . . .
>
> Basically, the Cominform (previously known as the Comintern) seeks to exploit American radio and TV to gain the following: Channels (known to the Communist Party as "transmission belts") for pro-Soviet, pro-Communist, anti-American, anti-democratic propaganda.
>
> The great prestige and crowd-gathering power that derives from having glamorous personalities of radio and TV as sponsors of Communist fronts and as performers or speakers at front meetings or rallies (which incidentally adds to the performer's prestige).
>
> Increasing domination of American broadcasting and telecasting, preparatory for the day when—the Cominform believes—the Communist Party will assume control of this nation as the result of a final upheaval and civil war.

The pamphlet made claims that were possible to believe by reframing known facts into a false narrative alleging Soviet communist infiltration into existing media. In a knowing tone, *Red Channels* let the reader in on the enormous Communist plot that was primed to flood the United States through its own radio and television system. The author invited the reader into the conspiracy through a review of the facts:

> Let us briefly examine Communist strategy and tactics in each of these categories.
>
> In indoctrinating the masses of people with Communist ideology and the pro-Soviet interpretation of current events, the Communist Party, with set purpose, uses not only Party members, but also fellow-travelers

and members of Communist adjuncts and periphery organizations. It is the Party's boast that for every Party member there are at least 10 "reliables," dupes or innocents who, for one reason or another will support its fronts. Our so-called "intellectual" classes—members of the arts, the sciences and the professions—have furnished the Communist Party USA with the greatest number in these classifications.

The anti-intellectual basis of this claim reflected the urban-rural divide that became prominent in the cultural conflicts surrounding the first red scare just after WWI. In that deeply polarized moment where conservatives rejected scientific approaches to social reality, clinging, instead, to traditional beliefs, including religion, intellectuals were regarded as unpatriotic threats to original American values. To succeed, the Communists needed insiders to help them undermine American culture and with the national government. *Red Channels* showed how:

> The importance of such accomplices has been emphasized by Stalin himself. In his classic, *Problems of Leninism*, a standard textbook and guide for Communists throughout the world, he quotes Lenin in support of his position: "The dictatorship cannot be effectively realized without 'belts' to transmit power from the vanguard (the Communist Party) to the mass of advanced class (the 'progressive' writers, actors, directors, etc.), and from this to the mass of those who labor (the public)" (*Problems of Leninism*, 29, 30).
>
> Dramatic programs are occasionally used for Communist propaganda purposes. A few documentary programs produced by one network in particular have faithfully followed the Party line. Several commercially sponsored dramatic series are used as sounding boards, particularly with reference to current issues in which the Party is critically interested: "academic freedom," "civil rights," "peace," the H-Bomb, etc. These and other subjects, perfectly legitimate in themselves, are cleverly exploited in dramatic treatments which point up current Communist goals.
>
> Perhaps the acme of the Party success in this field was reached when one program, sponsored by the advertising industry and American business, supposedly portraying the benefits of our economic system, turned out to be—in the words of one reviewer in the trade press—"more nearly a plea for collectivism!"
>
> With radios in most American homes and with approximately 5 million TV sets in use, the Cominform and the Communist Party USA now rely more on radio and TV than on the press and motion pictures as "belts to transmit pro-Sovietism to the American public.

The notion that the American broadcast media could be used to effect the communist overthrow of the United States frightened and alarmed the public. *Red Channels* expanded the blacklist from film to television and radio and greatly added to the number of people under suspicion—listing 151 actors, writers, broadcast journalists, and musicians. Appearing on that list ended the careers of many established figures in US broadcasting. It also changed the tone and tenor of broadcast industries for years to come. A tide of anticommunist fervor was rising, and one of its most prominent figures had emerged just months before the publication of *Red Channels*.

Lists, Lies, and Loyalties: Joe McCarthy's Media Strategies

Joseph McCarthy's career as a national figure started in an unlikely place. On February 9, 1950, Frank Desmond, a reporter from the *Wheeling Intelligencer* (West Virginia) arrived at Wheeling's McClure Hotel to cover the annual Lincoln Day speech hosted by the Republican Women's Club of Ohio County, West Virginia. The speaker that day, although a US senator, was rather undistinguished. In the four years since he had surprised the political establishment by winning election to the US Senate from Wisconsin in 1948, McCarthy's short career as a national politician had shown signs of weakness. He was isolated from his Republican colleagues, he was dogged by scandal, and he had recently been named "America's worst senator" by the Washington Correspondents' Association.[7]

McCarthy and his advisers had been searching for a strategy to reverse his flagging fortunes. In Wheeling, McCarthy displayed the new strategy, setting in motion a series of events that would define national politics in the United States from 1950 to 1954 and beyond. In his speech, McCarthy claimed that he had a list of 205 names of known communists serving in the US State Department. The papers McCarthy waved before the crowd that day did not, in fact, contain a list. The number was probably based on a letter from former secretary of state James Byrnes, in which he recommended against the permanent employment of 284 people in the department for a variety of reasons. When 79 were removed from their jobs, 206 remained. (McCarthy was prone to sloppy errors such as this.) By 1950, the list showed only 65 names of people from the original list who were still employees of the state department.[8]

The suggestion of communist infiltration was not a new idea, nor was the use of such fear appeals by government officials. In the first Red Scare in 1919–20, the Woodrow Wilson administration had passed current versions of the Espionage and Alien and Sedition acts of 1798 to revive century-old fears of an antidemocratic invasion by foreigners. The actual threat was minimal. In the 1920s, the Communist Party of the USA (CPUSA) had made its presence felt by trying to organize white and Black southern sharecroppers in the 1920s. In one particular case, seeking to prevent a miscarriage of justice, the CPUSA prominently stepped in to provide legal defense for the Scottsboro Boys, nine young Black boys and men falsely accused and infamously tormented for allegedly raping two white women in Alabama in 1931.[9]

Even as external threats came and went—the Russian Revolution of 1917–23, the rise of the Soviet Union after World War II, and the Korean War from 1952 to 1954—the fear of an anti-American insurgency from within the nation's borders by labor and Blacks was never out of the mainstream imagination. In the South, in particular, agitation for civil rights was often attacked as a communist plot.[10]

With that history for context, McCarthy's baseless charges made ready sense to many in the public. In Wheeling, Desmond followed a typical journalistic tradition of deference to a senator's authority. As a result, without asking for any evidence to support McCarthy's explosive claims, Desmond reported a wholly descriptive—and uncritical—account of the speech. The story he wrote appeared on the *Wheeling Intelligencer*'s front page the next day, with McCarthy's claims reported but unverified. Like the bombshell that it was, the story sounded alarms across the nation:

M'CARTHY CHARGES REDS HOLD U.S. JOBS
TRUMAN BLASTED FOR RELUCTANCE TO PRESS PROBE
WISCONSIN SENATOR TELLS LINCOLN FETE HERE 'CHIPS DOWN'

Joseph McCarthy, junior US Senator from Wisconsin, was given a rousing ovation last night when, as guest of the Ohio County Republican Women's Club, he declared bluntly that the fate of the world rests with the clash between the atheism of Moscow and the Christian spirit throughout other parts of the world.

More than 275 representative Republican men and women were on hand to attend the colorful Lincoln Day dinner of the valley women which was held in the Colonnade room of the McLure hotel.

In this setting, McCarthy turned his folksy Wisconsin charm to deliver chilling news about the government:

Disdaining any oratorical fireworks, McCarthy's talk was of an intimate, homey nature, punctuated at times with humor.

But on the serious side, he launched many barbs at the present setup of the State Department, at President Truman's reluctance to press investigation of "traitors from within," and other pertinent matters.

He said that recent incidents which brought traitors to the limelight is the result of an "emotional hangover" and a temporary moral lapse which follows every war. However, he added: The morals of our people have not been destroyed. They still exist and this cloak of numbness and apathy needs only a spark to rekindle them.

Referring directly to the State Department, he intimated that there was more to the story than he could disclose: "While I cannot take the time to name all of the men in the State Department who have been named as members of the Communist Party and members of a spy ring, I have here in my hand a list of 205 that were known to the Secretary of State as being members of the Communist Party and who, nevertheless, are still working and shaping the policy in the State Department."

The speaker dwelt at length on the Alger Hiss case and mentioned the names of several others who, during the not so many years, were found to entertain subversive ideas but were still given positions of high trust in the government. "As you hear of this (Hiss) story of high treason, he said, 'I know that you are saying to yourself well, why doesn't Congress do something about it?"

McCarthy presented himself the seer and savior of this threat to their conservative ideals of American life. He explained: "Actually, ladies and gentlemen, the reason for the graft, the corruption, the disloyalty, the treason in high government positions, the reason this continues is because of a lack of moral uprising on the part of the 140 million American people. In the light of history, however, this is not hard to explain.

It is the result of an emotional hangover and a temporary moral lapse which follows every war. It is the apathy to evil which people who have been subjected to the tremendous evils of war feel."

McCarthy's rhetorical approach to framing questions of "good and evil" depended on casting the U.S.-Soviet relationship in the starkest terms. He also spoke as a man with experience of war: "As the people of the world see mass murder, the destruction of defenseless and innocent people and all of the crime and lack of morals which go with war, they become numb and apathetic. It has always been thus after war."

At another time, he intoned that an American apocalypse at the hands of the communists already among them was imminent: "Today, we are engaged in a final all-out battle between Communistic atheism and Christianity. The modern champions of Communism have selected this as the time and, ladies and gentlemen, the chips are down—they are truly down."[11]

The way that the story was reported mattered. By describing, rather than presenting the story within its available interpretive context, the reporter effectively conceded the definition of the story's meaning to McCarthy. In

Senator Joseph McCarthy in 1954.

fairness, the reporter was outmatched, both by McCarthy and by the pre-vailing reporting conventions. For the rest of McCarthy's four-year assault on the press, journalists would reset their approaches to include interpretive reporting as they tried to remain both objective and truthful in the face of a dedicated liar. And, for a while, McCarthy held them at bay.

The public fear of being accused of communist leanings by McCarthy grew within a specific and volatile cultural dynamic. Fueled by his genius for media manipulation, McCarthy's self-serving version of anticommunism tapped into fear-based themes dating back to the nation's earliest days. By investigating alleged Reds in the State Department, Hollywood, and even in the military, he used Americans' traditional worries about outside threats to the nation as a way to gain power over them. Armed with subpoena power, he used his campaign of propaganda and disinformation to destroy citizens' careers with blacklists that banned suspected communists from working.[12]

Understanding the various roles played by the news media in the McCarthy era depends on understanding the origins of the anticommunist fear that McCarthy used to intimidate the nation so well from 1952 to 1956. The roots of anticommunism go deep into our founding beliefs about who can claim legitimate citizenship and a deep-seated fear of an invisible insurgency.

In Wheeling, McCarthy's allegations of spies invoked a fear that would later be expressed in the 1956 film *Invasion of the Body Snatchers*, in which a town's population is silently and almost imperceptibly taken over by an invading alien species. As the protagonist's friends are taken over, they creepily try to convince the heroes to succumb, promising they'll awaken into a utopia, "an untroubled world," where "everyone's the same."[13]

For McCarthy, projecting these fears was a path to unchallenged power. His platform was made more powerful by his mastery of journalists' deadlines and news cycles. At a time when most daily newspapers were printed in multiple editions, competitive editors were desperate for fresh leads and headlines for each new edition. "That's where Joe came in," said Charles Seib, ombudsman for the *Washington Post*. "Call him, and he'd have something for the new lead."

George Reedy of the UPI and, later, President Lyndon Johnson's press secretary, said, "We had to take what McCarthy said at face value. Joe couldn't find a Communist in Red Square—he didn't know Karl Marx from Groucho—but he was a United States Senator." According to Seib, "The competition was tremendous. We'd get a two-minute beat on a new name and Joe McCarthy rode this." He added, "If he said it, we wrote it."

McCarthy also exploited reporters' daily publication schedule. One favorite tactic was to deliver his allegations just prior to the filing deadlines for journalists. This ensured, at least initially, that his charges would be published without the possibility of rebuttal. As a result, rather than derailing the senator's lies, the wire services allowed McCarthey to co-opt them, leading their network of subscribing newspapers and radio stations into facilitating his disinformation campaign. Not all journalists saw the risks. Seib said, "It was sort of a game for us, as it was for McCarthy." He added, "That was true of the whole American press. It was a hysterical time. Practically all of us realized what McCarthy was, but we felt powerless."[14]

When the *Intelligencer* story appeared in 1950, public anxiety about communist subversion was already at a fever pitch. The treaties ending World War II had granted a large sphere of influence to the communist Soviet Union to the consternation of many Western nations. In 1949, after a long struggle, communist forces had seized control of China. Communists attempting to win control of the Korean peninsula would shortly lead to the deployment of US troops, intent on stopping the advance of the so-called "Red tide."

In 1948, Alger Hiss, a high-ranking State Department official, had been publicly accused of passing secrets to the Soviet Union. Hiss forever maintained his innocence. But to many, the charges seemed to have been confirmed when Hiss was convicted of perjury after the spectacular revelation of stolen government information. For many conservatives, the Hiss affair demonstrated that communists were, indeed, working secretly within the US government to undermine the American effort against communism.

In the days that followed McCarthy's Wheeling speech, journalists flocked to the senator, asking him to elaborate on his allegations. McCarthy proved a master at gaslighting the press, often by denying what he had been quoted as saying and then leveling new charges. When the State Department denied that any communists were employed there, McCarthy subtly shifted his language to describe "bad risks," whose names he claimed to have in bags that he was not then carrying with him. He constantly changed the number of the accused on his list from 205, to 207, to 57, to 81. When public officials repudiated his claims or denounced him, McCarthy went on the offensive, calling his critics' loyalty into question.

As a result of these tactics, McCarthy rose from relative obscurity to become one of the most visible and powerful members of the Senate. His accusations drew constant headlines. And in the hyperpartisan atmosphere of the Cold War, many of his fellow Republicans viewed him as a valuable asset to the party's efforts to dominate the elections in 1952. Some Republicans openly supported McCarthy, and few would publicly oppose him. Democrats, meanwhile, organized and published the report by Maryland Democratic Senator Millard Tydings to document their firm rebuke of McCarthy's reckless tactics.

Events, however, were on McCarthy's side. On July 14, 1950, the day the Tydings report was made public, the FBI announced that it had arrested Julius Rosenberg, an American citizen accused of (and later convicted and executed for) passing secrets to the Soviet Union relating to the atomic bomb. In the weeks that followed, the FBI arrested three other members of the alleged spy ring, including Rosenberg's wife, Ethel, and his brother-in-law. For many observers, the arrests of these Soviet spies underlined the importance of McCarthy's anticommunist crusade. After a contentious partisan debate about whether to approve the recommendations of the Tydings report, not a single Republican voted for the measure. Meanwhile, McCarthy continued to make new charges with extraordinary boldness.

Another point of vulnerability for the press lay in the ongoing disagreement about which practices produced objectivity and truth in the news. At the time, the news media's more conservative sense of objectivity held that the "straight" news should report only information that was descriptive of events, rather than offering more analytical or interpretive reports. This professional standard was intended to prevent bias in the news.

Alternately, many journalists and editors believed that the news should lend context to ongoing stories. According to historian Edwin Bayley, "It is clear that in these years convictions about objectivity were related to opinions about McCarthy. All of the 'fundamentalists' on objectivity were from newspapers that supported McCarthy editorially, and all of the editors who defended interpretive reporting were from newspapers that were critical of McCarthy."[15]

McCarthy's power grew throughout the 1952 campaign as he campaigned for fellow Republicans nationwide. He was so popular among his party that he received twice as many requests for speaking engagements as any other Republican. He drew huge crowds to his rallies and helped lead a Republican sweep of Congress and the White House in that year's elections. In recognition of his newfound importance, he was named chairman of the Senate's Government Operations Committee, as well as head of the Permanent Investigations Subcommittee. But challenges to his seemingly unstoppable power were also developing.

Edward R. Murrow: Exposing the Tactics of the Red Scare

Of the most enduring media myths of the Second Red Scare, which lasted from 1947 to 1957, the most common holds that McCarthy was solely responsible for the scare. Another myth identifies Edward R. Murrow as the only journalist brave enough to face McCarthy down. While each man played a key role in the Second Red Scare, Murrow was neither the only nor was he the first to react against McCarthy, and anticommunism can be traced back to the nineteenth century. McCarthy was opportunistic in building a crisis that was already part of the national imagination.

On February 18, 1950, *Washington Post* columnist Drew Pearson became the first journalist to identify and challenge McCarthy's lies. He would continue to attack McCarthy frequently and directly from then on.[16] Indeed, he would remain the senator's most vociferous critic. According to historian Edwin Bayley, "The *Washington Post*'s coverage of McCarthy was probably the best in the nation."[17] Because both Murrow and Pearson were opinion journalists, not news reporters, their criticisms could be more pointed than either descriptive or interpretive styles of news reporting.

On March 3, 1951, a column drafted by Pearson's staff, "McCarthyism Becomes a Menace," ran in the *Post* in Pearson's column, "Washington Merry Go Round." By then, McCarthy and Pearson were well acquainted: The year before, after making threats against the writer in Senate speeches, McCarthy had physically assaulted Pearson at a Washington social club in revenge for his criticisms in print.[18]

Attacks on McCarthy were common, but few were as outsize as the seventeen-part series published in September 1951 by the *New York Post*. Not obligated to news conventions of objectivity, the tabloid ridiculed and rebuked him from its first installment: "In the course of his careening, reckless, headlong dive down the road to political power and personal fame, he has smashed the reputations of countless men, destroyed Senate careers, splattered mud on the pages of 20 years of national history, confused and distracted the public mind, bulldozed press and radio."[19]

By the time Murrow turned his eye toward McCarthy three years later, most Americans had bought televisions. If the criticisms were not new, the shift from radio and newspapers to television was driven by Murrow's artful delivery. In 1950, Murrow teamed with producer Fred Friendly to produce *Hear It Now*, an hour-long CBS radio program in a magazine format sponsored by the aluminum company Alcoa. *Hear It Now* aimed to provide in-depth reporting on current events and to present the "sound of history in the making."

After only a few months, CBS convinced Murrow and Friendly to adapt their radio expertise to the emerging medium of television. The result was *See It Now*, a pioneering, prime-time news program that featured in-depth reporting on current events. "This is an old team, trying to learn a new trade," Murrow explained at the start of the first episode. "My purpose will be not to get in your light anymore than I can, to lean over the camera-man's shoulder occasionally and say a word which may help to illuminate or explain what is happening. . . . We're impressed with the importance of this medium. We shall hope to learn to use it, and not to abuse it."[20]

Murrow and Friendly produced a series that offered viewers an opportunity they had never had before: to be eyewitnesses to national dramas great and small. The series showed local men and women working around the clock to protect their Kansas town from a flooding Missouri River, members of southern communities struggling for and against racial integration, and GIs fighting the Korean War. Through these feature stories and profiles, *See It Now* created national news with an emphasis on the struggles of working people, gaining a loyal and growing audience.

Aware of television's power, many of Murrow's colleagues in radio and television began to call on Murrow and Friendly to expose McCarthyism's dishonest and heartless tactics. As Friendly later remembered, Murrow would respond by insisting: "We're not preachers. We cover the news. When there's a good news story about McCarthy that will give us a little picture, we'll do it, but we're not going to go out and make a speech against McCarthy."[21]

In late 1950, Murrow came across a news story in the *Detroit Free Press* announcing the firing of a reserve Air Force lieutenant named Milo Radu-lovich. As Friendly would later remember, Murrow showed him the article and told him, "This may be our McCarthy program." Radulovich had been labeled a "security risk" by McCarthy, because his father, a Serbian immigrant, subscribed to a newspaper from his homeland in the former Yugoslavia that was published by a communist organization there. The Air Force lieutenant's case helped to dramatize how hundreds, if not thousands, of loyal, productive, and talented citizens had been drummed out of public life by McCarthy on the flimsiest evidence in order that others might build political careers.

After some investigative reporting, which compared various sources to lend context to the story, the Murrow team was convinced. Even a source whom they thought would be a sure-fire pro-McCarthy supporter, the head of the local chapter of the conservative Veterans of Foreign Wars (VFW), offered a heated defense of Radulovich. The hosting CBS television network and ALCOA, the program's major sponsor, were decidedly less enthusiastic They were wary of alienating viewers with a controversial topic or of even attracting the unwanted attentions of McCarthy and his followers.

The report aired on October 3, 1953, under the title "The Case of Milo Radulovich, A0589839." Murrow did not defend the right to hold communist views. Instead, he criticized the decision to punish Radulovich for his family's unpopular political views and he highlighted the lack of evidence in the case. As Murrow explained, Radulovich was seen as a security risk solely on the basis of his father's and sister's reading habits. At the end of the piece, the reporter insisted, "We believe that 'the son shall not bear the inequity of the father,' even if that inequity be proved, and in this case, it was not." The program prompted eight thousand letters and telegrams to CBS, and numerous citations in the press. The reaction was largely sympathetic to the Air Force officer's case. The resulting outcry against McCarthy and the ensuing reinstatement of Radulovich by the Air Force emboldened Murrow and Friendly.

The pair quickly set to work on an exposé of McCarthy's tactics. The episode, "A Report on Senator Joseph R. McCarthy," aired on March 9, 1954. It showed mostly clips of McCarthy's questioning technique, including his oddly aggressive, yet monotone, speaking habit, his blatant hypocrisy, and his habit of twisting innocent statements by his witnesses into seemingly incriminating statements.

In the transcript that follows, Murrow introduced a television segment. It showed the curious American audience at home a glimpse of McCarthy at his worst. He was shading the Democratic presidential nominee, Adlai Stevenson, by intentionally confusing accused communist spy Alger Hiss's name with the senator's:

MURROW (LOOKING INTENTLY INTO THE TELEVISION CAMERA):
    And upon what meat doth Senator McCarthy feed? Two of the staples of his diet are the investigation, protected by immunity, and the half-truth. We herewith submit samples of both.
        First, the half-truth. This was an attack on Adlai Stevenson at the end of the 1952 campaign. President Eisenhower, it must be said, had no prior knowledge of it.
McCARTHY: I perform this unpleasant task, because the American people are entitled to have the coldly documented history of this man who says, "I want to be your President."
        Strangely, Alger—I mean, *Adlai* [laughter]—But let's move on to another part of the jigsaw puzzle. Now, while you think—while you

may think there can be no connection between the debonair Democrat candidate and a dilapidated [Maryland] barn, I want to show you a picture of this barn and explain the connection.

Here is the outside of the barn. Give me the pictures of the inside, if you will. Here is the outside of the barn up at Lee, [Maryland]. It looks as though it couldn't house a farmer's cow or goat. Here's the inside: a beautifully paneled conference room with maps of the Soviet Union. Well, in what way does Stevenson tie up with this?

My . . . my investigators went out and took pictures of this barn after we had been tipped off of what was in it, tipped off that there was in this barn all the missing documents from the Communist front—IPR—the IPR which has been named by the McCarran Committee[22] . . . named before the McCarran Committee as a cover shop for Communist espionage.

In this exchange, McCarthy tried to confirm his allegation that Adlai Stevenson, governor of Illinois and presidential candidate on the Democratic ticket in 1952 and 1956, was a communist. The hidden "documents" referred to here became known as the "pumpkin papers" for the unlikely place McCarthy said a film cannister containing them was found in a Maryland barn.[23]

McCARTHY: Now, let's take a look at a photostat of a document taken from the barn—one of those documents which was never supposed to see the light of day. Rather interesting it is. This is a document which shows that Alger Hiss and Frank Coe recommended Adlai Stevenson to the Mount Tremblant Conference, which was called for the purpose of establishing foreign policy in Asia. Now, as you know, Alger Hiss is a convicted traitor. Frank Coe has been named under oath before congressional committees seven times as a member of the Communist Party. Why? Why do Hiss and Coe find that Adlai Stevenson is the man they want representing them at this conference? I don't know. Perhaps Adlai knows.

MURROW: But Senator McCarthy didn't permit his audience to hear the entire paragraph. This is the official record of the (Senator Pat) McCarran (D.-Nevada) hearings. Anyone can buy it for two dollars. Here's a quote: "Another possibility for the Mount Tremblant conferences on Asia is someone from Knox's office or Stimson's office." (Frank Knox was our wartime Secretary of the Navy; Henry Stimson our Secretary of the Army, both distinguished Republicans.) And it goes on: "Coe, and Hiss mentioned Adlai Stevenson, one of Knox's special assistants, and Harvey Bundy—former Assistant Secretary of State under Hoover, and now assistant to Stimson—because of their jobs."

Standing up for journalism and for the place of television in it, Murrow added, "We read from this documented record, not in defense of Mr. Stevenson, but in defense of truth," he argued. "Specifically, Mr. Stevenson's identification with that red barn was no more, no less than that of Knox, Stimson, or Bundy. It should be stated that Mr. Stevenson was once a member of the Institute of Pacific Relations. But so were such other loyal Americans as Senator Ferguson, John Foster Dulles, Paul Hoffman, Harry Luce, and Herbert Hoover. Their association carries with it no guilt, and that barn has nothing to do with any of them."[24]

By challenging McCarthy, Murrow showed his audience the lengths that McCarthy would go to in order to fabricate an obviously far-fetched scenario. By showing, as well as telling, this story, Murrow's television program, *See It Now*, Murrow produced dramatic video spectacles showing the nation McCarthy's demagoguery.

In a typical McCarthy hearing, the senator would interrogate a witness for dramatic effect until the news deadlines were met. Then he would often dismiss them. In this example, the witness was Reed Harris, for many years a civil servant in the State Department, where he directed the Information Service. Harris was accused of helping the communist cause by curtailing some broadcasts to Israel. As in most cases, the ties to communism alleged by McCarthy dated from the 1920s and 1930s. Here the senator summoned Harris to question him about a book he had written in 1932:

HARRIS: At the time I wrote the book, the atmosphere in the universities of the United States was greatly affected by the Great Depression then in existence. The attitudes of students, the attitudes of the general public, were considerably different than they are at this moment, and for one thing there certainly was generally no awareness, to the degree that there is today, of the way the Communist Party works.

McCARTHY: You attended Columbia University in the early thirties. Is that right?

HARRIS: I did, Mr. Chairman.

McCARTHY: Will you speak a little louder, sir?

HARRIS (SPEAKING LOUDLY): I did, Mr. Chairman.

McCARTHY: And were you expelled from Columbia?

HARRIS: I was suspended from classes on April 1st, 1932. I was later reinstated, and I resigned from the University.

McCARTHY: And you resigned from the University. Did the Civil . . ., Civil Liberties Union provide you with an attorney at that time?

HARRIS: I had many offers of attorneys, and one of those was from the American Civil Liberties Union, yes.

McCARTHY: The question is, "Did the Civil Liberties Union supply you with an attorney?"

HARRIS: They did supply an attorney.

McCARTHY: The answer is yes?

HARRIS: The answer is yes.

McCARTHY: You know the Civil Liberties Union has been listed as a front for, and doing the work of the Communist Party?

HARRIS: Mr. Chairman this was 1932.

McCARTHY: Yeah, I know it was 1932. Do you know that they since have been listed as a front for and doing the work of the Communist Party?

HARRIS: I do not know that they have been listed so, sir.

McCARTHY: You don't know they have been listed?

HARRIS: I have heard that mentioned or read that mentioned.

McCarthy then moved on to two key favorite themes: The liberal decadence of the professoriate and the danger of allowing professors the academic freedom to challenge social norms in their work. He hammered Harris on a book the witness had written in 1932. Harris distanced himself from the opinions he had stated more than two decades earlier:

HARRIS: Mr. Chairman, two weeks ago, Senator Taft took the position that I took twenty-one years ago, that Communists and Socialists should be allowed to teach in the schools. It so happens that nowadays I don't agree with Senator Taft, as far as Communist teaching in the schools is concerned, because I think Communists are, in effect, a plainclothes auxiliary of the Red Army, the Soviet Red Army. And I don't want to see them in any of our schools, teaching.

McCARTHY: I don't recall Senator Taft ever having any of the background that you've got, sir.

HARRIS: I resent the tone of this inquiry very much, Mr. Chairman. I resent it, not only because it is my neck, my public neck, that you are, I think, very skillfully trying to wring, but I say it because there are thousands of able and loyal employees in the federal government of the United States who have been properly cleared according to the laws and the security practices of their agencies, as I was—unless the new regime says no; I was before.

Having shown McCarthy's interrogation techniques, Murrow then added his commentary, demonstrating the bad faith of McCarthy's arguments:

MURROW: The Reed Harris hearing demonstrates one of the Senator's techniques. Twice he said the American Civil Liberties Union was listed as a subversive front. The Attorney General's list does not and has never listed the ACLU as subversive, nor does the FBI or any other federal government agency. And the American Civil Liberties Union holds in its files letters of commendation from President Truman, President Eisenhower and General MacArthur.

Now let us try to bring the McCarthy story a little more up to date. Two years ago Senator Benton of Connecticut accused McCarthy of apparent perjury, unethical practice, and perpetrating a hoax on the Senate. McCarthy sued for two million dollars. Last week he dropped the case, saying no one could be found who believed Benton's story. Several volunteers have come forward saying they believe it in its entirety.

By the end of the program, Murrow and Friendly had shown McCarthy to have been a manipulative, opportunistic bully, whose actions were undermining the very principles on which Murrow believed the United States stood. In his closing statement, Murrow again looked his viewers in the eye and reminded them that "the line between investigating and persecuting is a very fine one, and the Junior Senator from Wisconsin has stepped over it repeatedly. His primary achievement has been confusing the public mind as between the internal and the external threats of communism. We must not confuse dissent with disloyalty. We must remember always, that accusation is not proof, and that conviction depends upon evidence and due process of law. We will not walk in fear, one of another, we will not be driven by fear into an age of unreason."

He concluded by accusing McCarthy in the same language made ominous by the junior Senator, the charge of giving "comfort to our enemies." Then, borrowing language directly from a *New York Times* column published two days before by *Times* editor James "Scotty" Reston, Murrow looked into the camera and asked, "And who's fault is that? Not really his; he didn't create this situation of fear, he merely exploited it, and rather successfully. Cassius was right: the fault, dear Brutus, is not in our stars, but in ourselves."[25]

After that episode, McCarthy accepted Murrow's invitation to respond on the April 13, 1954, edition of the program. And, predictably, he again accused Murrow of harboring communist sympathies. But his career as a power broker in the Senate had already begun its spectacular decline.

Conclusions: "At Long Last, Have You Left No Sense of Decency?"

The last straw in McCarthy's career came from his imprudent decision to accuse US Army officials of communist sympathies. The charges stemmed from the unusual efforts by McCarthy's chief counsel, Roy Cohn, to have the Army relocate his close friend, Army Private David Schine, to the Washington area where they could be together. In a clear case of over-reach, McCarthy saw his usual charges of communist leanings against the US Army backfire as the Army complained about McCarthy's interference in their internal personnel matters. Nonetheless, the investigation of these charges and countercharges became a national showdown between McCarthy and the Pentagon.

As the US Senate's Subcommittee on Investigations hearings drew on from April through June of 1954, the three television networks covered the story closely. NBC focused on the hearing's onset, CBS gave a nightly review of the proceedings, and ABC aired the hearings live from start to finish. In a move designed to bolster the network's audience and market, ABC devoted some 180 hours to the spectacle.[26]

On June 9, the Army's special counsel, Joseph Welch, shocked the nation when he stood up to the senator during the nationally televised hearings. From his seat at the conference table in the cavernous hearing room, a visibly agitated Welch rebuked McCarthy for attacking one of Welch's staff attorneys, Fred Fisher. As Welch explained, decades before, Fisher had belonged to the Lawyers' Guild, an organization that McCarthy alleged was communist. Prior to the hearing, McCarthy had agreed to overlook Welch's junior colleague, whose leftist history was thin and out of date.

When he reneged, attacking Fisher, anyway, Welch said, "Until this moment, Senator, I think I never really gauged your cruelty or your recklessness." When McCarthy ignored him, Welch uttered the words that sealed McCarthy's fate with the public: "Senator, may we not drop this? We know he belonged to the Lawyers Guild. . . . Let us not assassinate this lad further, Senator; you've done enough. Have you no sense of decency, sir? At long last, have you left no sense of decency?"

As McCarthy tried to rein the discussion in, Welch talked over him, saying, "Mr. McCarthy, I will *not* discuss this further with you. . . . You have seen fit to bring it out, and if there is a God in heaven, it will do neither you nor your cause any good! I will not discuss it further. . . . You, Mr. Chairman, may as you will, call the next witness!"

As the vast room absorbed the blow, the spectators erupted in cheers and applause. Moreover, a national television audience saw and heard the improbable scene explode around a stunned McCarthy.[27]

With his public appeal crumbling, McCarthy's many enemies closed in. In December, McCarthy was censured by the Senate and was stripped of his power to direct US anticommunist efforts. Impotent and humiliated,

McCarthy spun out of control. He died of alcoholism less than three years later at the age of 48.

Although Murrow proved to be a giant killer, setting television journalism's high-water mark led to Murrow's own disillusionment with the possibilities of television news. *See It Now* sponsor Alcoa withdrew its sponsorship after Murrow refused to avoid controversial, politically (and, from Alcoa's perspective, economically) divisive topics. As a result of this controversy, *See It Now* aired its final regular weekly episode in July 1958. Speaking that same year to the Radio-Television News Directors Association and Foundation, Murrow commented on the perils and promise of the still new medium. In spite of its potential, it was, he thought, organized in ways that privileged distraction over information and entertainment over illumination at a time when the public needed enlightenment more urgently than ever. He said,

> Our history will be what we make it. And if there are any historians about fifty or a hundred years from now—and there should be preserved the kinescopes [pre-video tape recording media] for one week of all three networks—they will there find recorded in black and white, or perhaps in color, evidence of decadence, escapism, and insulation from the realities of the world in which we live. I invite your attention to the television schedules of all networks between the hours of 8:00 and 11:00 p.m., Eastern Time. Here, you will find only fleeting and spasmodic reference to the fact that this nation is in mortal danger. There are, it is true, occasional informative programs presented in that intellectual ghetto on Sunday afternoons. But during the daily peak viewing periods, television, in the main, insulates us from the realities of the world in which we live. If this state of affairs continues, we may alter an advertising slogan to read: "LOOK NOW and PAY LATER.[28]

He ended his remarks with another reminder that his criticisms about television were not about the medium, per se, but rather about how it was being utilized: "This instrument can teach, it can illuminate; yes, and it can even inspire," he said. "But it can do so only to the extent that humans are determined to use it to those ends. Otherwise, it is merely wires and lights in a box. There is a great and perhaps decisive battle to be fought against ignorance, intolerance and indifference. This weapon of television could be useful."[29]

10

Civil Rights and the Spectacle
of Southern Racism

On September 6, 1955, the devastated body of Emmett Till, a fourteen-year-old Black boy, lay in a casket in the Roberts Temple Church of God in Christ. There on the South Side of Chicago, thousands of people waited hours to pay their respects. Many mourners had to be helped out of the building after seeing the sight of his muddied, unrecognizable face. After his captors had tortured and shot him, they dumped his body into the Tallahatchie River near Money, Mississippi. They then tied a large cotton gin fan around his neck with barbed wire to sink his corpse to the river's muddy bottom.

His "crime" was typical of the false charges that had been made against Black lynching victims for decades: A local white shopkeeper, Carolyn Bryant, had accused him of speaking to her disrespectfully at her general store. It was not true. In 2017—sixty-two years later—Bryant would confess to a reporter that she had told a lie that had cost this child his life.[1]

Till's lynching came as such violent attacks had been declining for years. Racial change had seemed imminent in 1954 when the Supreme Court had ruled in *Brown v. Board of Education of Topeka* that separate-but-equal racial segregation was unconstitutional. Immediately, white supremacists reasserted southern states' rights to local political leadership. James O. Eastland (1904–86), recently elected to the US Senate from Mississippi, protested the court's ruling with the familiar argument that segregation in the South helped maintain racial "harmony." While ignoring the unequal effects of white supremacy, he argued that separate-but-equal statuses for whites and Blacks was the remedy for the social, political, and racial harms done to white southerners by the North during Reconstruction. He wrote,

> The southern institution of racial segregation or racial separation was
> the correct, self-evident truth which arose from the chaos and confusion

of the reconstruction period. Separation promotes racial harmony. It permits each race to follow its own pursuits, and its own civilization. Segregation is not discrimination. Segregation is not a badge of racial inferiority, and that it is not recognized by both races in the Southern States. In fact, segregation is desired and supported by the vast majority of the members of both races in the South, who dwell side by side under harmonious conditions.

The negro has made a great contribution to the South. We take pride in the constant advance he has made. It is where social questions are involved that Southern people draw the line. It is these social institutions with which Southern people, in my judgment, will not permit the Supreme Court to tamper.[2]

Mamie Till, Emmett's mother, knew better than to stand for Eastland's excuse for segregation. When she saw her son's decomposed face and ruined body, she insisted on an open-casket funeral. "There was just no way I could describe what was in that box," she said later. "No way. And I just wanted the world to see." To tell the world about her son, she invited the *Chicago Defender* and *Jet*, both nationally distributed, Black-owned publications based in Chicago, to send photographers. The nightmarish images of Till's mutilated body ran in their pages.

Civil rights organizers would consistently repeat this strategy of using news media coverage to unveil the brutal violence that supported the romanticized "Southern way of life." This chapter examines how that strategy was deployed by various groups and focuses on how the technique of media management was mastered by Martin Luther King Jr.'s (1929–68) Southern Christian Leadership Conference (SCLC) and John Lewis's (1940–2020) Congress of Racial Equality (CORE). Through mass civil disobedience and a sustained, clear demand for change, these groups exposed the antidemocratic violence inherent in the political systems of the South.

To consider the role of white journalism and related mainstream public opinion as it often unwillingly changed during this period, we also describe the evolving views of Ralph McGill (1898–1969), a white, conservative editor at the *Atlanta Journal-Constitution*, who came to support the movement. As we shall see, the movement's tactics were effective, until they turned their critique toward the North to challenge federal domestic and international priorities.

Emmett Till, Martyr for the Movement

Jet's feature on Till's murder gave the magazine's editors pause, as they looked toward the upcoming trial. They asked whether "Mississippi

The Bryant Grocery & Meat Market in Money, Mississippi, where Emmett Till encountered Carolyn Bryant.

(would) whitewash its latest and most fiendish atrocity when the accused kidnapers go on trial September 19." They were right to be concerned. Just weeks later in Mississippi, national and international correspondents would report on the trial of Bryant's husband, Roy Bryant (1931–94), and his half-brother, J. W. Milan (1919–80), who had been accused of murdering Till.

The world watched as the casual, everyday denigration of Black lives was laid bare for all to see there in the trial. The judge segregated the courtroom and casually referred to Black people in the courtroom as "n*****s." Two black men—Willie Reed and Moses Wright, at the risk of torture and death—stepped forward in the courtroom to identify the killers—and then quietly and immediately left Mississippi for the rest of their lives. But their courageous testimony was of no use. In his closing argument, the lead defense attorney made a naked racial appeal, telling the all-white jury: "Every last Anglo-Saxon one of you has the courage to free these men." The jury found Bryant and Milan not guilty after deliberating for only sixty-seven minutes. It wouldn't have even taken that long, one jury member later bragged, if they hadn't stalled to keep up the appearance of serious deliberation.

With the trial settled and their freedom secured, Bryant and Milan agreed to be interviewed by journalist William Bradford Huie (1910–16) for $4,000. The resulting story, published in *Look* magazine, revealed the truth of their actions, as well as their complete lack of remorse. As Dave Tell details in *Remembering Emmett Till*, Huie had identified two additional men who had participated in Till's lynching, but he could not get them to sign a release, which would protect *Look* magazine from litigation. So Huie's story shrank the lynching party to the two legally accused perpetrators, essentially shielding from justice two other accessories to murder, or at least what passed for justice in Mississippi at that time.

A Media Strategy for the Movement

Resistance to such violence took many forms. Just months after the verdict, in December 1955, a seamstress named Rosa Parks was arrested on a Montgomery, Alabama, city bus for declining to give her seat to a white passenger. Parks, who was an active and respected member of the NAACP chapter, became the focus of the civil rights movement's first exercise of the protest strategy of civil disobedience. Her arrest led to a nearly year-long boycott of the city's buses—an act of remarkable endurance, nonviolence, and coordination led by the Bethel St. Baptist Church's new, twenty-six-year-old pastor, Dr. Martin Luther King Jr. The boycott was ultimately a success, achieving the integration of Montgomery's buses among a number of other demands. Encouraged, King and his partners formed the SCLC to organize social action against segregation and in favor of civil rights.

As the movement grew, so did white mob violence against movement participants. The campaign against desegregation was called massive resistance. It presented an unflinching refusal to cooperate with court-ordered changes to the southern way of life. These actions would invoke the states' lawful defense of segregation, frequently spilling over into violence. With national television and print journalists summoned to the scene by the SCLC and other organizers, national and international coverage of a new generation of what Ida B. Wells had called "southern horrors" was displayed for the nation and the world to see.

In 1957, in Little Rock, Arkansas, for example, segregationist governor Orval Faubus (1910–94) defied a federal court order based on the *Brown* decision by refusing to allow nine Black children to attend the all-white Central High School. President Dwight Eisenhower (1890–1969) was not particularly sympathetic to the aims of the civil rights movement, but the former five-star army general and commander of the Allied Forces in World

War II recognized the importance of enforcing federal orders. So, after delaying for weeks, he sent the 101st Airborne Division of the Army to the Little Rock high school to ensure that the federal mandate was followed. As a large crowd stood jeering outside the school on September 23, 1957, the day a federal court had designated for the school's integration, network cameras recorded a gang of white men hitting, kicking, and choking L. Alex Wilson, editor of the Black *Tri-State Defender*.[3]

The mainstream white press who had mostly come from the North also became targets of the white southern resistance to integration in Little Rock and beyond. This intimidation came from both everyday citizens and, more ominously, law enforcement officials. While photographing the attempt to integrate Little Rock Central, *Life* magazine photographer Francis Miller was attacked by a member of the crowd. When police arrived on the scene, instead of protecting him from the mob, they threw him in the back of a police van.

In 1961, when Freedom Riders organized by the Congress of Racial Equality (CORE) rode a bus caravan through Mississippi in buses full of mixed-race groups of college student-activists, they were threatened by the Ku Klux Klan. While they were on the highway, their thirty-vehicle escort by the Alabama State Police suddenly vanished. When the bus pulled into the depot, a crowd of two thousand angry white people was waiting for them with baseball bats, chains, and lead pipes. Unchecked by the police, the seething mob assaulted the Freedom Riders, including NBC News's Moe Levy, whose leg was permanently injured in the attack.

A year later, network cameramen were at the University of Mississippi, or "Ole Miss," as it was known, when that all-white campus erupted into two days of armed riots. The militant white students intended to keep James Meredith from becoming the first Black person to enroll there, even if it took violence. Faced with Mississippi governor Ross Barnett, who was as intent on stopping racial integration as was Arkansas's Orvil Faubus and Louisiana's Jimmy Davis, President John F. Kennedy called in thirteen thousand federal troops to quell the violence. In the running battle with the federal troops on the Ole Miss campus, the rioters targeted journalists. A thirty-year-old French journalist named Paul Guihard was murdered by a gunshot to the back. Karl Fleming of *Newsweek* was nearly killed by a sniper. Associated Press reporter Bill Crider was shot in the back with a pellet gun.[4]

The southern press reacted to the movement as if the protesters were the cause of the police violence, instead of its victims. At the same time that Joe McCarthy was terrorizing the nation at large, the threat of racially integrated schools was treated by southern government officials and newspaper editors as nothing less than a Soviet plot to end southern democracy.

Ralph McGill, "Conscience of the [White] South"

A clear exception to that Second Red Scare–like fear was the *Atlanta Journal-Constitution*'s editor, Ralph McGill. An opponent of demagoguery, especially among the racist White Citizens' Councils and the Ku Klux Klan, he also took on Senator Joseph McCarthy's national red-baiting attacks on innocent citizens. During the anxious period known as the Second Red Scare (1947–57), most Americans feared the senator from Wisconsin and his frequent, but unfounded, charges against anybody he chose to bully of sympathizing with Soviet communism. Writing against that harassment, McGill's nationally syndicated columns routinely censured McCarthy for his "un-American" extremism. McGill was so secure in his position at the *Constitution* that he once publicly compared McCarthy to Hitler.[5]

Not averse to facing bigots down, McGill earned the tag "Conscience of the South" for his daily editorials on the *Constitution*'s front page. There, nearly every day, he wrote to whites about the ills of their treatment of Blacks, describing the costs of those behaviors to whites themselves. Over time, McGill used his awareness in ways that earned him recognition from outsiders. He was awarded the Pulitzer Prize in 1959 and the Presidential Medal of Freedom in 1964. Still, to the white southern mainstream, his willingness even to mention racial violence marked him as a subversive, even a communist, to conservative bigots, including the Ku Klux Klan and its daylight version, the White Citizens' Council.

A product of the southern mainstream, McGill changed his beliefs about racial equality and equity gradually, using his role as an opinion journalist to reflect on the inequalities and inequities visited on Black southerners by whites.

His early difficulty speaking against white culture in any fashion is evident in this 1946 column titled "The Criticisms Coming to the South." The column shows McGill struggling to separate himself from a racially violent southern culture that was also his home.

In the column, McGill used a persuasive strategy to set up his rejection of outsider's criticisms. In this brief essay, he joined and then criticized white culture at a time when many whites were still offended by the echoes of Reconstruction. He used the pronouns, *we* and *us*, to align himself with his readers' resentment at being the object of outsiders' judgment. In conclusion, he identified himself as an opponent of lynching. He even asserted that the South deserved to be investigated, even if some of the attention was mistaken.

He wrote, "We with our lynchings and our politics are a national story. We will continue to be. . . . They are going to continue to examine us critically. I am all for that." He concluded by acknowledging that, "while the rest of the nation has its share of crime, ours is different and is too often un-American."[6] The degree of care McGill had to take to speak out against lynching shows his own early racism beginning to change as much as it shows the violent culture that the movement was working to stop.

Exposing the Violence behind "the Southern Way of Life"

Meanwhile, on the legal front, resisters of integration and civil rights sought to inflict financial pain on the institutions that employed journalists. When the *New York Times* published a paid advertisement titled "Heed Their Rising Voices," which described the difficulties protesters were facing, L. B. Sullivan, the Montgomery, Alabama, public safety commissioner seized on a few minor errors of fact in the advertisement. He sued the *Times* for defamation, and a sympathetic all-white jury awarded him $500,000.

Faced with a severe financial penalty and the looming threat of many similar lawsuits that might endanger the future of the paper, the *Times* appealed the judgment. Eventually, *New York Times v. Sullivan* reached the US Supreme Court. Their 1960 verdict was one of the most consequential in the history of First Amendment law. The court saw that capricious and opportunistic suits like *Sullivan* could endanger people's ability or willingness to inform the public. In his opinion, Justice William Brennan, Jr., defended the notion "that public discussion is a political duty, and that this should be a fundamental principle of the American government." This discussion, he added, should be "uninhibited, robust, and wide-open," and "may well include vehement, caustic, and sometimes unpleasantly sharp attacks on government and public officials."[7] Therefore, Brennan explained, it was not enough for public officials to show that the defamatory statements about them were false. They must also show that the defamation met a new standard: "actual malice." Actual malice referred to the decision to publish even when the information was known (or very likely) to be false. It is a high standard that protects journalistic organizations to this day.

In the spring of 1963, King and the SCLC launched "Project C" in Birmingham, Alabama. Birmingham was selected as the site of the movement's problems, because it was, in King's words, "probably the most thoroughly segregated city in the United States." A mining city in north central Alabama, Birmingham had been the site of dozens of racially motivated murders, many by the use of dynamite, which had earned the city the ominous nickname "Bombingham."

King and the other SCLC leaders had planned a campaign of civil disobedience to protest the segregation of downtown businesses. After a boycott of downtown businesses failed, a peaceful demonstration was planned. When the city refused to permit the march, the activists defied the order and fifty of them, including King, were jailed. Adjusting their strategy, they planned peaceful demonstrations, intending to get arrested and to overwhelm the city's jails. In that way—with the press present—they could expose the state violence on which segregation rested.

From his prison cell, King responded to his moderate critics who thought he was moving too quickly. In his "Letter from a Birmingham Jail," he countered that the movement was, instead, in danger of stalling. In a bold and controversial move, the organizers recruited school children, some as young as six, to demonstrate. Thousands heeded the call, filling the city's jails. Although the local *Birmingham News* ignored the tumult burying it in its back pages, journalists from around the nation and the world increasingly turned their gaze to the city. What they saw on May 3 shocked and horrified them. With no room in the jails and protesters continuing to flood the downtown district, Commissioner of Public Safety Bull Connor sought to clear the streets with brutal force. He ordered his deputies to use high-pressure fire hoses on the crowds and to unleash their attack dogs.

One iconic image of that day seemed to illustrate both the controversy of this violence and the tactics of the protesters. The image shows a young, smartly dressed young Black man standing stoically while a white police officer holds him still, allowing his German shepherd to tear into the boy's abdomen. The youth was Ullman High School student Walter Gadsden. While he appeared to be practicing principles of nonviolent resistance, he was, in fact, merely an observer. Indeed, he was one of many middle-class Black people who resented King and his tactics. That reaction was not uncommon among Black southerners. C. A. Scott, publisher of the Black newspapers the *Atlanta World* and *Birmingham World*, for example, was an outspoken critic of the Birmingham campaign. And so, his papers had a blanket rule against picturing King on their front pages.

While critics questioned the methods, the success of the movement was difficult to dispute. As the protests continued for days, city officials agreed to most of the protestors' demands. A month later, President John Kennedy addressed the nation, endorsing the movement's basic goals. He argued that resistance to civil rights had created embarrassment for the United States in it struggles in the Cold War. "We preach freedom around the world, and we mean it," Kennedy said. "But are we to say to the world, and, much more importantly, to each other, that this is the land of the free except for the Negroes?"[8]

Kennedy knew that news of institutional racism fed communist propaganda and hurt US influence in Africa and in many other spheres of ideological conflict. King knew it, too. Upon the news that their terms had been accepted, King told the assembled crowd, "The United States is concerned about its image. When things started happening down here, Mr. Kennedy got disturbed, for Mr. Kennedy is battling for the minds and the hearts of men in Asia and Africa—some one billion men in the neutralist sector of the world, and they aren't going to respect the United States of America if she deprives men and women of the basic rights of life because of the color of their skin."[9]

The behavior of the Birmingham police had not only shamed the United States internationally, it had disgusted southern liberals such as Ralph McGill, whose May 9, 1963, column, "A Matter of Costs," again stressed the constitutional questions at stake:

> Birmingham's barbarism of dogs and water hoses, following hard on the heels of that at Oxford [Mississippi], and the many instances of discrimination in other states, highlights an inescapable conclusion. It is the nation's single most internal problem at this place and time in history is how we deal with the minorities. To say that the security of the nation is in the final balance is no overstatement. . . . The constitutional requirement had been there all along. It no longer may—or should be—ignored. No 'rights' are being taken away. But the public rights of each U.S. citizen are being affirmed.[10]

Despite McGill's evolving views, the *Journal-Constitution* was not an ally of the movement. Instead, Cold War politics proved to be a double-edged sword. On July 25, 1963, the *Journal-Constitution* ran a story headlined "One-time Communist Organizer Heads Reverend King's Office in New York." The story, based on tips from sources within a hostile FBI, revealed that Jack O'Dell, director of the SCLC, had belonged to the Communist Party USA. Only a decade removed from the McCarthy-fueled purges, these charges fueled the claim, popular among southern white conservatives, that the civil rights movement was a communist plot to embarrass and undermine US interests. Activists in the movement, they argued, were either communists or manipulated by them.

The story was not news; many of the allegations had been published in the *Birmingham News* a month before. But, as historian Taylor Branch noted, "It was an unmistakable declaration of war on King in his hometown, by a newspaper, Ralph McGill's *Constitution*, that was regarded as a beacon of liberalism in the South." King quickly issued a statement calling the story "packed with half-truths and vicious innuendos," but the damage had been done. The allegations also disrupted planning for a new demonstration—this one in the nation's capital.[11]

Framing the March on Washington

The March on Washington for Jobs and Freedom took place on August 28, 1963, a Wednesday. A quarter-million people gathered in the summer heat on the national mall for what became a landmark moment in the nonviolent movement. The march had been planned to demonstrate public support for a proposed civil rights bill, which John Kennedy had described in a nationally televised address in response to the Birmingham campaign. Passing such a bill would be a heavy lift, because it would have to overcome resistance from southern Democrats. The march offered an opportunity to make the case for such a bill and to demonstrate the peacefulness of their cause.

But to many in the mainstream white press, the march loomed as an ominous and potentially violent date. The extraordinary coordination by the NAACP's executive secretary, Roy Wilkins, and King's SCLC signaled that something unusual was about to happen. After all, the two organizations were rivals. When the pair appeared on the NBC program, *Meet the Press*, two days before the march, they encountered concerns together that the massive rally would descend into violence. Moderator Lawrence Spivak began the questioning by expressing the view that "[It] would be impossible to bring to bring a hundred thousand militant negroes into Washington without incident and possibly rioting."[12] Wilkins responded that "I do not think there will be any rioting. I don't think a hundred thousand people just assembling is cause for apprehension about a riot. The city of Washington has accommodated much larger crowds, and nobody has talked up in advance the possibility of violence."[13]

Later, when Robert McNeil of NBC News pressed the issue, Wilkins responded again that he did not anticipate any violence. Rejecting claims that the movement had been uncivil at times and that there had even been a few scattered moments of violence, King pushed back: "I think we must see that we are in the midst of a great social revolution in this nation, and no social revolution can be neat and tidy at every point. I think the amazing thing is that it has been as neat and tidy as it has been, and that it has been as non-violent as it has been. This reveals that there is a great deal of discipline in this movement and a great deal of dignity."[14]

King and Wilkins were also asked to respond to the charge leveled in the *Atlanta Journal-Constitution* and elsewhere that their movement was riddled with communists. In this exchange, Frank Van der Linden of the *Nashville Banner* targeted one of the march's key organizers, Bayard Rustin, for his alleged ties to US-based communist groups. King objected to the line of questioning, arguing that Rustin had already distanced himself from communism.

It was obvious from these exchanges that members of the mainstream press were deeply skeptical of the movement's potential to manage threats of radicalism. King was invited to assuage these anxieties by endorsing moderation. He replied, "if moderation means slowing up at any point and capitulating to the undemocratic practices of many of the forces that are against democracy, then I think it would be tragic and certainly immoral to slow up at this point."[15]

It did not require an encounter with *Meet the Press* to impress on march organizers that the public was deeply suspicious of the event. A Gallup poll had found that only 23 percent of respondents had favorable expectations of the march.

On Monday, August 26, two days ahead of the planned march, the City of Washington began shutting down in anticipation of unrest. Thousands of military personnel were assembled to enforce order, liquor sales were suspended, and Washington's major league baseball team, the Senators, postponed its upcoming games.

As a gay, leftist Black man living at a time when all three of his identities were viewed as threatening, Bayard Rustin knew how readily public sympathy could turn to fear and disgust. In his tactical preparation, he was determined to let nothing detract from the powerful impression that the organizers hoped to make on a national and international television audience. He organized thousands of volunteer marshals to keep the crowds moving and orderly. He arranged for eighty thousand bag lunches to feed attendees. He kept speakers on a tight schedule.

He also knew that most marchers would need to be escorted back to their buses and out of town before nightfall. Not only would they not have anywhere to stay, but the threat of violence or mischief would increase after dark. Rustin knew that, despite Black people's being the overwhelming targets of attacks by white supremacists, most Americans still accepted traditional views that aligned Blackness, and especially Black attempts to gain freedom, with violence. He worked to avoid that prejudice.

At the march, Martin Luther King Jr. was the last speaker of the day. NBC News had been covering the event from the start. By now, all three networks had departed from their afternoon programming to carry King's address live. What viewers witnessed was perhaps the greatest and best-known moment of oratory in American history. King began from his prepared text, invoking the metaphor of Blacks' need to redeem the "bad check of liberty" promised but not delivered to Black Americans. Nearing the end, he paused, scanning the sweltering audience. Then he departed from his prepared remarks. Perhaps he had overheard the renowned singer Mahalia

Jackson, sitting just behind him, encouraging him to "tell them about the dream, Martin!" She was referring to a theme that King had visited in various versions over the past several months. Whatever the inspiration, King's speech galvanized the assembled crowd. Even President Kennedy was impressed. "He's damn good," he told his staff.[16]

Despite such a widespread audience, the impact of the speech was not immediately evident to everyone. The *Washington Post*, for example, did not even mention King's speech in its coverage of the event. All observers in the mainstream press remarked, sometimes with surprise, but always with approval, that the march had been peaceful. Nevertheless, the white public remained skeptical. A May 1964 Gallup poll found that 74 percent of respondents thought that mass demonstrations were more likely to hurt the cause of racial equality than to help it.

On November 22, just three months after the March on Washington, President Kennedy was assassinated in Dallas. Five days after the assassination, President Lyndon B. Johnson addressed a joint session of Congress, at which he argued that "No memorial oration or eulogy could more eloquently honor President Kennedy's memory than the earliest possible passage of the Civil Rights Bill for which he fought so long."[17] Johnson's bid to pass federal laws that could overcome states' racist legislation provoked the longest filibuster in the history of the Senate. By July 1964, the Civil Rights Act would stand against segregation and discrimination on the basis of race.

Johnson's Republican opponent in the presidential election of 1964, Arizona senator Barry Goldwater, opposed the bill. In September, South Carolina senator Strom Thurmond announced that he was leaving the Democratic party to join the Republicans. Many southern politicians and voters followed in the months and years that followed. In the presidential election of 1964, Johnson won in a landslide. But, notably, Thurmond's home state, along with Georgia, Alabama, Mississippi, and Louisiana, went for Goldwater—the first time former confederate states had ever gone for the party of Lincoln.

Although the Civil Rights Act included provisions designed to protect voting from racial discrimination, many in Congress and in the movement demanded stronger protections. Throughout the summer of 1964, activists had worked to register Black voters in the South as part of the Freedom Summer campaign. The murders of northern college student-activists, James Cheney, Andrew Goodman, and Mickey Schwerner by the Ku Klux Klan in Neshoba County, Mississippi, punctuated the dangers facing those who sought to facilitate the simple act of voting. Beginning in 1963 in Selma, Alabama, the SCLC had been promoting a voting-rights campaign that had drawn increasingly violent responses from the local police. In front of network cameras, Blacks who lined up at a county building to register to vote were arrested.

Judgment at Selma

In February 1965, as the movement leadership continued to agitate for voting rights, violence erupted in Selma when a teenager, Jimmie Lee Jackson, was killed there by a police officer. The youth had placed himself in front of his mother to protect her from the officer's shot. This tragedy changed the direction of the protests from local voting registration to a protest march from Selma to the state capitol in Montgomery. The SCLC joined with CORE and the Student Non-violent Coordinating Committee (SNCC) to stage a march from Selma, Alabama, to the state capitol in Montgomery through the most Klan-infested countryside in the state.

The march was planned for March 7, 1965. More than five hundred marchers gathered in Selma to cross the Edmund Pettus Bridge. Named to honor a Confederate general and Ku Klux Klan leader, the bridge marked the start of a dangerous fifty-mile march to Montgomery. Instead, they would be embroiled in what would come to be known as "Bloody Sunday."

Across the nation, millions of television viewers tuned in to watch ABC's Sunday night broadcast of *Judgment at Nuremberg*, a film that dramatized the legal reckoning with the Holocaust. The film was interrupted so that ABC News could show footage of helmeted and masked Alabama state troopers on horseback attacking peaceful adults with tear gas and truncheons. The melee had actually happened hours earlier, but the film had to be flown from Alabama to New York in order for it to be developed and shown—by then, in prime time.

Weeks earlier King had admonished *Life* magazine photographer Flip Schulke for assisting wounded protestors, instead of taking photographs of police brutality. King told Schulke, "The world doesn't know this happened because you didn't photograph it. I'm not being cold-blooded about it, but it is so much more important for you to take a picture of us getting beaten up than for you to be another person joining in the fray."[18]

But the media, Schulke included, had ensured that the world knew about Bloody Sunday. For ABC viewers who had been watching a searing account of Nazi war crimes, "the juxtaposition struck like psychological lightning in American homes."[19]

In Atlanta, Ralph McGill's sensibilities had been rocked by the depravity of what he saw. In "Take a Good Look," March 11, 1965, he admonished southern whites to see the moral crisis they were provoking. He wrote, "Now the whole world will see the pictures of the angry, sullen-faced Alabama 'peace' officers stopping nuns, ministers, and other peaceful men and women of all races walking calmly along a road—or demonstrating that this nation, 'under God,' must guarantee dignity and equal protection of the law." And further, "No southerner who loves his region and nation can rationalize this story."[20]

Eight days after Bloody Sunday, President Johnson, a south Texan, addressed a joint session of Congress. There he likened the thwarted march from Selma to Montgomery to the battles of Lexington and Concord in the American Revolution. He called for new legislation to protect voting. Then he delivered a surprising conclusion that stirred a television audience of millions that included King:

> What happened in Selma is part of a far larger movement which reaches into every section and State of America. It is the effort of American Negroes to secure for themselves the full blessings of American life.
>
> Their cause must be our cause too. Because it is not just Negroes, but really it is all of us, who must overcome the crippling legacy of bigotry and injustice.
>
> And we shall overcome![21]

Watching on television from Alabama and hearing the president of the United States invoke the motto of the civil rights movement was a profound moment for King, who was moved to tears. Organizers tried a second march but were persuaded to wait for federal protection. On March 21, after a federal court order protecting the protest and under the watchful eye of the National Guard, the marchers left Selma on their third try.

By then, they had been joined by tens of thousands who had mobilized in mass support of voting rights protections. Five months later, the Voting Rights Act of 1965 passed (again over the objections of many white southerners who were turning away from the Democratic party), offering strengthened protections for Black voters in the South.

In the last years of his short life, Martin Luther King Jr. grew more openly critical of the Johnson administration's war effort in Vietnam and of the disparities of wealth that he linked ever more explicitly to capitalism. He challenged *de facto* segregation in northern cities, where he encountered vitriol to rival anything he had seen in the South. King's critique, which tied racism with imperialism and capitalism, would become themes adopted by other civil rights activists.

King's critique of mainstream America's treatment of Black citizens did not make him popular among mainstream observers. Indeed, his relentless criticism of the long history of racism angered many who heard it, even among those who had supported his earlier calls for desegregation. In 1966, Gallup reported that 63 percent of Americans had a negative opinion of him. In 1967, he did not appear among Gallup's poll of the nation's ten most admired men, but George Wallace, the former segregationist governor of Alabama, ranked eighth.[22] King was assassinated by a white supremacist in Memphis, Tennessee, on April 4, 1968, an event that fueled violent anger and grief in many of the nation's Black neighborhoods.

Contentious though it was (and would continue to be for several decades), King's legacy had left an indelible mark on many people. Writing within hours of King's death, Ralph McGill aimed his pen directly at his mainstream white readers. Free of the racial gradualism of his earlier career, he unleashed a moral indictment of white racism and called for peace in his hometown. He wrote,

> White slaves killed Dr. Martin Luther King [Jr.] in Memphis. At the moment the trigger man fired, Martin Luther King was the free man. The White killer (or killers) was a slave to fear, a slave to his own sense of inferiority, a slave to hatred, a slave to the bloody instincts that surge in the brain when a human being decides to become a beast.
>
> In the wake of this disaster in Memphis, a great many such slaves must consider if they wish to continue serving their masters of fear, hate, inferiority, and beastliness. It is something of an irony that Dr. King was free and was hated by so many slaves. It is perhaps too much to hope, but much of the reaction to this bloody murder could be blunted if in every city and town there would be a resolve to remove what remains of injustice and racial prejudice from schools, from training and job opportunities, from housing and community life in general.
>
> Dr. King would not want his death to arouse an emotion that brought on what he had all his life had opposed—violence and death. Atlanta's mayor, Irv Allen, who drove his car through a rain-swept city to the home of Dr. King and took the stunned wife to the airport where she learned that death had come in Memphis, was another symbol of the South. He, too, was a free man. He was not a slave to hate and fear. His city is not a slave city bound by such terrible chains as held the killers in Memphis.
>
> The Memphis killer and his associates have done their own race a grave and hideous injustice. They have made it possible for blind violence to be loosed. They have elevated the beast in man. They may have imperiled the negotiations that, hopefully, may be arranged to end the war in Vietnam. The slave beast does not reason. The beast, unless chained, is only a beast.
>
> The white South—the white population in the whole country—must now give answer. From injustice and inequity, if racist prejudices and discriminations now become the targets of all decent men and women, Dr. King's death may bring about what he sought for himself, his people, and country.

If this does not happen, then slaves who serve masters of hatred, fear, and evil will have to be put down mercilessly and immediately.

Out of martyrdom must come the right answer.[23]

A Strategy of Media Coverage

The civil rights movement is remembered almost universally as a just cause, and one that widened the scope of American freedom. But, then as now, race sparks American dissension like no other issue. In the unfolding civil rights movement, journalism played a fundamental role by making it possible for individual citizens to connect with each other as they saw, read about, and found themselves within the events of the day. Where the new medium of television shocked viewers with the immediacy of the police riots against nonviolent protesters in southern cities, newspapers brought them the details, background, and complexity needed to understand what happened and what the implications were.

Taken as a contested site and process, televised news images, both live and recorded, gave people, especially white people, a sense of the brutal system of segregation in the American South. Coordinating planned actions with the desired media exposure brought two key kinds of resources: volunteers and money. The news coverage of these crisis events reflected the intentions of movement organizers. Often learning on the fly, movement media strategists understood the value of publicizing the violence, dehumanization, and death that undergirded the system of southern white supremacy.

A key asset of this media strategy came from the presence of northern news reporters in the Deep South. When reporters from the North reflected the violence visited on the movement back to their readers and viewers, the movement gained support from outside the region. As the movement developed, major national news agencies committed increasing resources to the crisis. *Newsweek* even devoted a section of its weekly magazine to covering the "race beat." In all, the ability to access favorable news coverage by bypassing the opposition of most southern newspapers and television stations played a pivotal role in the movement's success.

The Black Panthers and the Young Lords

Anti-imperialist and Anti-capitalist Journalism

As the social protest movements of the 1960s developed, a range of activists seeking a different vision of liberation began to form. These new protest movement organizations bypassed the strategy of gaining acceptance by the mainstream. Instead, they intended to fundamentally change or even to destroy it, a radical politics that represented a different kind of challenge to the mainstream, which viewed them as an existential threat. These movement organizations used journalism to frame and network their beliefs and actions. In some ways, this development echoed the abolition and suffrage movements, both of which had included elements that became increasingly radical.

To show this direct challenge to US authorities, this chapter focuses on the uses of journalism by two nationally organized organizations founded in 1968 at the height of what became a broader civil crisis. In part 1, we present the Black Panther Party, founded in Oakland, California. In part 2, we present the Young Lords, founded in Chicago. Both cases highlight the fundamental role journalism played in promoting the movements and in attempting to reframe their vision freeing themselves of a four-hundred-year legacy of slavery and its effects.

Part One: The Black Panthers

On August 11, 1965, Marquette Fry (1944–86) was driving to his home in Watts, a poor, mostly Black section of Los Angeles, when he was stopped by police. Frye had been drinking and failed a sobriety test. As the police tried to arrest him, he resisted, and one officer struck him in the face with a baton. By this time, an angry crowd that included Fry's mother and brother had gathered. The pair were also taken into custody. Fry's car was towed and impounded.

As word spread of the incident, many residents of Watts considered the news a breaking point. In the chaos, rumor spread that the police had kicked a pregnant Black woman in the stomach. A long history of police violence in the neighborhood made that believable. In the hours and days that followed the incident, Watts exploded in violence. Over the next six days, thirty-four people would lose their lives. Property damage would total $40 million. And some fourteen thousand members of the California National Guard were deployed to quell the unrest.

Network television coverage brought the scene to the nation through a new innovation, a CBS news helicopter equipped with a live-feed camera that flew over the burning neighborhoods. Until the mid-1960s, television news footage had been typically recorded, transported, and aired hours later. The live footage lent itself to what historian Rick Perlstein has called newscasting done "like a demonic sports play-by-play." The CBS reporter in the helicopter relayed the chaotic scene on the ground:

> There is little that they can do. These buildings will be a total loss before they can get the first drop of water on the building and another fire just erupted about a block away! And the spectators do not seem to be concerned with what's going on. Here are two kids running away from the fire right now! If the command center can see our picture, I would check the parking lot next to the National Dollar Store for three individuals. And now there's another building on fire on the north side of the street. There's another group of spectators. All they're doing is standing around and looking. They couldn't be less concerned. And now we have orders to climb higher into the air as pot shots are being taken from the ground. Rifle fire and small arms fire, so we're pulling up and out.[1]

Like this news reporter, many white Americans watched the uprising with a sense of confusion. Why were these Black people destroying their own neighborhood? What were they so angry about, anyway? After all, the Voting Rights Act had been signed into law less than a week earlier. Mystified by the apparent self-destruction of Watts, white commentators and observers failed to understand the riots as a rebellion against longtime institutional oppression.

In many ways, the story of the Watts riots capped a much deeper history that had seen Black Americans bring their dreams of equality out into America with them. Their mass emigration from the rural South between 1915 and 1970 became known as the Great Migration. At its peak after

World War II, generations of Black families fled the overt white supremacy of the southern United States to start new lives in towns and cities across the nation.[2]

Many placed their hopes on southern California, where the number of Black people living in Los Angeles had grown dramatically. Gathered in Watts and other unofficially segregated neighborhoods, what these new arrivals found there in 1968 was hardly equal treatment with whites. Black-owned industries and businesses had been underdeveloped. Black neighborhoods had been neglected by city officials, except for the all-too-attentive police. What many of these migrants found in California was not an absence of racism, but racism in a different, subtler form. California was not the South, but even there the newcomers found a backlash against them that was made worse by the civil rights movement. As the movement grew in 1968, for example, California voters overwhelmingly voted to repeal the 1963 Rumford Fair Housing Act, which was intended to protect Black buyers from housing discrimination.

Huey Newton (1942–89) and Bobby Seale (b. 1936) knew this experience intimately. Prior to meeting in California, each had left the South while young to migrate to the Bay Area with their families. There they had found a different life, but one with familiar echoes of oppression. If the racial order in the South was overt, the unspoken rules for Blacks in the cities of the North and West was nevertheless pronounced. Instead of easing discrimination, arcane federal housing policies often ensured racial segregation of neighborhoods. Most of the businesses and dwellings in Black neighborhoods were not locally owned. Police routinely harassed residents of Black communities, and acts of brutality were commonplace.

Newton and Seale met in 1961 through the Afro-American Association at Merritt College, a recently opened community college in Oakland. There they encountered a vibrant international community of thinkers and activists. Students there began thinking of themselves not as oppressed minorities, but as representatives of a dark-skinned global majority. Malcolm X's (1925–65) Islamist-based values, his insistence on self-defense, and his radical black internationalism contributed important influences to this new global perspective, as were Marxist critiques of colonialism. The critical theories of power that they studied and developed in their resistance helped them to recognize the systemic and structural barriers they faced as they sought their own self-determination. Guided by these insights, they developed a more local organization based on direct action.[3]

Seale and Newton soon came to see their local circumstances in the context of global struggle. They also began to view the police presence in Black neighborhoods as an occupying force, a colonial army enforcing its unjustified and abusive dominance. Armed both with a meticulous knowledge of the law and firearms, which were legal to carry under California law as long as they were not concealed, Seale and Newton began to monitor police interactions in their neighborhoods, while openly carrying weapons. These police patrols were meant to warn the local police against committing acts of brutality and to signal to the community the importance of local self-determination.

The concerns that Seale and Newton had about police harassment and poverty in the Watts neighborhood led them to form the Black Panther Party. Their dramatic uniforms with black berets, dark glasses, black leather jackets and boots, shotguns, and bandoliers of live shells crossing their chests made an impression on the streets and, soon, in the halls of power as well. Aesthetics were only part of their local appeal, however. Their primary program sponsored a community service organization that was prepared to do what the establishment seemed uninterested in doing: protecting and advancing the lives of local citizens of color.

An American Manifesto: The Panthers' Ten-Point Program

In October 1966, the Black Panther Party published its Ten-Point Program. Effectively the organization's constitution, their document drew on long-standing demands from Black nationalist and anti-imperialist groups. Like the abolitionists and suffragists before them, the manifesto created by the Panthers laid claim to the freedoms called for in the Declaration of Independence. Although it would be hard to imagine two groups of people less alike, the most direct comparison to the Panthers' Ten-Point Program might be the suffragist "Declaration of Rights and Sentiments." Like the call to revolution issued by Elizabeth Cady Stanton and Lucretia Mott at Seneca Falls 120 years before, the Panthers' manifesto claimed the truths of American history. In that spirit, it expressed the sometimes chaotic, but surely foundational, creed of individualism and antigovernment sense of freedom that actively drives our political life today. The manifesto called for freedom, employment, and introduced the concept of reparations, compensation they believed due to the descendants of enslaved people from the US government. They highlighted the urgent need for affordable housing for Black and brown Americans. Housing policies that made federally backed loans widely available in white neighborhoods were largely inaccessible to Black families. The unspoken policy of denying loans to non-white would-be borrowers is still a common practice by American lending institutions. It is known as "red-lining" for the way that lending institutions draw boundaries in red around neighborhoods where they refuse to make home and business loans. They called for the end of police brutality, claiming that "The Second Amendment to the Constitution of the United States gives a right to bear arms. We therefore believe that all Black people should arm themselves for self-defense." Relatedly, they critiqued the justice system, asserting that Black people in prison had not received fair trials, nor had been truly judged by a jury of their peers, as required by the Fourteenth Amendment because "A peer is a person from a similar economic, social, religious, geographical, environmental, historical, and racial background. To do this the court will be forced to select a jury from the Black community from which the Black defendant came." Their final demand asserted "We Want Land, Bread, Housing, Education, Clothing, Justice, and Peace."[4] Having spelled out unconditional demands based on historical wrongs, the Panthers laid claim to their American heritage. And so, invoking the Declaration of Independence to show their self-determination, they wrote, "When, in the course of human events, it becomes necessary for one people to dissolve the political bands which have connected them with another, and to assume, among the powers of the earth, the separate and equal station to which the laws of nature and nature's God entitle them, a decent respect of the opinions of mankind requires that they should declare the causes which impel them to the separation."[5]

The Panthers argued that the language of the Declaration of Independence should have made them equals among all other Americans. Failing that prospect, they took charge. Like Samuel Adams's fight with the Crown, they sought to break with the institutions of white America. This position defined them as "Black nationalists" because they "looked at Black America as separate and distinct from white America."[6]

In the language of the declaration's assertion of the right to life, liberty, and the pursuit of happiness, the Panthers regarded the right to secede from the nation as inherent. Having declared their revolutionary independence, the Panthers turned to a strategy of creating spectacles that the press would cover. Instead of writing the news, they would manage it.

Mediated Direct Action

The Panthers wanted to connect with the most alienated and oppressed citizens of Oakland. To reach them, they organized local programs that addressed basic needs in their communities, including a daycare center and a food pantry. Their efforts also built goodwill within the broader Black community. By implication, the Panthers' outreach program highlighted the degree to which these places had been neglected by the white power structure.

At the national level, the Panthers lacked the resources to publicize their community-building goals. And so they orchestrated spectacles, events designed to appropriate national news media attention that would spread awareness about their existence and goals. Although their actions were in most cases legal, the Panthers anticipated, even provoked, their condemnation by the mainstream press as outlaws. With a clear understanding of how the nightly news often focused on the dramatic and the unusual, they also knew that thousands of people would find common cause with the Panthers and their struggle through the mainstream news.

One example of how the Panthers orchestrated publicity unfolded on May 2, 1967. Republican Don Mulford of the California legislature, who objected to the Panthers' police patrols, had introduced a bill that would to repeal the state's open-carry law. In a response that shocked officials and observers, two dozen Panthers entered the California state capitol in Sacramento fully armed and dressed in their revolutionary garb of sunglasses, black leathers, and berets. They announced their intention to read a statement to the legislature.

Barred from the House floor, they returned to where the press had gathered to read their prepared statement. Seale declared, "The American people, in general, and the Black people, in particular, must take careful note of the racist California legislature aimed at keeping the Black people disarmed and powerless. Black people have begged, prayed, petitioned, demonstrated, and everything else to get the racist power structure of America to right the wrongs which have historically been perpetuated against Black people. The time has come for Black people to arm themselves against this terror before it is too late."[7]

As they had expected, their actions got the press's attention. The *New York Times* published an article on the protest under the headline "The Spirit of Lawlessness." Ignoring the fact that the Panthers' actions—which were clearly intended to provoke—had been perfectly legal at the time, the newspaper compared the group to the Ku Klux Klan.[8] As historian Jane Rhodes has argued, "The Panthers had deliberately fashioned themselves as a paradox—on one hand claiming a constitutional right to bear arms, while on the other hand abandoning the tactics of nonviolence and reconciliation."[9]

Their dramatic actions led California governor Ronald Reagan to quickly sign Representative Mulford's bill outlawing the right to carry a weapon openly in the state. At the time, Reagan commented that "there's no reason why on the street today a citizen should be carrying loaded weapons."[10] To the Panthers, his response came as a predictable response from a government they saw as bent on subjugating Black communities.

The Panther Community News Service

In 1967, Huey Newton and Bobby Seale founded a weekly newsletter, the *Black Panther Community News Service*. Renamed *The Black Panther Intercommunal News Service* in 1971, it published the *Black Panther* weekly newspaper until 1980, which was central to the Panthers' global consciousness-raising strategy. First, operating their own media brought framing their revolutionary worldview more under their control. Second, that sweeping vision linked the local community to global allies, and the revolutionary struggles of the present to those of the past. Perhaps too ambitiously, the Panthers reported circulation numbers between one and three hundred thousand copies weekly.[11]

One of their first published issues included a reprinting of "The Tactic of Persuasion," an argument for abolitionist strategy that had been published in the pages of William Lloyd Garrison's *The Liberator* well over a century before. The inclusion of a nineteenth-century text was a departure from the Panther's usual editorial voice. In its normal practice, the *Black Panther* was characterized by a distinctive use of Black English.

As Donna Murch notes, "The Black Panther Party's symbolic invocation of the 'pig,' vernacular forms rooted in black southern idiom became essential to building popular support."[12] The term, *pig*, which referred to the police, was intended to offend "defenders of the ruling class." At the same time, it was used to express their revolutionary ideology in everyday terms, especially for an urban Black public, many of whom had recently left southern farming for life on the West Coast. In that way, the Panthers used Black dialect that could be widely shared and easily recognized to build their movement's community. Of equal importance, their insiders' language defined the gulf between the Panthers and their daily adversaries, the police.

As Bobby Seale explained, the direct language with which the Panthers communicated their goals came from a calculated strategy to reach Black people on their own terms and offer them clear alternatives:

> We don't want to go real elaborate with all these essays and dissertations and all this stuff 'cause the brother going to look at that, he going to say, man, I ain't got time for that. I got to go see what I can do for myself. Just a basic platform that the mothers who struggle hard to raise us, that the fathers who worked hard, that the young brothers in school who come out of school semi-literate—say, all—we just want a basic platform to outline Black people's basic political desires and needs.[13]

The Panthers' media strategy sought to convey the understanding that racism in the United States was part of a historical, global, and colonial struggle. Rather than seeing distinctions between the police in local areas, the National Guard at the state and national level, and the US Marines in the international arena of conflict, the Panthers sought to connect them, encouraging their audience to see the struggle against local police as tied to their opposition to armed invasions of foreign countries populated by people of color.

By framing their struggle in global terms, the Young Lords linked policing within segregated Black communities to the state's use the National Guard to control antiwar protests on American college campuses, to quell urban rebellions, and to fight unjust American wars abroad. The military draft remained a crisis for Black Americans. The percentage of Blacks in the US population sent to fight in Vietnam (16.3 percent) exceeded their percentage of the American population (11.1 percent).

For the Panthers, each aspect of this problem reflected part of a larger whole. Their conception of what American democracy was failing to give them led them to believe that white supremacist governments at every level in America were actively working to subjugate and oppress communities of color at home and abroad.

In order to change local conditions in their communities, the Panthers needed a global imagination. This strategy called for forming cross-racial coalitions with similarly oppressed groups, both in the United States and internationally. Fred Hampton (1948–69), a Black Panther leader stationed in Chicago, sought to create a Rainbow Coalition of antiracist working-class movements. Hampton connected the Panthers' project with the work of other groups, such as the American Indian Movement and the white, southern-identified Young Patriots Organization. His organizing efforts also included the radical Puerto Rican revolutionary nationalists, the Young Lords.

Part Two: The Young Lords

In 1968, the founder of the Young Lords, José ("Cha Cha") Jiménez, transformed a neighborhood gang on the North Side of Chicago, the Young Lords Organization, into a revolutionary organization that advocated for community needs. From his local position, the Panthers' Fred Hampton quickly recognized that these young radicals shared the Panthers' radical global worldview. Like so many others, Jiménez had what he referred to as a "conversion experience" after encountering radical political thinkers in prison.[14] Part of his inspiration was the Black Panther Party, who, in turn, looked to Malcolm X.

As Jiménez explained in an interview with the *Black Panther*, "We're still looking for that way in which we can help our people. Now we're starting to realize who our people really are, who our friends are and who our enemies are. And as we read and studied other organizations that are appearing now in the United States, we see and we recognize the Black Panther Party as a vanguard party, a vanguard revolutionary party. And we feel that as revolutionaries we should follow the vanguard party, this is why we follow them."[15]

Later in the interview, Jiménez elaborated on the position shared by the Young Lords and the Black Panthers. He explained that the structural, race-based inequalities in the United States could be overcome only if people of different races recognized their common interests and their common enemies:

> I can't relate to black people hating white people and Puerto Ricans getting hated by anybody, you know, and people can't relate to that, you know, we look to see which is our enemy, which is our commonest enemy and we just see that the pigs are the body guards of the capitalist pigs that are oppressing and exploiting our people. We look to see that this octopus, the United States, has been sucking all the resources from Puerto Rico and we see who our enemy is. We see that the United States is our enemy. And we look out for allies, you know, we look at Cuba, we look at Mao, we look at all these other countries that have liberated themselves from the monsters.[16]

Like the Black Panthers, the Young Lords Organization presented itself as a revolutionary outfit, but their most connected work focused on improving the lives of people in their neighborhood. Dedicated to their communities, they sought immediate, local ways to effect such changes. In the long view, they also worked to publicize their activities and worldview with the aim of creating coalitions with like-minded groups and individuals to their cause. Movement journalism would give them the forum for that networking and outreach. The first issue of the Young Lords Organization's newspaper, *The Latin Liberation News Service*, which was modeled on *The Black Panther Intercommunal News Service*, included an editorial that sought to answer the question, "Why a YLO Newspaper?" They began by announcing that, like the Panthers, the YLO sought to bring about a socialist society and demanded an end to police brutality, community control of community institutions and "an end to the colonization of Puerto Rico and all other Third World countries."[17] The editors explained that one goal of the movement was to convince other activists that radical, rather than reformist, aims were necessary for transforming society in meaningful ways. They envisioned the newspaper as occupying a central role in the movement, asserting that it could provide:

the focus of a permanent organization . . . a bridge between the peaks of activity. It creates an organization and organizes the division of labor among activists. It creates the kind of division of labor needed not just for the newspaper, but also the guidelines for action and study of an organization interested in radical change. And it develops a necessary network throughout the city. [18]

The paper published many stories in both Spanish and English and covered the movement's activities, as well as efforts to which it lent its support. It backed the expansion of a local hospital, for example, laying out the case for the expansion. It also served to strengthen the connections with the Black Panthers. This was made clear when the YLO newspaper published the Panthers' Ten-Point Program in full.[19]

The newspaper also reprinted "Puerto Rico: 'Island Paradise' of U.S. Imperialism," a long essay by Patricia Bell that documented the fraught colonial relationship between the US government and the island. In it, Bell asserted,

> The fact is that the monopolists of this country derive enormous benefits from the bondage of Puerto Rico, and this in three principal ways:
> Puerto Rico as a market for the US.
> Puerto Rico as a source of super-profits for US investors.
> Puerto Rico as a strategic military, naval and air base.[20]

By linking these economic and military objectives, the YLO offered an understanding of the relationship between the US federal government and its "protectorate," Puerto Rico as colonial. Though their points of emphasis were different, they shared this basic outlook with the Black Panthers.

New York City, 1969–1976: Reproach and Reform

As the Young Lords Organization began to spread its message, they attracted the attention of a group of young intellectuals in New York City. In the summer of 1969, some of them drove to Chicago to meet with Jiménez and to secure his blessing. They wanted to begin organizing a Young Lords chapter in New York. Soon after, they began promoting direct actions in their local community of East Harlem, which they referred to as "El Barrio." They began by reaching out to their neighbors and asking what they needed. "This place is filthy, man. It stinks. There's garbage all over," was a refrain one former member remembered hearing over and over.[21] Sanitation service was sporadic in the neighborhood. Garbage was often piled high on the street corners, providing a constant health hazard.

After the Young Lords were rebuffed in their appeals to the Department of Sanitation, they began bagging the garbage themselves. But, after the bags sat uncollected, the Young Lords took a more confrontational approach, relocating the garbage to the street, blocking traffic, disrupting the flow of goods and services, sometimes setting the garbage on fire. Frustrated with the city's refusal to extend garbage collection to the brown and Black citizens of el Barrio, they became more militant, demanding, instead of requesting, attention from city authorities.

The Garbage Offensive, as the protest came to be named, was not simply an attempt at reform. It aimed instead to "trash the system" by exposing what they saw as the structural shortcomings of the current system's ability to meet basic needs of their community. In place of the current system, the Young Lords advocated for socialism. The offensive was a crucial first step in this mission. As the scholar Darrel Wanzer-Serrano notes, "Just by being there—on the streets—the Young Lords performed resistance by reclaiming and redrawing their own public space by performing a sense of ownership and even separatism. . . . Exploding such a 'mind bomb' was a critical step in jarring fundamentally the consciousness of Barrio people to get them to imagine a world beyond inaction."[22]

Within this escalating dynamic, publishing their own newspaper offered the group another way for the Young Lords Party in New York to act for change in on-the-ground conditions and within the community's consciousness. To do so, they used the printing press of the RAT, an underground newspaper published by a feminist collective with whom the Young Lords had cooperated. In May 1970, the YLO newspaper *Palante* debuted, with artwork and layout by Denise Oliver in her role as communications secretary. Pablo "Yoruba" Guzman edited the content, and Juan González served as production editor. Their bimonthly paper would become a major source of fundraising for the organization, with circulation routinely reaching the tens of thousands.

A month later, the Young Lords of New York split with the YLO in Chicago and declared themselves the Young Lords Party. Relations between the Young Lords Organization in Chicago and the New York chapter had become strained over differences of vision and ambition. The New York–based Young Lords Party claimed the mantle of the national party and announced their new name on the cover of their newspaper, *Palante*.

Inside, the editors explained that "consistent leadership is necessary to set a revolutionary example for the members and the people. The members were not disciplined and many did not report regularly, so that important political work could not be done in this community all the time. This is one of the main reasons that National Monthly newspaper (YLO) came out only six times in 18 months."[23]

Taking that lesson to heart, *Palante* dedicated itself to a more regular and robust presence. Closely modeled on the Black Panthers' journalistic strategy, *Palante* published a Thirteen-Point Program in every issue, echoing the Panthers' Ten-Point Program. Demonstrating an understanding of their own local fight with larger, global struggles, the newspaper linked the issues of "Self-Determination for Puerto Ricans" and "Community Control" to another demand, the "Liberation of All Third World People." The Young Lords also emulated the Panthers by critiquing gender relations. "We Want Equality for Women," read one demand. "Machismo Must Be Revolutionary . . . Not Oppressive."[24]

Palante highlighted the work in the community in which the Young Lords were engaging and explained their goals. Writing of the garbage offensive, for example, *Palante* explained: "They've treated us like dogs for too long. When our people came here in the 1940's, they told us New York was a land of milk and honey. And what happened? Our men can't find work . . . they won't even give us brooms to sweep up the rubbish in our streets."[25]

The Young Lords' interventions were intended to ameliorate the conditions of el Barrio, but also to highlight how the powers that be failed their communities. For example, the Young Lords Party in New York conducted tests for lead poisoning in el Barrio and discovered several positive cases. They also tested for tuberculosis, capturing a city-owned mobile testing site to take to their neighborhood. They documented these actions in the pages of *Palante*, framing them as an attempt to transform life in el Barrio through a socialist health-care plan in action. They explained their program as a corrective to the injustices they saw in their communities, noting that "Even though t.b. has been eliminated among the rich, the middle classes, and white people in general, it is alive and spreading in the Puerto Rican and Black colonies of amerikkka, the 'richest' country in the world." To address this imbalance, they reported that "During the last 3 months, in El Barrio, and the last month in the South Bronx, we have given over 800 tests for tuberculosis. One out of every three people tested has had a positive reaction. Why aren't the hospitals doing anything to prevent t.b. in our communities? Because the hospitals do not serve the needs of our people. They exist only to make a profit." After detailing their work, the authors critiqued systemic issues that limit access to health care for poor people of color. They noted that access to proper care relies on income and race. "The racism of the health empire must be exposed," they wrote, noting that, while drugs had plagued their communities for years: "it wasn't until a few white kids in the suburbs started getting strung out, that the health empire 'discovered' drugs, and a big stink was made in the press. This is like Columbus 'discovering' Puerto Rico. The 70,000 Taino Indians had always been there, but just like the drug problem, until the man feels it directly, in his pocket or in his home, it doesn't exist and he doesn't give a damn."

The article closed with a defiant declaration of their commitment to community action. "The YLP will fight until hospitals, police, schools, etc. are run by the people, especially those who work in and are affected by these institutions. FREE HEALTH CARE FOR ALL! LIBERATE PUERTO RICO NOW!"

On July 14, 1970, the Young Lords took over the dilapidated Lincoln Hospital, which served communities of color in the South Bronx. The Butcher Shop, as the hospital was known to many locals, had alienated the local community by ignoring their complaints and requests.[26] The Young Lords walked into the lightly guarded hospital and escorted the leadership and security out. For twelve hours, they occupied the hospital and pressed their demands for a new hospital building, local control of health care, and universal access. Most significant, they composed the first-ever Patient's Bill of Rights, a template that has since become standard practice in hospitals in the United States.

The police eventually raided the hospital and arrested fifteen activists, but the movement was not over. In November, when the hospital hesitated to implement a heroin treatment program, the Young Lords again occupied the hospital and, after negotiations, won the right to run a local methadone clinic with volunteer staff.[27]

Repression and Redirection

For all their talk of revolution, the Black Panthers and the Young Lords remained relatively small organizations at the national level. Their programs actually posed no threat to the government, aiming instead to improve living conditions for their local communities. At their peak, the Young Lords claimed a membership of one thousand; the Panthers had closer to five thousand members. Most of these activists were teenagers and young adults. Nevertheless, the US government treated both groups as existential threats to the nation's internal security.

The FBI attempted to gain the cooperation of *New York Times* African American reporter Earl Caldwell, who had been reporting on the Black Panthers closely for several months, as well as other journalists who had covered the group. When Caldwell and the other journalists refused, the

FBI sought to force their cooperation with a lawsuit. A federal court sided with the government, finding that journalists did not have a constitutional right to refuse cooperation with the government, but the decision was reversed by the US Supreme Court on appeal in *United States v. Caldwell* in June 1972.[28]

Through various methods, the FBI infiltrated the Black Panthers and Young Lords, disrupting operations and sowing dissent among the leadership. Members were repeatedly surveilled, charged with crimes, and imprisoned. As declassified files would later show, federal and local law enforcement routinely broke laws and violated the rights of activists by attempting to subvert their efforts at change. Fred Hampton, the Chicago Black Panther who formed a partnership with the Young Lords Organization as part of the Rainbow Coalition, was killed in his bed by police during a 4 a.m. raid on December 4, 1969.

Eventually, both the Black Panthers and Young Lords collapsed under the relentless campaign of government repression. Some of their members entered more mainstream channels of influence. Some moved into politics. Bobby Seale ran for mayor of Oakland in 1973, losing in a runoff election. Bobby Rush, cofounder of the Illinois chapter of the Black Panthers, was elected to the US House of Representatives in 1993 and still represents his district today. Others found careers in journalism and other media. Denise Oliver-Vélez of the Young Lords co-founded the community radio station WPFW, and Juan González became a newspaper and television journalist and wrote a column for the *New York Daily News* for nearly thirty years.

Though they were active only for a short time and never exceeded a few thousand members, the Black Panthers and Young Lords had an outsized cultural influence. Their berets and revolutionary maxims have entered popular consciousness, often as parody. Less well understood has been their actual work—their community programs and their coalition building across racial lines. When mainstream journalism, which was generally hostile to the aims of these revolutionary groups, shaped public (mis)perceptions of them, the Panthers and Young Lords argued for their own positions. Their efforts to find a place in the American public are apparent in the journalism they produced. By publishing their own newspapers, they helped consolidate their movement and clarify their aims.

Recently, a new wave of interest in these groups has arisen, and public perceptions about them are showing signs of change. A spate of new books, documentaries, and even Hollywood films are providing a reappraisal of these groups and their work. In that sense, at least, their common goal of transforming how people understand their relation to power and to one another remains unfinished.

12

The American Indian Movement and Indigenous Peoples' Media Strategies

The practice of journalism is entwined in every aspect of the long struggle by Native Americans against the theft of their lands by whites. Beginning with the colonial requirement that Indians be literate in English in order to be "civilized," the Indians' embrace of the white cultural conventions of journalism only furthered their losses of their land, their identity, and their self-determination. Indians have engaged in an array of strategic writing genres in English in their attempts to engage, appease, and cope with the awful costs of assimilation. Through strategic speeches, manifestos, and newspaper and magazine journalism, they have tried to stop the erosion of their culture. Tracing the historical uses of journalism by American Indians offers a way to understand their long fight against colonization.

Establishing that history in the first half of this chapter sets the stage for describing the twentieth-century protest movement, the American Indian Movement (AIM), which formed in 1968 in Minneapolis. The US government's legacy of drafting, signing, and ratifying treaties—some 371 between 1776 and 1871—was matched only by their willingness to break each one. Instead of working from a self-determined place among whites, which was the Indians' lasting goal, they experienced a sustained program of genocide by the US government. From an estimated population in 1492 of 10 million, the indigenous population had, by 1922, dropped to 222,000. In the years between, Indians had faced forced removal from their native lands to reservations and attempts to erase their native cultures.[1] The Indians' nineteenth-century turn toward journalism showed their hopeful—if, ultimately, unsuccessful—reliance on the press as a buffer, a resource, and a gateway to a place like American citizenship.

This chapter describes the long train of historical events that culminated with AIM in the late 1960s and early 1970s. Their media strategies used conventional and creative means to frame their historical grievances against the national mainstream. The chapters explains the central role of Indian journalism in that long fight, demonstrating a diversity of tactics and viewpoints across and within the multiple nations and tribes.

The scale and scope of the American Indians' losses is incalculable. In the documentary "A Good Day to Die," AIM cofounder Russell Banks reflects on those costs, asking, "What is the sacrifice that we native Americans have made? We can't tell it by the amount of land that they have taken from us. We can't tell it by the massacres that they've committed. But the totality of all of it—that's where the pain is."[2]

It is important to consider that there was, in some terrible sense, a moral logic used by those responsible to justify their actions at the time. In seventeenth-century Pennsylvania and Ohio, to take one example, the British colonials considered migratory patterns of tribes like the Shawnees in the Ohio River Valley to be evidence that the Indians were morally treacherous, "because they did not own land and live in one place." Based on this disqualification, by the mid-eighteenth century the British had "laid claim to superiority over the Shawnees." Further, they turned to their belief in "science and technology to support their essential superiority." Over time, the whites' program to extinguish native cultures through the process of "termination" seemed not only necessary, but natural.[3]

Even more, the language differences between colonizer and colonized privileged whites as English dominated all treaties and related negotiations. In his study of the Shawnee, historian Stephen Warren described the English-driven colonization of native lands as a "literary assault." Begun even before Jamestown in 1607, Warren reports, the British soon realized that the potential to "lawfully divest American Indians of their lands" lay in their monopoly on English literacy. The British belief that they were on a "civilizing mission" justified writing treaties written by "the British and their Iroquois allies (who) used the power of the written word to define what the "'chaos of colonization' meant."[4] The weaponization of English literacy left the Shawnee tradition of oral communication at a complete disadvantage. Moreover, their British colonizers knew that their superior English literacy gave them greater power to define the Indians' reality by writing treaties, framing the news, drawing new maps—all to their advantage.[5]

This inequality extended to other facets of colonial behavior, including access to the wealth required to mount modern armies. But more than traditional military aspects of combat, turning the tools of literacy into weapons of war meant building beliefs about Anglo superiority that could sustain their dominance. In terms that add up to structural racism, that meant writing Anglocentric histories of events that could justify two centuries of genocide. So it was that contemporary British historians wrote Anglocentric accounts of events and British mapmakers recorded the boundaries and contours of the Crown's colonies with future conquests in mind.

The linguistic dynamic between the Shawnee and the British explains why the Indians continued to use English. Briefly, their public writing and newspaper journalism acted as a "site and a process" intended to show them as "civilized" enough to live peacefully alongside whites.[6] Being "civilized" meant "assimilating to Anglo-American norms, including . . . widespread Christianity, written constitutions, centralized governments, intermarriage with white Americans, market participation, . . . animal husbandry, patrilineal descent, and even slaveholding. None of these attributes characterized all the nations or all the citizens that they encompassed. The term was also used to distinguish these five nations from other so-called 'wild' Indians who continued to rely on hunting for survival.[7]

In this context, newspaper journalism was not a specific criterion for British recognition of civilized status, but it demonstrated the elite practice of English by four of the so-called Five Civilized Tribes. This set included the Cherokee, Chickasaw, Choctaw, and Creek tribes. The fifth, the Seminoles, did not write or publish newspapers.[8]

Still, newspaper journalism played a prominent role in a highly developed indigenous culture from very early on. In describing what he called the century of Indian journalism, historian Richard LaCourse reported that by "the time the first Indian newspaper was brought off the press in 1828, [Indians] had already developed court systems and already had a series of tribally administered schools. I think there were approximately forty in Cherokee country alone. They had a bicameral legislature; they had popular elections. This isn't the stereotyped image you may have of Indians." In the first century of Indian journalism from 1828 to approximately 1910, there were about one hundred Indian newspapers published across the present fifty states.[9]

Such sophisticated communication methods were not new to Indian culture. Indeed, most of the natives' newspapers mentioned were officially recognized tribal outlets in routine communication with each other. Historian Jeanette Henry described a "complex system of native communications (that) covered most of North America before white contact. It was a unique network of trails and footpaths used by tribally recognized messengers that crisscrossed the continent, passing through dense forests, over rivers and streams, across mountains and meadow." In spite of prevalent assumptions by white Europeans, who ignored this sophistication among native people, Henry reports that "a *system* of communications existed among the native tribes as a traditional, historical and necessary part of their society." She added that "news moved more slowly following white expansion."[10]

In 1828, a Cherokee silversmith named "George Guess" or "Gist," whose Cherokee name was "Sequoyah," created an eighty-six-character Cherokee writing system. Simple enough to become widely used by the tribe—even by his six-year-old daughter—Sequoyah's syllabary addressed a need. In his military service in the US Army in the War of 1812 fighting against the Creek Indians, "He realized that white society possessed in written language a power his people lacked."[11]

Embracing Journalism: Boudinot and the Cherokee *Phoenix*

In 1828, when Elias Boudinot, a college-educated Cherokee teacher and missionary, learned of Sequoyah's success, he was inspired to found a bilingual newspaper for the tribe. The first issue of the *Cherokee Phoenix* was printed in the Cherokee capital, New Echota, Georgia, on February 21, 1828. The newspaper's name was changed to the *Cherokee Phoenix and Advocate* the next year. The five-column, four-page newspaper was valued by tribal leaders as a vehicle for tribal education. The newspaper also served the civilizing goals of colonization. In particular, it presented the articles of the Cherokee constitution in English and Cherokee. Rich with local advertisements, the articles there also carefully aligned the Indians' religious beliefs with the prevalent Christianity of the Americans. To signal the newspaper's mission for its Indian readership, its masthead showed a Phoenix rising from the flames over the legend "Protection." The *Phoenix's* last issue was published on May 31, 1834.[12]

The *Cherokee Phoenix* sparked a new era in Indian newspapers. In 1843, the Cherokee National Council commissioned a new national newspaper, the *Cherokee Advocate*. Led by principal chief John Ross and edited by his nephew, William P. Ross, a Princeton graduate, the *Advocate* published a bilingual paper using the Cherokee alphabet.[13]

The importance of journalism to Cherokee survival was made clear in "An Address to the Whites" by Boudinot on May 26, 1826. Speaking to an audience at the First Presbyterian Church of Philadelphia, he promoted equal parts of a fundraising appeal for Cherokee advancement, promotion of the new Cherokee alphabet, and pleas to white Philadelphians for the chance to survive "fostered, regulated and protected by the generous government of the U.S."

Then, in language that sounded like other challengers to white hegemony of that moment—including the abolitionist voices of his contemporaries, Sojourner Truth, Maria Stewart, David Walker, and Frederick Douglass—Boudinot argued against stereotyping and for racial equality. He said, "Some there are, perhaps even in this enlightened assembly, who at the bare sight of an Indian, or at the mention of the name, would throw back their imaginations to ancient times, to the ravages of savage warfare, to the yells pronounced over the mangled bodies of women and children, thus creating an opinion, inapplicable and highly injurious to those for whose temporal interest and eternal welfare, I come to plead. What is an Indian? Is he not formed of the same materials with yourself?"

Having made his case for their common humanity, he settled on his reason for being there—to raise funds for a printing press for a Cherokee newspaper and to found a Christian seminary. Emphasizing the ways in which those two projects would enhance a shared life with white Americans, he used words that his audience would register: "Christianization and civilization."

In his effort to persuade his white audience, he promised that the Cherokee would become more assimilated to white culture through the often-twinned practices of not just civilization and Christianity, but of *journalism* and a *seminary*. The virtue of each would come from its practice, he explained. "You will . . . be convinced of three important truths. First, that the means which have been employed for the Christianization and civilization of this tribe, have been greatly blessed. Second, that the increase of these means will meet with final success. Third, that it has now become necessary, that efficient and more than ordinary means should be employed. Sensible of this last point, and wishing to do something for themselves, the Cherokees have thought it advisable that there should be established, a Printing Press and a Seminary of respectable character; and for these purposes your aid and patronage are now solicited."

Boudinot knew that the American Board of Commissioners for Foreign Missions in New England had already set aside funds for an offset printing press using English and Cherokee writing systems. He assured his audience that having the resources to produce a newspaper would do much to settle the differences between whites and Indians. He said, "Such a paper could not fail to create much interest in the American community, favorable to the aborigines, and to have a powerful influence on the advancement of the Indians themselves.[14]

But there was another message to convey about the ever-nearer threat of relocation and even extermination. And so he told of the perils already decimating the Indians:

There are, with regard to the Cherokee and other tribes, two alternatives; they must either become civilized and happy, or sharing the fate of many kindred nations, become extinct. . . . There is, in Indian history, something very melancholy, and which seems to establish a mournful precedent for the future events of the few sons of the forest, now scattered over this vast continent. We have seen every where the poor aborigines melt away before the white population. I merely speak of the fact, without at all referring to the cause. We have seen, I say, one family after another, one tribe after another, nation after nation, pass away; until only a few solitary creatures are left to tell the sad story of extinction. Shall this precedent be followed? I ask you, shall red men live, or shall they be swept from the earth? With you and this public at large, the decision chiefly rests. Must they perish? Must they all, like the unfortunate Creeks, (victims of the unchristian policy of certain persons), go down in sorrow to their grave? They hang upon your mercy as to a garment. Will you push them from you, or will you save them? Let humanity answer.[15]

Although Boudinot argued in this speech in 1827 against the relocation of the Cherokee, in 1835 he sided with the US government's relocation program by signing the controversial Treaty of New Echota. That switch cost him his life: In 1839, he was axed to death by Cherokees who were incensed at his disloyalty to the tribe.[16]

A Legacy of State Violence

Between 1830 and 1850, the US government evicted some one hundred thousand Indians from their ancestral lands in Georgia, Tennessee, Alabama, North Carolina, and Florida. As many as a quarter of the sixteen thousand Cherokee men, women, and children died on that tortured journey. The Indian Removal Act of 1830 signed by Andrew Jackson deployed federal forces to remove Indians from Georgia, Alabama, North Carolina, and Tennessee to Oklahoma."[17] According to LaCourse, "the deportation of the Cherokee people along the Trail of Tears meant they were thrown on the back of a buckboard, or they were put on a small raft, floated up a river, forced to walk here or there. It reminds me very much of the more recent Nazi experience."[18]

Historian Jeffry Ostler drew a broader picture of the Indian experience of being driven from their lands, writing that

Although the Cherokee Trail of Tears is the most well known removal, there were dozens of other such evictions. Creeks, Seminoles, Chickasaws, Choctaws, Senecas, Wyandots, Potawatomis, Sauks and Mesquakies,

Ojibwes, Ottawas, Miamis, Kickapoos, Poncas, Modocs, Kalapuyas, and Takelmas represent only a partial list of nations that suffered trails of tears. Not all experienced the same mortality as the Cherokee, but many did, and for some, the toll was even higher. The allied Sauks and Mesquakies were forced to move four times from their villages in western Illinois—once to central Iowa, once to western Iowa, once to Kansas, and finally to Oklahoma. In 1832, the time of the first expulsion, the Sauks and Mesquakies numbered six thousand. By 1869, when they were finally sent to Oklahoma, their population was only nine hundred, a staggering loss of 85 percent.[19]

The US government committed these acts while "ignoring treaties, property deeds, and the sacredness of their ancestral homes and burial grounds." Contrary to popular stereotypes, "These emigrants were not the whooping naked savages of Hollywood," historians James and Sharon Murphy explained. "They were civilized and well established people. . . . Many of their leaders were college-educated; many owned large plantations, others were skilled teachers, outstanding craftsmen, successful tradesmen." Indeed, in spite of their English-based civilization, the Five Civilized Tribes made up most of the first deportees.[20]

The American policy that followed relocation was called termination. It was designed to erase Indian culture in the nineteenth and twentieth centuries by assimilating Indian children into white society. To that end, the US government often forcibly took infants and children from their parents. The children were placed in boarding schools that were often too far for their parents to visit them. Banned from speaking their native languages, forced to cut their hair, and required to wear school uniforms instead of their tribal clothes, the children were often emotionally, physically, and sexually abused.

During this period, some hundred thousand Indian children were sent to 367 schools across the nation. Most of them never saw their parents again. One scholar estimated that as many as four thousand children died in American boarding schools during this period, a number that compares to the death toll of the Trail of Tears relocation march in the late 1830s-1850s.

Indian boarding schools practiced journalism, too, albeit often as a kind of propaganda for termination. The cover of *The Youth's Companion* published in October 1881 (more later) reflects the combination of Christianity and journalism that supported the aims of termination. The front cover was presented as a way to display Indians' efforts to adapt to white culture. The cover also begins a tale of a small boy, "René Placide Bonnet, Pupil of the Christian Brothers of Poitiers." Faced with his own death from an unidentified illness and surrounded by his adoring family, the boy demonstrated the ideal qualities of Christian nature that the Catholic administrators worked so hard to instill in the Indian children they kept. Written in the voice of one of the Catholic teachers, the maudlin story began thus: "René had scarcely attained the use of reason when he gave marks of virtue and piety. To cultivate this happy disposition, his good parents placed him at the Brother's Boarding School at Poitiers. His teachers soon recognized in him one of those privileged, worthy of being proposed as a model to all the others."[21]

In the stark circumstances most often associated with the Indian boarding schools, the truth behind such a story likely lay with the staff's need for cover.

The most overt feature of the Indian experience with the United States was the series of wars in the nineteenth century over territory. In 1816–1818 and 1835–1842, the Seminoles lost two wars with the United States, leading to their forced walk on the Trail of Tears from the Everglades to Oklahoma. After the US Civil War, legal and military harassment continued. The Sand Creek Massacre of 1864 in present-day Colorado saw US soldiers slaughter 148 Cheyenne and Arapahoe men, women, and children. At the Battle of the Little Bighorn in 1876, General George Custer and his six hundred

The *Youth's Companion*, published by the Sisters of Charity.

men were killed when they engaged three thousand Sioux and Cheyenne led by Chief Crazy Horse. Of all these armed conflicts, the massacre on December 29, 1890, of seven hundred Lakota Sioux by the 7th US Calvary at the village of Wounded Knee proved to be the deadliest. Its memory among Indians would also spark the Red Power protest movement.[22]

By the mid-nineteenth century, the basis of the US government's violence against Indians and their responses was fixed. After a delay for the Civil War, a steady torrent of federal Acts, court decisions, and federal lying further poisoned Indian-American relations. What had begun as whites' control over native peoples in the Articles of Confederation in 1781 and Article I of the US Constitution in 1788 gave way to an ever-shifting pattern of plots and lies by the US government. Every solution proposed by the government returned to one outcome: The Indians' loss of land to whites. These false negotiations often followed the discovery of natural resources such as coal and uranium lands.[23]

As Indians' losses fed westward expansion seemed to validate the myth of Manifest Destiny, the torrent of federal actions aimed at the Indian nations only continued. The Homestead Act of 1862 "turned over lands within the American public domain to private U.S. citizens." The Pacific Railway Act authorized the construction of a transcontinental railroad through tribal lands. "In 1887, the General Allotment Act . . . and its subsequent amendments created the general framework for removing reservation land from communal tribal ownership and allotting parcels to individual members. . . . This formed the basis for modern land trust status, land fractionation, checkerboard land ownership and on-going land loss." In 1903, in *Lone Wolf v. Hitchcock*, the US Supreme Court "ruled that treaties may be unilaterally breached or modified by Congress." In 1906, the Burke Act gave the secretary of the interior authority to "administer Indian trust property."

From 1946 to 1978, the Indian Claims Commission sought to end the government's traditional ties to Indians in order to obligate them to assimilate to white culture. Like the Indian boarding schools, the government intended to do away with indigenous cultures by immersing Indians in white culture and then taking their land. The program featured an "adversarial court process to [hear] land claims brought by tribes for wrongful dispossession of their lands. Although tribes won about two-thirds of these cases, they were settled with inadequate cash payments rather than the return of their lands.

In 1953, Congress formalized the policy of tribal termination by passing House Concurrent Resolution 108. One of the most destructive laws passed to separate Indians from their lands, the resolution "set up the process whereby a tribe's political status could be dissolved, tribal lands be taken out of trust and sold to non-natives, and imposed state laws on former tribal members." In *Tee-Hit-Ton v. U.S.*, the Supreme Court held that aboriginal title is "not a property right but amounts to a right of occupancy which the sovereign grants and . . . may be terminated and such lands fully disposed of by the sovereign itself without any legally enforceable obligation to compensate the Indians." From 1953 to 1970, more than 11.4 million Indians lost their lands and with them, their tribal identities.[24]

It was in their struggle against this constant checkmate that the Indian movement would begin a transition to self-determination in the last quarter of the twentieth century. They would even find a kind of sovereignty in the years to follow. But as the founders of the American Indian Movement knew in 1968, the damage was done.

AIM, 1968: Reclaiming Identity, Demanding Justice

By 1968, protests against the Vietnam War, authoritarianism and police violence, and the white Establishment, and for Black civil rights, Black Power, Latino farmworkers' rights, women's rights, gay rights, and the environment coalesced into a general climate of protest. Referred to collectively as the "Movement," each of these groups made claims against religious, corporate, and governmental institutions for their contributions to long-held structural inequities. Adding to these claims against American cultural norms was the Red Power movement—a movement umbrella organization—and its most prominent member organization, AIM, the American Indian Movement.[25] Unlike the Prairie Power hippies or other countercultural protest groups of the era, AIM "was an indigenous, land-based spiritual movement, a call for Indian people to return to their sacred traditions, and at the same time, to stand firm against the tide of what they call European influence and dominance."[26]

AIM was formed in 1966 when a group of young Chippewa, including Dennis Banks, Edward Benton-Banai, and brothers Clyde and Vernon Bellecourt. They met in Oklahoma's Stillwater State Prison, where they were serving time for an assortment of property crimes. As they reflected on their shared experiences with poverty and prison, they developed a common understanding. They saw the inequalities and inequities that the American system had always visited on their people. They also saw that the profound lack of pride among their fellow Indians at this point led them to see that the Indian community needed a way to revive itself. Above all, they believed that Indians needed to reclaim lands lost to the United States. Their turn to the national media showed just how savvy they were.

In 1968, most Americans owned television sets and the founders of AIM were aware that media attention would be essential to their success.

Unlike in the nineteenth-century Indian press, media success called for a larger understanding of the immense space of a national and international broadcast system. It also depended on the movement leadership's sense of how to stage media events that would catch the television journalists' attention. What they did not understand was the impact of their historical relegation to reservations and the urban animosity it brought. This increased difficulty meant changing the longheld perceptions among the American viewing audience, a barrier they would overcome.

In his study of news coverage of the Students for a Democratic Society (SDS) in the antiwar protest movement of the 1960s and early 1970s, media sociologist Todd Gitlin explained that what becomes "news" out of this "struggle" depends on an ideological—and necessarily powerful process. This built-in cultural system works through a "selection, emphasis, and presentation composed of little tacit theories about what exists, what happens, and what matters."[27] That meant that AIM's campaign had to change not just audiences' beliefs but *journalists'* beliefs before them. That would be difficult, but getting covered on the national news produced free media that helped the Indians' fundraising and aided in the recruitment of volunteers.

In that sense, they understood that manipulating the news agenda offered a viable alternative to reporting it. AIM settled on a strategy of occupying buildings on sites of historic battles and abuses. "The only way we could get publicity was by threats," AIM's Russell Means recalled. "We had to threaten institutions we were trying to change."[28] For that reason, AIM was regarded as too radical by the other organizations in the new Red Power protest organization.

Red Power: Occupation as Media Strategy

From 1960 to 1980 dozens of Indian-led protests were staged by Indian organizations across the country. Most prominently, a week before Thanksgiving 1969, 89 Indian students reclaimed Alcatraz Island and its defunct prison off the coast of Sausalito, California. Although AIM was not involved in the Alcatraz siege, which lasted until June 1971, they directed media strategy for the Red Power organization from then on that called for occupying and reclaiming key federal buildings, parks, and monuments. The goal of this new Red Power protest initiative was "to draw attention to American Indian historical and contemporary grievances: unsettled land claims, poor living conditions on reservations, U.S. failure to recognize cultural and social rights or to allow tribal self-determination."[29]

The successful use of confrontational methods at Alcatraz led to a series of small actions staged at Milwaukee, the Twin Cities Naval Air Station in Minneapolis, Fort Lawton near Seattle, Sheep Mountain in North Dakota, and an attempted takeover of Ellis Island in 1970.[30] Occupations at more prominent sites besides Ellis Island were the Mayflower II and Plymouth Rock, the Bureau of Indian Affairs in Littleton, Colorado, all also in 1970. In 1971, they occupied Mount Rushmore.

In 1972, AIM staged its most prominent media event when it organized the Trail of Broken Treaties. Three caravans of Indians in cars and buses left Seattle, Los Angeles, and San Francisco to meet in Minneapolis in October. During their stay there, they drafted a six-thousand-word manifesto to deliver to the Bureau of Indian Affairs in Washington, DC. Featuring twenty demands, the "Preamble" spelled out the administrative and legal steps required to redress those crimes. The preamble read

> We need not give another recitation of past complaints nor engage in redundant dialogue of discontent. Our conditions and their cause for being should perhaps be best known by those who have written the record of America's action against Indian people. In 1832, Black Hawk correctly observed: You know the cause of our making war. It is known to all white men. They ought to be ashamed of it.
>
> The government of the United States knows the reasons for our going to its capital city.
>
> Unfortunately, they don't know how to greet us. We go because America has been only too ready to express shame, and suffer none from the expression—while remaining wholly unwilling to change to allow life for Indian people.

The document concluded with the Indians' centuries-old call for a peaceful coexistence with white culture:

> We seek a new American majority—a majority that is not content merely to confirm itself by superiority in numbers, but which by conscience is committed toward prevailing upon the public will in ceasing wrongs and in doing right. For our part, in words and deeds of coming days, we propose to produce a rational, reasoned manifesto for construction of an Indian future in America. If America has maintained faith with its original spirit, or may recognize it now, we should not be denied.
>
> Press Statement issued: October 31, 1972[31]

The seventy-one-day armed standoff at Wounded Knee resulted from local Lakota Indians' deep dissatisfaction with Lakota Sioux tribal chairman

Richard "Dickie" Wilson, whom they accused of being a pawn of the Bureau of Indian Affairs. Unlike previous AIM occupations, Wounded Knee turned violent. By the end, two Indians would be shot dead and one FBI agent would be wounded. Described as "arbitrary and dictatorial,"[32] Wilson faced impeachment for allegedly colluding with the BIA to deprive the local Oglala Sioux tribe of mineral and grazing fees owed to the Indians who owned the land. To effect this swindle, the BIA had created a leaselike form that falsely led individual landowners to sign control of their property to the BIA.

Prior to the February 27, 1973, occupation, the charges against Wilson piled up. Among other points, he had agreed to cede 153,000 acres from the reservation—an eighth of its land—to the US government. The land had been promised to the Indians as compensation for their prior loss of the Black Hills. True to previous experiences with the government, the Indians understood that the land's suddenly increased value came because it was "believed to be rich in uranium and oil deposits."[33] To protest these events, hundreds of local Lakota Sioux massed in Pine Ridge fifteen miles northeast of Wounded Knee on the Pine Ridge reservation to attend Wilson's impeachment. All knew that they were being cheated out of their land by the government's self-dealing agreement with Wilson. Others were not being paid for their mining leases. Many resented the presence of non-Indian forces in Pine Ridge.

As tensions mounted, tribal leaders—"Oglala Sioux chiefs, medicine men and headsmen"—called for AIM to "take a stand" against the Americans. At a meeting on February 27, according to Dennis Banks, two older Oglala Sioux women asked, "What was AIM going to do about it—the injustices that were happening that very minute—allowing the federal people, the federal officers, the FBI and the (federal) marshals . . . to turn the village of Pine Ridge into an armed camp.[34]

When more than three hundred citizens came to the first impeachment hearing, the BIA reacted by sending in seventy counterinsurgency Special Operations Group soldiers. As Wilson's trial on February 14, 1973, drew near, units began to take positions around the village. Delaying the hearing a week only gave military and police forces more time to set up for a siege. By the time AIM appeared, the BIA police, the FBI and "Wilson's burgeoning goon squad" had set up roadblocks on all routes to Wounded Knee.[35]

As the conflict drew reporters to the scene, the US Department of Justice issued an order that read "Do not let newspaper personnel in the Wounded Knee area. . . . No TV coverage of the Wounded Knee Area, authority Attorney General [Richard Kleindienst. . . . No photos of [military] personnel."

This order was intended to mask the first ever use of US troops against American citizens.[36]

The attorney general did not need to have been so concerned about the journalists gathering at Wounded Knee. Many national media outlets had already been compromised by their relationships with the FBI's Counter-intelligence Program (COINTELPRO). In the same sort of domestic spying used by J. Edgar Hoover against Martin Luther King Jr. during the Civil Rights Movement, the FBI investigated AIM, its leaders, and its members as threats to national security. It even planted a spy within AIM. The bureau also cultivated relationships with "friendly" media to collect evidence against AIM, as they had in King's case. Allegations of communist influence were common in both cases.

As it worked against the press, COINTELPRO took two approaches: "the manipulation of general information to the general media" and "the feeding of stories to the willing and cooperative media." The list of coop-erating media produced by the National Lawyers Guild in 1978 showed that "the list included the Hearst Newspaper chain, Associated Press, *New York Daily News, Chicago Tribune, Milwaukee Journal, Los Angeles Examiner, U.S. News and World Report, Arizona Daily Star*, and other newspapers and radio and television stations."[37]

Despite this attempt by the government to control the media narrative about the standoff, AIM nevertheless found a way to put its cause before the American public. A young Apache actress named Sacheen Littlefeather approached screen legend Marlon Brando to seek his assistance in raising awareness of the standoff at Wounded Knee, and to confront Hollywood about its complicity in creating and disseminating dehumanizing depictions of native people.

Brando, who had been a prominent supporter of the civil rights move-ment, agreed to cooperate. When he was announced as the winner of the Best Actor honor for his iconic role in *The Godfather*, Littlefeather took the stage in Brando's place, wearing Apache buckskin. Upon taking the stage, she was informed that she would be given only one minute to deliver her remarks before she would be removed from the stage. She declined the Oscar, and said the following:

> Hello. My name is Sacheen Littlefeather. I'm Apache and I am presi-dent of the National Native American Affirmative Image Committee. I'm representing Marlon Brando this evening, and he has asked me to tell you in a very long speech which I cannot share with you presently, because of time, but I will be glad to share with the press afterwards, that he very regretfully cannot accept this very generous award. And the

reasons for this being are the treatment of American Indians today by the film industry—excuse me—and on television in movie re-runs, and also with recent happenings at Wounded Knee. I beg at this time that I have not intruded upon this evening, and that we will in the future, our hearts and our understandings will meet with love and generosity. Thank you on behalf of Marlon Brando.

Littlefeather's remarks were interrupted by a mix of boos and cheers, and many in attendance seemed outraged by the protest. John Wayne, waiting backstage, had to be restrained from taking the stage to confront her. When Clint Eastwood took the stage to present the award for Best Picture, he remarked that he was presenting it "on behalf of all the cowboys shot in John Ford westerns over the years." But in spite of the outrage and dismissals, the message was delivered to millions of people.

After the show, Littlefeather delivered Brando's full remarks to the press, which were published the next day in the *New York Times*. His remarks began by noting that American authorities had repeatedly encouraged native people to lay down their arms. He then noted that "when they laid down their arms, we murdered them. We lied to them. We cheated them out of their lands. We starved them into signing fraudulent agreements that we called treaties which we never kept. We turned them into beggars on a continent that gave life for as long as life can remember. And by any interpretation of history, however twisted, we did not do right."[38]

He decried the "kind of moral schizophrenia" that allowed the United States to declare itself as a beacon of freedom while denying freedom to the land's native inhabitants and their descendants. He then turned his focus toward the movie industry itself, criticizing Hollywood's role in creating a consistently dehumanizing depiction of native people. "Recently," he added, "there have been a few faltering steps to correct this situation, but too faltering and too few." He revealed that the reason he was not present at the Academy Awards was because he had traveled to Wounded Knee "to help forestall in whatever way I can the establishment of a peace which would be dishonorable as long as the rivers shall run and the grass shall grow."[39]

The occupation of Wounded Knee in 1973 signaled the end of the protest movement led by AIM. In its aftermath, little changed in the press as journalists continued to differ about the meaning of the occupation. Most mainstream commentators continued to see the modern standoff at Wounded Knee as an aberration in a nation of laws. As James and Sharon Murphy put it, "Wounded Knee did not coincide with the belief that America was a democratic country where the courts dispensed justice, government agencies dealt benevolently with Indians, and all people had opportunities to match their ambition and willingness to work hard."[40] It was not that simple.

Many indigenous people also differed on AIM's tactics and their status as outsiders to the Pine Ridge community. Opinions varied about the possibility of unifying the North American tribes with or without AIM. In the historical swirl of internal Indian perspectives, the mainstream media's tendency to rely on stereotypes and culturally blindered frames to characterize AIM offered the Indian community a point of consensus. At a remove, it can be said that AIM stood up to the mainstream media's preconceptions in a solitary fashion, even if the white press turned a blind eye.

This history of Indian journalism and the media strategies of the American Indian Movement show the importance of journalism both as it was used by and, at once, against native people. If the Indian experience with journalism failed to overcome colonization, it was because the more powerful colonists had no intention of cooperating. Instead, their false promise of learning English failed the Indian people at every point. After native journalism failed to produce the equal (or even humane) treatment, AIM took a different approach. They understood the power of the press, for such marginalized people, came from their ability to make news of their own.

But there were limits to that strategy. The immediate, hostile reaction to Sacheen Littlefeather at the Academy Awards demonstrated the durability of mainstream attitudes. Many of the people in that auditorium that evening had a stake in preserving inequality; they had enriched themselves by creating a consistent image of native people that denied them the equity required for full humanity and cast them in the role of violent villains or—at best—compliant helpmates. What Hollywood and mainstream journalism were missing was an understanding of native people as full, complex human beings.

Conclusions

The Indian experience with media from Elias Boudinot's *Phoenix* onward was a cosmic trick sustained by mainstream white journalism. The white press aided and abetted the government's oppression of indigenous peoples by creating and always recreating the mirage of equality that depended on Indians having to play by white rules. The colonial notion that acquiring English literacy would make Indians the peers of their white adversaries was never really a possibility. So, rather than "using the master's tools (English) to tear down the master's house," mainstream whites inverted the equation of "using the master's tools to *build* the master's house"—the very definition of hegemony for Indians who thought they had seen a way out of centuries of racist abuse. It was not so.

To recall the historian Steve Warren's idea of "weaponized words," the Anglo insistence that Indians adapt to the English language meant that the natives were not encouraging Indians to build access for the whites to the Indians' culture. They wanted land. They wanted all the Indians had, and genocide was the system for getting it. To facilitate that process, journalism often served as an ally of the state. This structural pattern was clear.

By contrast, it was not that Indians sought out white culture. They were given nowhere else to go. At that, their systemic embrace of English and journalism reflected a trap laid by whites. That left Indians nowhere else to go, in time. Their efforts to assimilate might have brought a kind of parity, if not equality. But their goal was not to become white. It was to return home. Instead—unknowingly, they wrapped themselves in the service of a white supremacy more effective than the plague.

In terms of the use of journalism as an equalizing tactic, only AIM varied from the historical obligation that earlier Indians faced in colonial English. The momentary advantage they realized came not from their producing journalism in the traditional mode of the *Cherokee Phoenix* and its progeny, but through their understanding themselves as contemporary, mass media newsmakers. What they did *not* fully appreciate was how hard it is to change cultural meanings. In this power struggle, hints of control were never enough. Getting covered by the news was not the same as controlling the news.

Conclusion

The Ongoing Struggle to Define the Public

Journalism in all of its practices offers a site of struggle to define the public and the public interest. As we have shown, this struggle has been engaged in variously at different moments in American history. The forms of journalism that we have described show where, when, and how the definitions of the public and its interests have been contested. Outsiders have usually found themselves facing certain structural disadvantages in comparison with the mainstream-defined systems of power they sought to change. We have shown how historical attributes of nation, race, gender, class, and enslaved status worked to slow, but not stop, their calls for reforms and revolutions. Those making the claims on the public—from the earliest American colonists to the Black Panthers, Young Lords, and AIM—have used journalism to do so.

Over the same period, mainstream news has benefited from a growing range of institutional structures that the historian John Nerone calls "news formations." These formations shaped the information systems. In the early nineteenth century, for example, most newspapers were subsidized by political parties. They were run by small staffs or even individuals, targeted particular, rather small audiences and delivered political developments through a partisan lens. By the end of the century in New York and other places, that form of the news was being replaced with a whole set of institutional arrangements that were very different. In both cases, however, mainstream newspapers had access to other institutions and to their money. From their prominent cultural and political positions, the mainstream press also helped to set the terms of public debate. They established norms for evidence and helped to define which kinds of arguments got taken seriously and which did not. This implicit strategy was often to conserve the power of the institutional status quo.

Movement news in general has had much less access to these institutions and their sources of funding and authority. Their existence as news sources were typically precarious and brief. Their claims and their tone were often radical and so could be dismissed more easily. When broadcasting emerged as a major medium, the problem of access became even more acute. Broadcasting was limited to the select few who could gain access to the expensive technology and the broadcasting license from the government. Nevertheless, outsider groups found ways to use radio and television to get their messaging in front of the public, either by staging protests that the broadcasters would feel compelled to cover, as did the movement for civil rights that Martin Luther King Jr. led, or by gaining the cooperation of media insiders with special access, as in AIM's Academy Awards protest. Occasionally, media insiders like Mark Twain, Walter Lippmann, and Edward R. Murrow used their access to power to expose bad-faith arguments, propaganda, and other obstacles to democracy. Often, media insiders used their power and access to silence and delegitimize dissenters, but the dissent is always there and the outcome has never been assured.

In each chapter of this book, people engaged in disagreements about the proper contours of public life. And at each urgent turn, a pattern has emerged. People with the access and privilege to lay claim to the public interest have repeatedly struggled against those who had no such privilege. The distribution of privilege has not been random. It flowed from deeply embedded values of racial, national, gender, and class identity. In particular, Anglo-white males have consistently claimed to represent both the public and mainstream journalism. In most cases, they have had the power to deny outsiders access to public status, often by framing them as threats to the nation.

By focusing on the efforts of the poor, the dispossessed, the nonconformists, and the oppressed, this history offers a different, more equitable story about the role historically played by the mainstream press. Instead of the traditional view emphasizing journalism as a voice for progress and inclusion, this book has argued that it more often served as a support for the status quo. But never without challenges from those at the margins. Arguments for a wider public and a more pluralistic democracy have most often come from the margins, often from those excluded from public life. The multicultural chorus that that has so enriched life in the United States did not gain access because of the actions of the white mainstream but in spite of it. It came about because marginalized voices challenged limits set for them by the cultural and political majority. Working from outside the system, they adopted and adapted the technologies and conventions of the day in the service of their cause. Sometimes they succeeded in realizing their aims; often they did not. But by employing journalism to test the limits set by the mainstream, they held open the promise of an actualized democracy. Always a work in progress, this democratic ideal has been argued, written, and wrestled into view as "news" often by those with little access to power.

Because the words used in these struggles mattered, we have presented the actual language used to argue for and against changing visions of public life. It is important to see how their arguments were presented, with what language they were opposed, and what the outcomes of these conflicts were. This book has presented a range of voices to show how the practice of journalism has often worked hand in hand with other, less formal kinds of writing to provide strategically important resources to those who would argue for the right to freedom. Always involved in the politics of the moment, these tracts—pamphlets, broadsides, manifestos, speeches, sermons, newspapers—often showed that apparently different groups could have similar impulses to challenge dominant ideas about belonging to America. As the outsiders contributed to the civic debates of the day, their public language fed on the culture of argument and dissent that was otherwise promoted by newspapers.

Our perspective has not been to take sides or to referee or even to keep score in the ongoing fight between the conservatism of the mainstream press and the journalism used by outsiders to challenge it. Rather, we have worked to write a broader, more inclusive account of the past. By broadening the boundaries of US journalism history, we believe that we can all better understand how Americans have used journalism to accomplish key social changes. We have also found that that studying the past with power and struggle at the center helps us better understand trends and events in the present. We hope that reading this history leaves our readers better able to question, contextualize, and understand not only the past but also the many ongoing struggles that define the public today. When considering contemporary struggles for equality, rights, and human dignity, we hope to have exposed the legacies and strategies that contemporary movements are built on. We also hope to have exposed echoes of the past in the responses of the powerful.

Today it would be easy to write journalism off as a failing enterprise, underresourced and overwhelmed by the kaleidoscopic depths of the Web. It is true that many aspects of the importance, credibility, and sustainability of the news have been troubled. Propaganda has mushroomed in the forms of mis- and disinformation produced around the clock by enemies of democracy, both foreign and domestic. Profiteering social media megacorporations have monetized private data. News companies are hunted down by rapacious hedge funds hungry for their remaining assets. Still, as terrible as that sounds, we have seen crises before. And in response, new voices of democracy have arisen using new forms of journalism to reason with a nation that has often failed to honor its highest ideals. Therefore, history serves to remind us that we have survived trying times before. But it should also remind us of the terrible cost when the press fails.

In recalling a time when the world truly was not safe for democracy, Robert McChesney calls the lows of the 1919 postwar crisis for journalism "the last truly great defining crisis for journalism." Gamely facing the present, he writes, "Faced with crisis, our greatest thinkers often become more critical, creative, and original, providing us with insights for the ages."[1] So, here is what we want our readers to have gained from this book: In our nation's long history, the union of journalism and democracy has not been a given. It has been an unrealized *idea*. But there have always been people who believed in it. People who have turned their pain, their dispossession, and their outrage toward a vision of a better, fairer world. And ideas like that, thankfully, are very hard to extinguish.

Notes

Introduction

1. James W. Carey, "The Press and Public Discourse," *Center Magazine* 20, (March, 1987), 5.

2. David T. Z. Mindich, "Understanding Frederick Douglass: Toward a New Synthesis Approach to the Birth of Modern American Journalism," *Journalism History* 26, no. 1: 15–22.

3. Michael Warner, *Publics and Counterpublics* (New York: Zone Books, 2002), 114.

4. Jane Rhodes, "Diversity in Media History: A Call for Broader Study," *Clio in the Media* 29 (Spring, 1997): 1–4.

5. Mindich, "Understanding"; Ron Eyerman and Andrew Jamison, *Social Movements: A Cognitive Approach* (University Park: Pennsylvania State University Press, 1991); M. J. Heale, *American Anticommunism: Combating the Enemy within, 1830–1970* (Baltimore, MD: Johns Hopkins University Press, 1990).

6. Michael Rogin, *Ronald Reagan, the Movie: And Other Episodes in Political Demonology* (Berkeley, CA: University of California Press, 1988), xiii.

7. Nell Irvin Painter, *The History of White People* (New York: W. W. Norton, 2010.)

8. Heale, *American Anticommunism*, 10.

9. Alexis de Tocqueville, *Democracy in America* (New York: Library of America, 2004), 285.

10. Tocqueville, *Democracy in America*, 211.

11. Tocqueville, *Democracy in America*, 601.

12. Tocqueville, *Democracy in America*, 211.

13. Tocqueville, *Democracy in America*, 212.

14. This section on the partisan press owes much to Jean Folkerts and Dwight Teeter, *Voices of a Nation*, 2nd ed. (New York: Maxwell Macmillan International, 1994): 101–3.

15. Folkerts and Teeter, *Voices*, 130; John Nerone, *The Media and Public Life: A History*, (Cambridge, UK: Polity, 2015), 92.

16. James W. Carey, *Communication as Culture*, 2nd ed. (New York: Routledge, 2008), 11–28.

17. Folkerts and Teeter, *Voices*, 130.

18. Nerone, *Media and Public Life*, 5.

19. Nerone, *Media and Public Life*.

20. Nerone, *Media and Public Life*, 5.

21. Nerone, *Media and Public Life*, 141.

22. Quoted in Jill Lapore, *A History of the United States* (New York: Norton, 2108), 422–23.

23. Folkerts and Teeter, *Voices*, 477.

24. Daniel Hallin, "The Passing of the High Modernism of American Journalism," *Journal of Communication* 42, no. 3 (1992): 14–25.

25. Thomas Jefferson, *Notes on the State of Virginia* (New York: Palgrave-MacMillan, 2002).

26. Tocqueville, *Democracy in America*, 596.

Chapter 1. Creating an American Public Interest

1. Jill Lepore, *These Truths: A History of the United States* (New York: Norton, 2018), 83.

2. Lepore, *These Truths*, 78.

3. Benjamin Harris, *Publick Occurrences Both FORREIGN and DOMESTICK*, Boston, Thursday, September 25, 1690.

4. Harris, *Publick Occurrences*.

5. John R. Vile, *Peter Zenger* (Murfreesboro, TN: Free Speech Center, Middle Tennessee State University), https://www.mtsu.edu/first-amendment/article/1235/john-peter-zenger; Isaiah Thomas, *The History of Printing in America with a Bibliography of Printers and Account of Newspapers*, 2nd ed., edited by Marcus A. McCorison (New York: Weathervane, 1970).

6. Jean Folkerts and Dwight Teeter, *Voices of a Nation: A History of Mass Media in the United States* (Minneapolis: Pearson, 2008), 42–45.

7. Anthony Fellow, *American Media History* (Boston: Thomson Wadsworth, 2005), 40–41; John Nerone, *The Media and Public Life: A History*, (Malden, MA: Polity, 2015), 44–45.

8. Fellow, *American Media History*, 40–41. See also Allen Weinstein and David Rubel, *The Story of America: Freedom and Crisis from Settlement to Superpower* (New York: DK Publishing, 2002), 91–92; Susan Thompson, "Origins of Advertising," in *The Age of Mass Communication*, edited by William Sloan (Northport, AL: Vision), 83.

9. Fellow, *American Media History*, 41.

10. *Boston Gazette*, May 26, 1755; Jeffery A. Smith, *Printers and Press Freedom: The Ideology of Early American Journalism* (New York: Oxford, 1988), 7.

11. *Boston Gazette*, May 26, 1755.

12. Isaiah Thomas, *The History of Printing in America with a Bibliography of Printers and Account of Newspapers*, 2nd ed., edited by Marcus A. McCorison (New York: Weathervane, 1970) 258–59.

13. Rodger Streitmatter, *Mightier than the Sword*, 2nd ed. (Boulder, CO: Westview), 14.

14. Oliver Morton Dickerson, *Boston under Military Rule, 1768–1769* (Boston: Chapman and Grimes, 1936, 2010), viii.

15. Dickerson, *Boston under Military Rule*, 2.

16. Jacques Ellul, *Propaganda: The Formation of Men's Attitudes*, translated from the French by Konrad Kellen and Jean Lerner (New York: Knopf, 1965).

17. Fellow, *American Media History*, 39–40; Dickerson, *Boston under Military Rule*, x–xi.

18. Fellow, *American Media History*, 34.

19. Fellow, *American Media History*, 1.

20. Fellow, *American Media History*, vii–viii

21. Streitmatter, *Mightier Than the Sword*, 9–10.

22. Dickerson, *Boston under Military Rule*, vii–viii.

23. Dickerson, *Boston under Military Rule*, x–xi.

24. Dickerson, *Boston under Military Rule*, x–xi.

25. *Boston Journal*, March 12, 1769.

26. Peter Messer, "'A Scene of Villainy Acted by a Dirty Banditti, as Must Astonish the Public'": The Creation of the Boston Massacre," *New England Quarterly* 90, no. 4 (December, 2017): 218–19.

27. Folkerts and Teeter, *Voices*, 66–68; Fellows, *American Media History*, 46; Nerone, *The Media*, 45.

28. Eric Foner, *Tom Paine and Revolutionary America*, 2nd ed. (Oxford: Oxford University Press, 2004), xxxii, 16.

29. Craig Nelson, *Thomas Paine: Enlightenment, Revolution and the Birth of the Modern Nation* (New York: Penguin, 2006), 92.

30. Thomas Paine, *Political Writings*, edited by Bruce Kuklick (Cambridge: Cambridge University Press, 1989).

31. "The Sedition Act of 1798," *Historical Highlights*, US House of Representatives, History, Art, and Archives, https://history.house.gov/Historical-Highlights/1700s/The-Sedition-Act-of-1798/.

32. Smith, *Printers and Press Freedom*, 59.

Chapter 2. Writing against Slavery

1. Benjamin Fagan, *The Black Newspaper and the Chosen Nation* (Athens: University of Georgia Press, 2016), 6.

2. Painter, *History of White People*.

3. Maria Stewart, "Address Delivered at the African Masonic Hall, Boston," February 27, 1833, accessed July 12, 2022, https://www.historyisaweapon.com/defcon1/stewartmason.html.

4. Fagan, *Black Newspaper*, 47; Leon F. Litwak, *Been in the Storm So Long: The Aftermath of Slavery* (New York: Knopf, 1980).

5. Fagan, *Black Newspaper*, 6.

6. Stephen David Kantrowitz, *More Than Freedom: Fighting for Black Citizenship in a White Republic, 1829–1889* (New York: Penguin, 2012), 4.

7. Kantrowitz, *More Than Freedom*, 4, 8.

8. Fagan, *Black Newspaper*, 6, 45.

9. Kantrowitz, *More Than Freedom*, 8.

10. John C. Nerone, *The Media and Public Life: A History* (Cambridge, UK: Polity, 2015), 56–58.

11. Nerone, *Media and Public Life*, 56–58.

12. Thomas Paine, "African Slavery in America" (March 18, 1775), *Pennsylvania Journal and the Weekly Advertiser* [online]. See also Stanley Harrold, *American Abolitionists* (New York: Routledge, 2001), 19.

13. "American Anti-Slavery Society," *Encyclopaedia Britannica online*, https://www.britannica.com/topic/American-Anti-SlaverySociety.

14. *Freedom's Journal,* https://www.pbs.org/blackpress/news_bios/newbios/nwsppr/freedom/freedom.html.

15. *Walker's Appeal, in Four Articles; Together with a Preamble, to the Colored Citizens of the World, but in Particular, and Very Expressly, to Those of the United States of America, Written in Boston, State of Massachusetts, September 28, 1829,* third and last edition (Boston: David Walker, 1830), accessed on March 28, 2024, at https://docsouth.unc.edu/nc/walker/walker.html; also quoted in the *Liberator*, May 14, 1831, 1.

16. John Nerone, "Elijah Lovejoy, Anti-Slavery and Freedom of the Press," unpublished manuscript, 2007, http://www.lib.niu.edu/2007/iht07140138.html.

17. "Anti-abolition Meeting," *Daily Commercial Bulletin and Missouri Literary Register* (St. Louis, Missouri), July 17, 1837.

18. "Declaration of Sentiments of the American Anti-Slavery Society Adopted at the Formation of Said Society, in Philadelphia, on the Fourth Day of 1833" (New York: American Anti-Slavery Society, 1844?).

19. William Lloyd Garrison, "To the Public," *Liberator*, January 1, 1831, http://www.pbs.org/wgbh/aia/part4/4h2928t.html.

20. "Declaration of the National Anti-Slavery Convention," December 14, 1833, 198.

21. H. Seldon (n.d.). "A Moment in Abolition History," The Liberator Files. https://www.theliberatorfiles.com/a-moment-in-abolition-history/.

22. "Declaration of Sentiments of the American Anti-Slavery Society Adopted at the Formation of Said Society, in Philadelphia, on the Fourth Day of 1833," Library of Congress, https://www.loc.gov/resource/rbpe.11801100/.

23. Ronald C. White Jr. and C. Howard Hopkins, "Christian Abolitionism," *The Social Gospel: Religion and Reform in Changing America,* 14–25 (Philadelphia: Temple University Press, 1976).

24. Frederick Douglass, *Narrative of the Life of Frederick Douglass, an American Slave. Written by Himself* (Boston: Published at the Anti-Slavery office, no. 25 Cornhill, 1845), http://docsouth.unc.edu/neh/douglass/douglass.html.

25. *Liberator*, September 21, 1841, 1.

26. Nerone, *Media and Public Life*, 74–79.

27. Patsy Brewington Perry, "Before the North Star: Frederick Douglass' Early Journalistic Career," *Phylon* 35, no. 1 (qtr. 1, 1974): 96–107.

28. Kantrowitz, *More Than Freedom*, 151.

29. Frederick Douglass, *North Star*, December 3, 1847, as reprinted in Philip Foner, ed., *Life and Writings of Frederick Douglass*, vol. 1 (New York: International, 1950), 280, http://docsouth.unc.edu/neh/douglass/support15.html.

30. *Liberator*, July 7, 1854, 1.

31. David Walker, "Walker's Appeal, in Four Articles; Together with a Preamble, to the Colored Citizens of the World, but in Particular, and Very Expressly, to Those of the United States of America," in *Slavery in America and the World: History, Culture and Law* (Boston: Printed for the Author, 1829).

32. Maria Stewart, "Religion and the Pure Principles of Morality," in *Words of Fire: An Anthology of African-American Feminist Thought*, edited by B. Guy-Sheftal (New York: Norton, 1995).

33. Shirley J. Yee, Black Women Abolitionists: *A Study in Activism, 1828–1860* (Knoxville: University of Tennessee Press, 1992), 115.

34. Jacqueline Jones, "Living the Examined Life in the Antebellum North, and in the Post–World War II United States," review of *The Grimké Sisters from South Carolina: Pioneers for Women's Rights and Abolition*, by Gerda Lerner," *American Historical Review* 123, no. 5 (2018): 1547.

35. Angelina Grimké, *Appeal to the Christian Women of the South* (New York: American Anti-Slavery Society, 1836), 17.

36. Sarah Moore Grimké and Angelina B. Grimké, "Appeal to the Christian Women of the South," *Anti-slavery Examiner* no. 2 (9), 1836: 1.

37. Theodore Dwight Weld, *American Slavery as It Is: Testimony of a Thousand Witnesses* (New York: Anti-Slavery Society of New York, 1839).

38. Jones, "Living the Examined Life:" 1549.

39. Weld, *American Slavery as It Is*, 120.

40. Jane Rhodes, "Overlooked No More: How Mary Ann Shadd Cary Shook Up the Abolitionist Movement," *New York Times*, June 6, 2018.

41. Carolyn Calloway-Thomas, "Mary Ann Shadd Cary: Crafting Black Culture through Empirical and Moral Arguments," *Howard Journal of Communication* 24, no. 3 (2013): 239–56; Fagan, *Black Newspaper*, 110, 98.

42. Mary Ann Shadd Cary, "The Voice of the Bondsman," Chatham, Canada West, March 7, 1858.

43. Alan Carden, "Religious Schism as a Prelude to the American Civil War: Baptists, Methodists and Slavery," *Andrews University Seminary Studies* 24, no. 1 (Spring 1986): 13–29.

Chapter 3. The Long Struggle for Women's Suffrage

1. Elisabeth Griffith, *In Her Own Right: The Life of Elizabeth Cady Stanton* (New York: Oxford University Press, 1984), 38.

2. Elizabeth Cady Stanton, *Eighty Years and More: Reminiscences, 1815–1897* (Boston: Northeastern University Press, 1993), 82–83.

3. Kathleen L. Endres (1997) Women and the "Larger Household," *American Journalism*, 14:3–4, 262–82.

4. Stanton, *Eighty Years and More*, 136, 147.

5. Elizabeth Cady Stanton, *Declaration of Sentiments, Report of the Women's Rights Convention Held at Seneca Falls, New York, July 19 and 20* (Rochester, NY: *North Star*, 1848), 7.

6. Carol Faulkner, *Lucretia Mott's Heresy: Abolition and Women's Rights in Nineteenth Century America* (Philadelphia: University of Pennsylvania Press), 140.

7. Philip Foner, ed., *Frederick Douglass on Women's Rights* (Westport, CT: Greenwood, 1976), 51.

8. Elizabeth Cady Stanton, Susan B. Anthony, and Matilda Joslyn Gage, eds., *History of Women's Suffrage*; vol. 1, *1848–1861*, 804.

9. Stanton, *Eighty Years and More*, 163.

10. "Elizabeth Cady Stanton Dies at Her Home; Noted Advocate of Women's Suffrage Nearly 87 Years Old. Her Championship of Her Political Belief Almost Lifelong—Her Companionship with Miss Susan B. Anthony," *New York Times*, October 27, 1902, 1.

11. Eric Foner and Joshua Brown, *Forever Free: The Story of Emancipation and Reconstruction* (New York: Knopf, 2005).

12. Ida Husted Harper and Carrie Chapman Catt, *The Life and Work of Susan B. Anthony: Including Public Addresses, Her Own Letters and Many from Her Contemporaries during Fifty Years* (Indianapolis: Bowen-Merrill, 1898), 1908.

13. Maurine H. Beasley and Sheila Gibbons, *Taking Their Place: A Documentary History of Women and Journalism* (Washington, DC: American University Press, 1993), 81.

14. Elizabeth Cady Stanton, "Infanticide and Prostitution," *Revolution*, February 5, 1868.

15. Abraham J. Johnston, "Some Account of the History of the Treatment of Syphilis: An Address to the Medical Society for the Study of Venereal Diseases," *British Journal of Venereal Diseases*, 24(4) (April 24, 1948), 153–60, https://sti.bmj.com/content/sextrans/24/4/153.full.pdf.

16. Harper and Catt, *Life and Work of Susan B. Anthony*, 441.

17. Julia Ward Howe, "Salutatory," *Woman's Journal*, January 8, 1870.

18. This section draws heavily from Linda Lumsden's article, "Suffragist: The Making of a Militant," *Journalism and Mass Communication Quarterly* 72, no. 3 (Autumn 1995): 525–40.

19. Richard Barry, "Why Women Oppose Women's Suffrage," *Pearson's*, March 1910, 319.

20. Barry, "Why Women Oppose Women's Suffrage," 320.

21. Barry, "Why Women Oppose Women's Suffrage," 320–21.

22. Barry, "Why Women Oppose Women's Suffrage," 325–26.

23. Barry, "Why Women Oppose Women's Suffrage," 329.

24. Jane Rhodes, "Woman Suffrage and the New Negro in the Black Public Sphere," in *Front Pages, Front Lines: Media and the Fight for Women's Suffrage*, edited by Linda Steiner, Carolyn Kitch, and Brooke Kroeger (Urbana: University of Illinois Press, 2020), 101.

25. Coralie Franklin Cook, "Votes for Mothers," *The Crisis*, August, 1915, 184.

26. Cook, "Votes for Mothers," 184–85.

27. Cook, "Votes for Mothers," 185.

28. Linda M. Grasso, "Differently Radical: Suffrage Issues and Feminist Ideas in *The Crisis* and *The Masses*," in *Front Pages, Front Lines: Media and the Fight for Women's Suffrage*, edited by Linda Steiner, Carolyn Kitch, and Brooke Kroeger (Urbana: University of Illinois Press, 2020), 122.

29. Quoted in Laura Ellsworth Seiler, "The Suffragists: From Tea Parties to Prison," Online Archive of California, http://texts.cdlib.org/view?docId=kt2h4n992z&doc.view=entire_text.

30. "Suffrage Paraders," *The Crisis* 5(6), April, 1913, 267.

31. Bethanee Bemis, "Mr. President, How Long Must Women Wait for Liberty?" *Smithsonian*, January 12, 2017, https://www.smithsonianmag.com/smithsonian-institution/scrap-suffrage-history-180961780/.

32. Alice Paul, "Editorial," *The Suffragist* 9, no. 1 (January–February, 1921): 339.

33. Paul, "Editorial," 339.

Chapter 4. The Haymarket Riot and the Rights of Labor

1. Timothy Messer-Kruse, *The Trial of the Haymarket Anarchists: Terrorism and Justice in the Gilded Age* (New York: Palgrave Macmillan, 2011); Timothy Messer-Kruse, *The Haymarket Conspiracy: Trans-Atlantic Networks* (Urbana: University of Illinois Press, 2012).

2. "Albert Parsons, Labor Leader and Martyr in His Own Words," Black Rose Anarchist Federation, posted May 10, 2019, https://blackrosefed.org/albert-parsons-anarchist-and-labor-martyr/.

3. "Attention working men!" in *Haymarket Scrapbook*, edited by David R. Roediger and Franklin Rosemont (Chicago: Charles H. Kerr Publishing, 1986), 27.

4. Messer-Kruse, *Trial of the Haymarket Anarchists*, 11.

5. James Green, *Death in the Haymarket: A Story of Chicago, the First Labor Movement and the Bombing That Divided Gilded Age America* (New York: Anchor, 2007), 126.

6. Green, *Death in the Haymarket*, 130–31.

7. Green, *Death in the Haymarket*, 39–41.

8. Quoted in Messer-Kruse, *Haymarket Conspiracy*, 6.

9. Green, *Death in the Haymarket*, 75.

10. Green, *Death in the Haymarket*, 130.

11. W. J. Harrell, "I Am an Anarchist: The Social Anarchism of Lucy E. Parsons," *Journal of International Women's Studies* 13, no. 1 (2012): 1–2; Gale Aherns, "Introduction" to *Lucy Parsons: Freedom, Equality and Solidarity: Writing and Speeches, 1878–1937* (Chicago: Charles H. Kerr), 1–26; "Anarchism," from *The Lucy Parsons Project*, http://www.lucyparsonsproject.org/anarchism.html.

12. Carolyn Ashbaugh, *Lucy Parsons: American Revolutionary* (Chicago: Illinois Labor History Society, 1976), 73.

13. "Anarchy's Red Hand," *New York Times*, May 5, 1886, 1.

14. Joseph E. Gray, "The Chicago Anarchists of 1886," *The Century Magazine* 45, 6 (April, 1893), 829.

15. Gray, "The Chicago Anarchists of 1886," 833; Messer-Kruse, *Trial of the Haymarket Anarchists*, 1–3.

16. Messer-Kruse, *Haymarket Conspiracy*, 2.

17. Gray, *The Chicago Anarchists of 1886*, 829; "Anarchy's Red Hand," *New York Times*, May 5, 1886, 1.

18. Quoted in Harry Barnard, *"Eagle Forgotten": The Life of John Peter Altgeld* (Indianapolis: Bobbs-Merrill, 1962), 45.

19. "The UnAmericanized Element," *Chicago Daily Tribune*, May 7, 1886, 4.

20. "Stamp Out the Anarchists," *Chicago Daily Tribune,* May 7, 1886, 4.

21. Albert R. Parsons and Lucy E. Parsons, *Anarchism: Its Philosophy and Scientific Basis as Defined by Some of Its Apostles* (Chicago: Mrs. A. R. Parsons, 1889), 8.

22. Green, *Death in the Haymarket*, 131; Eric Foner, *Tom Paine and Revolutionary America*, 2nd ed. (Oxford: Oxford University Press, 2005), xxxii, 16.

23. Albert R. Parsons and Lucy E. Parsons. "What Is Anarchism?" in *Anarchism*, ed. Parsons.

24. Messer-Kruse, *Trial of the Haymarket Anarchists*, 3–4.

25. Donald L. Miller, *City of the Century: The Epic of Chicago and the Making of America* (New York: Simon and Schuster, 2003), 477.

26. Green, *Death in the Haymarket*, 227.

27. Messer-Kruse, *Trial of the Haymarket Anarchists*, 3.

28. Stanley Turkel, *Heroes of American Reconstruction: Profiles of Sixteen Educators, Politicians and Activists* (Jefferson, NC: McFarland, 2005), 121.

Chapter 5. Reconstruction, Lynching, and Ida B. Wells's Crusade for Justice

1. Kantrowitz, *More Than Freedom*, 320–28.

2. Kantrowitz, *More Than Freedom*, 32–33.

3. Kantrowitz, *More Than Freedom*, 321.

4. Foner and Brown, *Forever Free*, 96.

5. Isabella Wilkerson, *The Warmth of Other Suns: The Epic Story of America's Great Migration* (New York: Vintage, 2010), 10.

6. Foner, *Forever Free*, 190.

7. Rayford Whittingham Logan, *The Betrayal of the Negro: From Rutherford B. Hayes to Woodrow Wilson* (New York: Macmillan, 1965).

8. Dwight D. Murphey, *Lynching: History and Analysis* (Washington, DC: Council for Social and Economic Studies, 1995), 8.

9. Richard Perloff, "The Press and Lynchings of African Americans," *Journal of Black Studies* 30, no. 3 (January 2000), 315–30.

10. Perloff, "Press and Lynchings," 320.

11. Ethan Michaeli, *The Defender: How the Legendary Newspaper Changed America* (New York: Houghton Mifflin, 2016), 27–28.

12. Wilkerson, *Warmth of Other Suns*, 8–9, 243.

13. Carol Stabile, *White Victims, Black Villains: Gender, Race, and Crime News* (London: Routledge, 2006), 78.

14. Stabile, *White Victims, Black Villains*; Henry Louis Gates, *Stony the Road: Reconstruction, White Supremacy, and the Rise of Jim Crow* (New York: Penguin, 2019), 136–47.

15. Painter, *The History of White People* (New York: Norton, 2010).

16. Anonymous, *Miscegenation: The Theory of the Blending of the Races Applied to the American White Man and Negro* (New York: Dexter, Hamilton, 1864), 1–11.

17. Anonymous, *Miscegenation*, 50–51.

18. "The Miscegenation Ball," *Smithsonian*. Available at: https://www.si.edu/object/nmah_325557

19. Quoted in Samuel L. Adams, "Ida B. Wells: A Founder Who Never Knew Her Place," *The Crisis*, 101, 1 (January, 1994), 43

20. Ida B. Wells-Barnett, *Southern Horrors: Lynch Law in All Its Phases* (Frankfurt, Germany: Verlag, 2018), 5.

21. Wells-Barnett, *Southern Horrors*, 6.

22. Christopher Waldrep, *Lynching in America: A History in Documents* (New York: New York University Press, 2006), 131.

23. Wells-Barnett, *Southern Horrors*, 17.

24. Wells-Barnett, *Southern Horrors*, 17.

25. Wells-Barnett, *Southern Horrors*, 18.

26. Wells-Barnett, *Southern Horrors*, 19.

27. Fagan, *Black Newspaper*, 6.

28. Wells-Barnett, *Southern Horrors*, 19.

29. Beverly Guy-Sheftall, *Words of Fire: An Anthology of African-American Feminist Thought* (New York: New Press, 1995), 74.

30. For more on this aspect of her argument, see chapter 2 in Gail Bederman, *Manliness and Civilization: A Cultural History of Gender and Race in the United States, 1880–1917* (Chicago: University of Chicago Press, 1995).

31. Gates, *Stony the Road*, 128.

Chapter 6. Dreams and Nightmares of Empire

1. Frederick Merk, *Manifest Destiny and the Mission in American History: A Reinterpretation* (New York, Knopf, 1963), 8.

2. Painter, *History of White People*, 132.

3. Merk, *Manifest Destiny*, 193.

4. Caroline Elkins, *Legacy of Violence: A History of the British Empire* (New York: Alfred A. Knopf, 2022).

5. Merk, *Manifest Destiny*, 3; Haynes Johannsen, Morris Johannsen, Robert Walter, Sam W. Haynes, and Christopher Morris, *Manifest Destiny and Empire: American Antebellum Expansionism*, edited by Sam W. Haynes and Christopher Morris, Walter Prescott Webb Memorial Lectures, 31 (College Station, TX: Texas A&M University Press, 1997), 9.

6. Andrew Griffiths, *The New Journalism, the New Imperialism and the Fiction of Empire, 1870–1900* (New York: Palgrave Macmillan, 2015), 5.

7. "Progress of the Englishman Stanley—Fierce Encounters with Arabs—Arrival at the Coast—The Great Explorer Remains Two Years More in Africa," *New York Times,* July 2, 1872, 1.

8. "Progress of the Englishman Stanley," 1.

9. "Another Attack on Stanley—Colonel Williams Strikes at Him from the Congo Region," *New York Daily Tribune,* April 14, 1891, 4.

10. Theodore Roosevelt, *American Ideals* (New York: Putnam, 1897), 259.

11. Theodore Roosevelt, *The Winning of the West: An Account of the Exploration and Settlement of Our Country from the Alleghanies to the Pacific,* Vol. IV (New York: Putnam's Sons, 1908), 52.

12. Richard Harding Davis, "The Death of Rodríguez," *New York Journal,* February 2, 1897.

13. Rudyard Kipling, "The White Man's Burden," *New York Tribune, New York Sun,* and *San Francisco Examiner,* February 5, 1899.

14. Whitelaw Reid, "Our New Duties: Their Later Aspects," address delivered at Princeton University, October 21, 1899.

15. For more on the Anti-Imperialist League and its activities, see Steven Kinzer, *The True Flag: Theodore Roosevelt, Mark Twain, and the Birth of American Empire* (New York: Henry Holt, 2017).

16. *New York Herald,* October 15, 1900; reprinted in James Zwick, ed., *Mark Twain's Weapons of Satire: Anti-Imperial Writings on the Philippine-American War* (Syracuse, NY: Syracuse University Press, 1992), 5.

17. Mark Twain, "To the Person Sitting in the Darkness," *North American Review,* February 1901.

18. William H. Walker, "The White(?) Man's Burden." *Life* 33 (March 16, 1899).

Chapter 7. La Raza and the Rangers

1. "Fall of San Antonio and Massacre of the Texian Troops," *Long-Island Star,* April 14 1836, 2.

2. "Fall of San Antonio."

3. David McDonald, *José Antonio Navarro: In Search of the American Dream in Nineteenth Century Texas* (Denton: Texas State Historical Association, 2010), 1828.

4. Gabriella González, *Redeeming La Raza: Transborder Modernity, Race, Respectability and Rights* (Oxford: Oxford University Press, 2018), 16.

5. González, *Redeeming La Raza,* 42.

6. Quoted in Nicholas Kanellos, *Herencia: The Anthology of Hispanic Literature of the United States* (Oxford: Oxford University Press, 2001), 142–43.

7. Roberto Lovato, "Juan Crow in Georgia," *The Nation,* May 26, 2008.

8. Doug J. Swanson, *Cult of Glory: The Bold and Brutal History of the Texas Rangers* (New York: Viking, 2020), 252.

9. Kelly Lytle Hernández, *Bad Mexicans: Race, Empire and Revolution in the Borderlands* (New York: W. W. Norton, 2022).

10. "What Is Sympathy Worth?" *Regeneración,* July 19, 1913, 4.

11. "A Dangerous Alien," *Laredo Weekly Times,* December 20, 1914, 10.

12. González, *Redeeming La Raza,* 25.

13. Quoted in González, *Redeeming La Raza*, 28.

14. Quoted in González, *Redeeming La Raza*, 28.

15. Quoted in González, *Redeeming La Raza*, 37–38.

16. Quoted in González, *Redeeming La Raza*, 41.

17. Quoted in Swanson, *Cult of Glory,*109–10.

18. Miguel Antonio Levario, *Militarizing the Border: When Mexicans Became the Enemy* (College Station, TX: Texas A&M Press, 2015), 18.

19. Quoted in Swanson, *Cult of Glory*, p. 271.

20. Aisha Harris, "BROW BEAT: What Do You Mean 'Kemosabe,' 'Kemosabe'?" *Slate*, June 26, 2013, https://slate.com/culture/brow-beat.

21. *The Alamo*, dir. John Wayne (United Artists,1960).

Chapter 8. What Is Democracy?

1. William E. Leuchtenburg, *The Perils of Prosperity, 1914–1932* (Chicago: University of Chicago Press, 1993).

2. Sue Curry Jansen, "Semantic Tyranny: How Edward L. Bernays Stole Walter Lippmann's Mojo and Got Away with It and Why It Still Matters," *International Journal of Communication* (2013): 1094–1111.

3. Walter Lippmann, *Liberty and the News* (New York: Macmillan, 1920).

4. Robert McChesney, Preface to Walter Lippmann, *Liberty and the News* (New York: Macmillan, 1920), 22.

5. Jansen, "Semantic Tyranny."

6. Jansen, "Semantic Tyranny."

7. Sue Curry Jansen, *Walter Lippmann: A Critical Introduction to Media and Communication Theory* (New York: Peter Lang, 2012).

8. Larry Tye, *The Father of Spin: Edward L. Bernays and the Birth of Public Relations* (New York: Henry Holt, 1998).

9. Quoted in Ronald Steel, *Walter Lippmann and the American Century* (New Brunswick, NJ: Paradigm, 1980), 141, 143.

10. Steel, *Walter Lippmann and the American Century*, 148.

11. Steel, *Walter Lippmann and the American Century*, 147; Jansen, "Semantic Tyranny," 1100.

12. Walter Lippmann, *Public Opinion* (New York: Free Press, 1997), 53.

13. Lippmann, *Liberty and the News*, 5.

14. Lippmann, *Public Opinion*, 125.

15. McChesney, Preface, xii.

16. Lippmann, *Liberty and the News*, 21.

17. Lippmann, *Public Opinion*, 217–18.

18. Walter Lippmann and Charles Merz, "A Test of the News," *New Republic*, August 4, 1920, 3.

19. Lippmann and Merz, "Test of the News," 43.

20. Lippmann, *Liberty and the News*, 16.

21. Lippmann, *Liberty and the News*, 144.

22. Lippmann, *Liberty and the News*, 33.

23. Lippmann, *Liberty and the News*, 28–29.

24. Lippmann, *Liberty and the News*, 30–31.

25. Lippmann, *Public Opinion*, 218.

26. Michael Schudson, *Advertising: The Uneasy Persuasion* (New York: Basic, 1984), 186–87.

27. Lepore, *These Truths*, 456.

28. Jansen, *Semantic Tyranny*, 1104.

29. McChesney, Preface, x.

30. Stuart Ewen, Introduction to Edward L. Bernays, *Crystallizing Public Opinion* (New York: Boni and Liveright, 1923), 30.

31. Jansen, *Semantic Tyranny*.

32. Jansen, *Semantic Tyranny*, 1107.

33. Jansen, *Semantic Tyranny*, 1104–7.

34. Edward L. Bernays, *Crystallizing Public Opinion* (New York: Boni and Liveright, 1923), 62.

35. Jansen, *Semantic Tyranny*; Edward L. Bernays. (1928). *Propaganda* (New York: H. Liveright, 1928).

36. Bernays, *Propaganda*, 10

37. Bernays, *Propaganda*, 11.

38. Bernays, *Propaganda*, 18.

39. Lippmann, *Phantom Public*, 13.

40. Lippmann, *Phantom Public*, 32.

41. Bernays, *Crystallizing Public Opinion*, 118.

42. Lippmann, *Phantom Public*, 67.

43. Jansen, *Semantic Tyranny*, 1011.

Chapter 9. What Is "Americanism"?

1. Edwin R. Bayley, *Joe McCarthy and the Press* (Madison: University of Wisconsin Press, 1981), 176.

2. Michael Newton, *The Ku Klux Klan in Mississippi: A History* (Jefferson, NC: McFarland, 2010), 102.

3. Thomas Doherty, *Show Trial: Hollywood, HUAC, and the Birth of the Blacklist* (New York: Columbia University Press, 2018), 197.

4. Humphrey Bogart, "As Bogart Sees It Now" *Milwaukee Journal*, December 3, 1947.

5. Humphrey Bogart, "I'm No Communist," *Photoplay*, May 1948, 53.

6. Bogart, "I'm No Communist," 53.

7. Larry Tye, *Demagogue: The Life and Long Shadow of Senator Joe McCarthy* (Boston: Houghton Mifflin Harcourt, 2020), 217.

8. Larry Tye, *Demagogue*, 118–19.

9. Dan T. Carter and the American Council of Learned Societies, *Scottsboro: A Tragedy of the American South* (Baton Rouge: Louisiana State University Press, 1979).

10. Glenda Elizabeth Gilmore, *Defying Dixie: The Radical Roots of Civil Rights, 1919–1950* (New York: Norton, 2008).

11. "Speech of Joseph McCarthy, Wheeling, West Virginia, February 9, 1950," *History Matters*, https://historymatters.gmu.edu/d/6456/.

12. David M. Oshinsky, *A Conspiracy So Immense: The World of Joe McCarthy* (New York: Oxford University Press, 2005).

13. *Invasion of the Body Snatchers*, dir. Don Seigel (Allied Artist Pictures, 1956).

14. Quoted in Bayley, *Joe McCarthy and the Press*, 68–69.

15. Bayley, *Joe McCarthy and the Press*, 85.

16. W. Joseph Campbell, *Getting It Wrong: Ten of the Most Misreported Stories in American Journalism* (Berkeley: University of California Press, 2010), 58.

17. Bayley, *Joe McCarthy and the Press*, 148.

18. Campbell, *Getting It Wrong*, 62.

19. Campbell, *Getting It Wrong*, 56.

20. *See It Now*, November 18, 1951.

21. Quoted in Al Tompkins, *Aim for the Heart: Write, Shoot, Report and Produce for TV and Multimedia* (Lanham, MD: Taylor Trade Publishing, 2004), 67.

22. The McCarren HUAC committee was chaired by McCarthy ally Patrick McCarran of Nevada.

23. Sam Tanenhaus, *Wittaker Chambers: A Biography* (New York: Random House, 1997), 301–2.

24. *See It Now*, March 9, 1954.

25. Campbell, *Getting It Wrong*, 64.

26. Rodger Streitmatter, *Mightier Than the Sword: How the News Media Have Shaped American History*, 2nd ed. (Boulder, CO: Westview), 169.

27. "Have You No Decency?" "McCarthy," *American Experience*, PBS, n.d. Transcribed from https://www.youtube.com/watch?v=svUyYzzv6VI.

28. Edward R. Murrow, "Wire and Lights in a Box Speech," Radio, Television, Digital News Association, https://www.rtdna.org/content/edward_r_murrow_s_1958_wires_lights_in_a_box_speech.

29. Murrow, "Wire and Lights in a Box Speech."

Chapter 10. Civil Rights and the Spectacle of Southern Racism

1. Timothy B. Tyson, *The Blood of Emmett Till* (New York: Simon and Schuster, 2017), 7.

2. W. Stuart Towns, *"We Want Our Freedom: Rhetoric of the Civil Rights Movement* (Ann Arbor: University of Michigan Press, 2002), 240–41.

3. Gene Roberts and Hank Klibanoff, *The Race Beat: The Press, the Civil Rights Struggle, and the Awakening of a Nation* (New York: Vintage, 2007).

4. Roberts and Klibanoff, *Race Beat*, 296.

5. Karen S. Miller, "'Typical Slime by Joe McCarthy': Ralph McGill and Anti-McCarthyism in the South," *American Journalism* 13, no. 3 (Summer 1996), 325.

6. Ralph McGill, "The Criticisms Coming to the South," in *The Best of Ralph McGill: Selected Columns*, edited by Michael Strickland, Harry Davis, and Jeff Strickland (Atlanta: Cherokee, 1980), 97–98.

7. *"New York Times v. Sullivan,"* The Oyez Project at IIT Chicago-Kent College of Law (Chicago: The Oyez Project at IIT Chicago-Kent College of Law).

8. Taylor Branch, *Parting the Waters: America in the King Years 1954–1963* (New York: Simon and Schuster, 1989), 791.

9. Branch, *Parting the Waters*, 791

10. Ralph McGill, "We cannot escape history," in *The Best of Ralph McGill: Selected Columns* Michael Strickland, Harry Davis and Jeff Strickland, eds. (Cherokee Publishing Company, 1980), 128–130.

11. Branch, *Parting the Waters,* 857.

12. Transcribed from "Remembering the Dream," *Meet the Press*, August 25, 1963, https://www.nbcnews.com/meet-the-press/video/remembering-the-dream -44521539537.

13. "Remembering the Dream."

14. "Remembering the Dream."

15. "Remembering the Dream."

16. Branch, *Parting the Waters*, 883.

17. "President Lyndon B. Johnson's Address to a Joint Session of Congress, November 27, 1963," Center for Legislative Archives, https://www.archives.gov/ legislative/features/civil-rights-1964/lbj-address.html.

18. Roberts and Klibanoff, *Race Beat*, 383.

19. Roberts and Klibanoff, *Race Beat*, 386.

20. Ralph McGill, "Take a Good Look!" *Atlanta Constitution*, March 11, 1965, 1.

21. Lyndon B. Johnson, "Special Message to the Congress: The American Promise," *The American Presidency Project*, https://www.presidency.ucsb.edu/documents/ special-message-the-congress-the-american-promise.

22. Frank Newport, "Martin Luther King Jr.: Revered More after Death Than Before," *Gallup*, January 16, 2006, https://news.gallup.com/poll/20920/martin -luther-king-jr-revered-more-after-death-than-before.aspx.

23. Ralph McGill, "A Free Man Killed by White Slaves" (April 5, 1968), in *The Best of Ralph McGill*, 145–47.

Chapter 11. The Black Panthers and the Young Lords

1. Rick Perlstein, *Nixonland: The Rise of a President and the Fracturing of America* (New York: Scribner, 2009), 10.

2. Isabel Wilkerson, *The Warmth of Other Suns: The Epic Story of America's Great Migration* (New York: Random House, 2010).

3. Joshua Bloom and Waldo E. Martin Jr., *Black Against Empire: The History and Politics of the Black Panther Party* (Berkeley: University of California Press, 2016).

4. "What We Want, What We Believe," *Black Panther*, May 4, 1969, 16.

5. "What We Want, What We Believe," *Black Panther*, May 4, 1969, 16.

6. Moore, *The Defeat of Black Power: Civil Rights and the National Black Political Convention of 1972* (LSU Press, 2018), 7.

7. Huey P. Newton, "Executive Mandate No. 1," (Black Panther Party: Oakland, 1968). Accessed on April 7, 2024, at: https://www.marxists.org/archive/ newton/1967/05/02.htm.

8. Jane Rhodes, *Framing the Black Panthers* (New York: New Press, 2007), 77.

9. Rhodes, *Framing the Black Panthers*, 75.

10. Laurel Rosenhall (July 3, 2022) "Commentary: Reagan embraced gun control in response to political extremism. This Supreme Court didn't." *Los Angeles Times*.

Accessed on April 7, 2024 at: https://www.latimes.com/opinion/story/2022-07-03/commentary-ronald-reagan-gun-control-political-extremism-supreme-court.

11. *The Black Panther Newspaper*, n.d., https://www.marxists.org/history//usa/pubs/black-panther/index.htm.

12. Donna Murch, *Living for the City: Migration, Education and the Rise of the Black Panther Party in Oakland, California* (Chapel Hill: University of North Carolina Press, 2010), 7.

13. Transcribed from Rund Abdelfatah, Ramtin Arablouei, Jamie York, Julie Caine, Laine Kaplan-Levenson, Lawrence Wu, Parth Shah, and Victor Yvellez, "The Real Black Panthers," *Throughline*, National Public Radio, April 15, 2021, https://www.npr.org/2021/04/12/986561396/the-real-black-panthers.

14. Johanna Fernández, *The Young Lords: A Radical History* (Chapel Hill: University of North Carolina Press, 2020).

15. "Interview with Cha Cha Jiménez—Young Lords Organization," *Black Panther*, June 7, 1969, 17.

16. "Interview with Cha Cha Jiménez," 17.

17. "Why a YLO Newspaper?" *YLO*, May 1969, 18.

18. "Why a YLO Newspaper?" 9–11.

19. "October 1966 Black Panther Party Platform," *YLO*, March 19, 1969, 8.

20. "Puerto Rico: 'Island Paradise' of U.S. Imperialism," *YLO*, March 19, 1969, 19.

21. Daniel José Older, "Garbage Fires for Freedom: When Puerto Rican Activists Took Over New York's Streets." *New York Times*, October 11, 2019. Accessed on April 8, 2024 at: https://www.nytimes.com/2019/10/11/nyregion/young-lords-nyc-garbage-offensive.html

22. Darrel Wanzer-Serrano, *The New York Young Lords and the Struggle for Liberation* (Philadelphia: Temple University Press, 2015), 130.

23. *Palante*, June 5, 1970.

24. *Palante*, May 22, 1970.

25. Quoted in Matthew Gandy, *Concrete and Clay: Reworking Nature in New York City* (Cambridge: MIT Press, 2002), 165–66.

26. Emma Francis-Snyder, "The Hospital Occupation That Changed Public Health Care," *New York Times*, October 12, 2021. Available at https://www.nytimes.com/2021/10/12/opinion/young-lords-nyc-activism-takeover.html.

27. Fernández, *Young Lords*.

28. "Writer Who Fought a Subpoena Wins; Grand Jury Ended," *New York Times*, December 24, 1972, https://www.nytimes.com/1972/12/24/archives/writer-who-fought-a-subpoena-wins-grand-jury-ended.html.

Chapter 12. The American Indian Movement and Indigenous Peoples' Media Strategies

1. Rex Weyler, *Blood of the Land: The Government and Corporate War against the American Indian Movement* (New York: Everest House), 64–66.

2. Mueller, Salt, Banks, Bellecourt, Harris, Hill, Mueller, David, et al. A Good Day to Die / a Yocha Dehe Winton Nation Production; produced and directed by

David Mueller and Lynn Salt. (New York, NY: Distributed by Kino Lorber, Inc., 2011.)

3. Stephen Warren, *The Worlds the Shawnees Made: Migration in Early America* (Chapel Hill: University of North Carolina Press), 224–29.

4. Warren, *Worlds the Shawnees Made*, 224–25.

5. Warren, *Worlds the Shawnees Made*, 224–25.

6. Warren, *Worlds the Shawnees Made*, 224–25.

7. David T. Z. Mindich, *Just the Facts: How "Objectivity" Came to Define American Journalism* (New York: New York University Press, 1998).

8. James Emmett Murphy and Sharon M. Murphy, *Let My People Know: American Indian Journalism, 1828–1978* (Norman, OK: University of Oklahoma Press, 1981), v.

9. Richard LaCourse, "An Indian Perspective—Native American: An Overview," *Journalism History* 6, 1979, Vol. 6(2), 34–38.

10. Jeannette Henry, Foreword to James Emmett Murphy and Sharon M. Murphy, v–xvi. *Let My People Know: American Indian Journalism, 1828–1978* (Norman, OK: University of Oklahoma Press, 1981), v.

11. Murphy and Murphy, *Let My People Know*, 20–21.

12. Murphy and Murphy, *Let My People Know*, 16–17, 24–25, 30–31.

13. Murphy and Murphy, *Let My Know*, 33.

14. Murphy and Murphy, *Let My People Know*, 24.

15. Elias Boudinot, *An Address to the Whites: Delivered in the First Presbyterian Church, on the 26th of May, 1826. Sabin Americana 1500–1926.* Philadelphia: Printed by W.F. Geddes, 1826, May 26, 1826, 5–6, 12–13, 19. https://acdc.amherst.edu/view/asc:427890/asc:428168.

16. Murphy and Murphy, *Let My People Know*, 30.

17. Elizabeth Prine Pauls, "Trail of Tears." *Encyclopaedia Britannica*, https://www.britannica.com/event/Trail-of-Tears, last updated January 11, 2024.

18. LaCourse, "Indian Perspective," 34–38.

19. Jeffrey Ostler, "Disease Has Never Been Just about Disease for Native Americans," *Atlantic*, April 29, 2020, https://www.theatlantic.com/ideas/archive/2020/04/disease-has-never-been-just-disease-native-americans/610852/.

20. Murphy and Murphy, *Let My People Know*, 32.

21. *The Youth's Companion*, October 1881, vol. 1, no. 5 (Tulalip Indian Reservation, Tulalip, Washington Territory: Indian Industrial Boarding Schools), 1.

22. A&E Television Networks, "American-Indian Wars," March 9, 2010, History.com, https://www.history.com/topics/native-american-history/american-indian-wars, last updated July 7, 2023.

23. Weyler, *Blood of the Land*, 66.

24. Bryan H. Widenthal, *Native American Sovereignty on Trial* (Santa Barbara, CA: Bloomsbury, 2003), 59

25. Joane Nagel, *American Indian Ethnic Renewal: Red Power and the Resurgence of Identity and Culture* (New York: Oxford University Press, 1996), 163–64.

26. Weyler, *Blood of the Land*, 36.

27. Todd Gitlin, *The Whole World Is Watching: Mass Media in the Making and Unmaking of the New Left* (Berkeley: University of California Press, 1980), 7.

28. Robert Burnette and John Koster, *The Road to Wounded Knee* (New York: Bantam, 1974), 196–97.

29. Nagel, *American Indian Ethnic Renewal*, 163–65.

30. Rolland Dewing, *Wounded Knee II* (Sioux Falls, SD: Pine Hill, 2000), 16–19.

31. Preamble to Trail of Broken Treaties twenty-point position paper "An Indian Manifesto: Restitution, Reparations, Restoration of Lands for a Reconstruction of an Indian Future in America," news release, October 31, 1972, Minneapolis: American Indian Movement, https://aimovement.org/ggc/trailofbrokentreaties.html.

32. John Kifner, "At Wounded Knee, Two Worlds Collide: At Wounded Knee, a Century-Long Conflict of Two Cultures Is Unresolved," *New York Times,* March 24, 1973, 1.

33. Weyler, *Blood of the Land*, 71–78.

34. Weyler, *Blood of the Land*, 76.

35. Weyler, *Blood of the Land*, 70–72.

36. Weyler, *Blood of the Land*, 79–80.

37. Weyler, *Blood of the Land*, 176.

38. Marlon Brando, "That Unfinished Oscar Speech," *New York Times*, March 30, 1973.

39. Brando, "That Unfinished Oscar Speech."

40. Murphy and Murphy, *Let My People Know*, 8.

Conclusion

1. Robert W. McChesney, "That Was Now and This Is Then: Walter Lippmann and the Crisis of Journalism," in *Will the Last Reporter Please Turn Out the Lights: The Collapse of Journalism and What We Can Do to Fix It*, edited by R. McChesney and V. Pickard (New York: New Press), 153.

Index

145–47, 153–54, 156–59, 160–61; public-relations counsel and, 154, 155–56, 160

Bernstein, Leonard, 166

Bibb, Henry Walton, 40, 48, 49

Birmingham (Alabama) *News,* 191, 192

Birmingham (Alabama) *World,* 191

Black Codes, 93

Black English dialect, 206

Black Panther Party, 200–208; *Black Panther Community News Service/ The Black Panther Intercommunal News Service,* 206–7, 208; cultural influence of, 213; FBI and, 212–13; founding in Oakland, California, 200, 202–3; Marxist critiques of colonialism and, 202–3, 207; mediated direct action outreach program, 204–5; repression and redirection of, 212–13; Ten-Point Program, 203–4, 209, 211; Watts riots and, 200–201

Blacks. *See* African Americans

Blatch, Harriot Stanton, 67–68

Bogart, Humphrey, 163–65

Bonfield, John, 77, 78, 80–81

Bonnet, René Placide, 220–21

Boston Gazette, 16, 17, 20, 22–24

Boston Massacre (1770), 11, 18, 24

Boston Post-Boy, 16

Boudinot, Elias, 217–19, 229

Bowie, Jim, 129

Bradford's *Gazette,* 13

Bradley, Richard, 14

Branch, Taylor, 192

Brando, Marlon, 227–28

Brennan, William, Jr., 190

broadcasting. *See* radio; television

broadsides, 17, 19, 24, 49–50

Bross, William, 90

Brown, John, 76–77

Brown v. Board of Education of Topeka (1954), 184, 187

Bryant, Carolyn, 184

Bryant, Roy, 186–87

Buffalo Bill's Wild West Show, 113

Bundy, Harvey, 178, 179

Burke Act (1906), 222

Burns, Lucy, 69

Byrnes, James, 169

cable television, 9

Caldwell, Earl, 212–13

Calhoun, John, 109

Canales, J. T., 141

Carey, James, 1

Carnegie, Andrew, 123

cartoons, 111–12, 116–17, 121–22, 126–27, 133–34

Cary, Mary Ann Chapman Shadd, 40, 47–49

censorship, 28, 149, 150, 155

Cheney, James, 195

Cherokee Advocate, 217

Cherokee Phoenix and Advocate, 217–19, 229, 230

Chesapeake and Ohio Railroad, 102

Chicago Daily Tribune, 83–84

Chicago Defender, 95–96, 185

Chicago labor movement, 73–91; anarchism and, 73–74, 78, 79, 81, 85–89; eight-hour day, 79, 83; First Red Scare and, 77–78; Haymarket affair, 73–74, 76, 79–85, 89–91; Albert Parsons and, 73–91

Chicago Times, 78, 83

Chicago Tribune, 50, 77, 90, 107, 227

China, communism in, 173

Christianity: Native Americans and, 216–21; slavery/enslaved people and, 46

Church of England, 13

cigarette smoking, 154

citizenship: Treaty of Guadalupe Hidalgo exclusions, 130; voting rights and, 54; whiteness as requirement for, 4. *See also* immigration

Civil Rights Act (1964), 195

civil rights movement (1954–68), 94, 184–99, 227; Birmingham civil disobedience campaign, 190–92, 193; "Bloody Sunday" march from Selma to Montgomery, 196–97; Central High School protests, 187–88; Congress of Racial Equality (CORE), 185, 188, 196; Freedom Riders bus caravan, 188; Freedom Summer, 195;

Paul, Alice, 63–68, 69–72
Pearson, Drew, 175
Pearson's Magazine, 64–66
pen names: abolitionist journalism
    and, 37; colonial journalism and,
    16–17
*Pennsylvania Journal and Weekly Adver-
    tiser*, 16
Pennsylvania Magazine, 25
penny press, 6, 7, 110
People's Grocery, 102
Perloff, Richard, 94, 95
Perlstein, Rick, 201
The Phantom Public (Lippmann),
    160–61
Philadelphia Inquirer, 122
Philippines, American imperialism
    and, 119–22
Phillips, Wendell, 41, 58
Photoplay magazine, 164
Pitt, William, 12
political participation: early partisan
    press and, 4–5, 6, 8. *See also* voting
    rights; women's suffrage
Polk, James K., 109, 110
Post Office Act (1792), 4, 32–34, 49
power: gender and, 5; whiteness and,
    3, 5
pregnancy, 60
press agents, 148–51
Preston, Captain, 23
Problems of Leninism (Stalin), 168
professionalization of journalism, 7–10,
    147–48, 152–53
Propaganda (Bernays), 156–59
propaganda/fake news: Alamo battle
    and, 129–30, 140, 142; Edward
    L. Bernays and, 145–47, 153–54,
    156–59, 160–61; in colonial journal-
    ism, 12, 17–19, 20–24; conspiracy
    theories, 24, 73; election of 1864
    and *Miscegenation* hoax, 97–102; of
    Hitler and Goebbels, 154; *Journal
    of Occurrences* and, 12, 17–19, 22;
    Walter Lippmann and, 8, 145–47,
    148, 160–61; objective journalism vs.
    (*see* objective journalism); in popular
    culture, 141–42; post–World War

I First Red Scare and, 77–78, 144,
    145, 150, 162, 168, 169–70; post–
    World War II Second Red Scare and,
    162, 167, 169–83, 188, 189; "reality"
    vs, 153–54; social media and, 9–10,
    233–34; sources of propaganda, 145
    (*see also* advertising; partisan press;
    public relations); Spanish-American
    War and, 7, 117–22; as threat to
    democracy, 144; "yellow journal-
    ism," 7
prostitution, as problem of patriarchy,
    59–61, 66–67
Provincial Freeman, 48
Publick Occurrences, 12–13
Public Opinion (Lippmann), 147–50,
    155, 160
public opinion, public relations vs.,
    6–10, 20, 25, 155–56
public relations, 2, 19, 143–61; Edward
    L. Bernays and, 143–47, 153–61;
    crisis of liberalism and, 160–61;
    defining "reality" and, 153–54;
    Walter Lippmann and, 8, 143–55,
    160–61, 232; press agents in, 148–51;
    as "private propaganda," 144,
    156–57, 160; public opinion and,
    6–10, 20, 25, 155–56
Puck (British magazine), 116
Puerto Rico, Young Lords and, 207–12
Pulitzer, Joseph, 7, 81, 100, 111–12

race: concept of La Raza and, 138; *Mis-
    cegenation* hoax, 97–102; nature of,
    in journalism, 3; in popular media,
    141–42; power and, 3, 5; skin color
    and, 109–10. *See also* African Ameri-
    cans; Latinos/Latinas; Native Ameri-
    cans; white Americans/whiteness
radio: Associated Press expansion to,
    162; *The Lone Ranger*, 141–42; as
    more objective than newspapers,
    9; objectivity and, 9; *Red Channels*
    report on communist influences in,
    166–69; rise in the 1920s, 9; Second
    Red Scare and, 166–69, 176
Radio-Television News Directors Asso-
    ciation and Foundation, 183

Wallace, George, 197–98
Wanzer-Serrano, Darrel, 210
War of 1812, 217
Warren, Stephen, 215, 230
Washington, Booker T., 123
Washington, George, 28, 122–23
Washington Correspondents Association, 169
Washington Post, 173, 175, 195
Wayne, John, 142, 228
The Weekly Advocate (The Rights of All), 34–35
Welch, Joseph, 182
Weld, Theodore, 40, 47
Welles, Orson, 166
Wells-Barnett, Ida, 68–69; as former enslaved person, 92, 102; lawsuit with Chesapeake and Ohio Railroad, 102; lynching and, 92, 94, 96, 101–8; NAACP and, 108; People's Grocery incident, 102–3; on "southern horrors," 187
Weston, Nancy, 47
Wheeling Intelligencer, 169–74
Whig party, proslavery stance, 36
white Americans/whiteness: Anglo-Saxon Protestant supremacy/exceptionalism and, 12–13, 97, 99, 110–13, 120, 121; assimilation and, 132, 214, 216, 218, 220, 222, 230; Black American vs. white American exceptionalism, 31, 49; Black Codes and, 93; colonial expansion worldwide and, 113–17 (*see also* colonies/colonial journalism); in dual system of white press/Black press, 95–97; election of 1864 and *Miscegenation* hoax, 97–102; immigration and (*see* immigration); Jim Crow and (*see* Jim Crow); lynching and the press, 92, 94, 96, 101–8, 189–90; *Miscegenation* hoax and, 97–102; paternalism of the abolitionist movement, 49; power and, 3, 4; as requirement for citizenship, 4; slavery as normal business practice and, 30–31, 38–42, 49; voting and (*see* voting rights); white male property ownership, 4, 27, 33, 52, 54; women's suffrage

movement and (*see* women's suffrage). *See also* civil rights movement
White Citizens' Councils, 189
Wilhelm, Kaiser, 144
Wilkins, Roy, 193
Williams, George Washington, 115–16
Wilson, L. Alex, 188
Wilson, Richard "Dickie," 225–26
Wilson, Woodrow, 68–71, 136, 146, 150, 169
Woman's Journal and Suffrage News, 61–63, 64
Women's Rebellion, 65
women's rights: abolitionist journalism and, 38, 43, 46–47; cigarette smoking "pseudo-events" and, 154; Liga Femenil Mexicanista (League of Mexican Women), 139–40; pregnancy and, 60; *The Revolution,* 58–62, 66–67, 72; Seneca Falls "Declaration of Rights and Sentiments," 53–57, 71, 203; as a social movement, 53–57; temperance movement, 43, 53, 56, 58; voting rights (*see* women's suffrage)
women's suffrage, 51–72; Susan B. Anthony and, 52, 57–61, 63; Mary Ann Shadd Cary and, 48; Cult of True Womanhood and, 52, 55–57, 65, 72; Lucretia Mott and, 51–53, 54–55; Alice Paul and, 63–68, 69–72; Reconstruction impact on movement, 57–63; *The Revolution,* 58–62, 66–67, 72; Seneca Falls "Declaration of Rights and Sentiments," 53–57, 71, 203; Elizabeth Cady Stanton and, 51–55, 56, 58–62, 63; Lucy Stone and, 58, 61–62, 63, 72; suffrage movement organizations, 58–59, 61–64; unity and dissent within the movement, 68–72; *Woman's Journal and Suffrage News,* 61–63, 64; Women's Suffrage Procession, 68–70; World Anti-Slavery Convention and, 51–52
World Anti-Slavery Convention (1840), 51–52
World Columbian Exposition (1893), 116–17

FRANK D. DURHAM is an associate professor in the School of Journalism and Mass Communication at the University of Iowa.

THOMAS P. OATES is an associate professor in the department of American Studies and an associate professor in the School of Journalism and Mass Communication at the University of Iowa. His books include *Football and Manliness: An Unauthorized Feminist Account of the NFL*.

The University of Illinois Press
is a founding member of the
Association of University Presses.

———————————————————

Composed in 11.5/13 Adobe Garamond Pro
with New Century Schoolbook LT Std display
by Lisa Connery
at the University of Illinois Press

University of Illinois Press
1325 South Oak Street
Champaign, IL 61820–6903
www.press.uillinois.edu